OL
SHANGHAI

GANGSTERS IN PARADISE

LYNN PAN

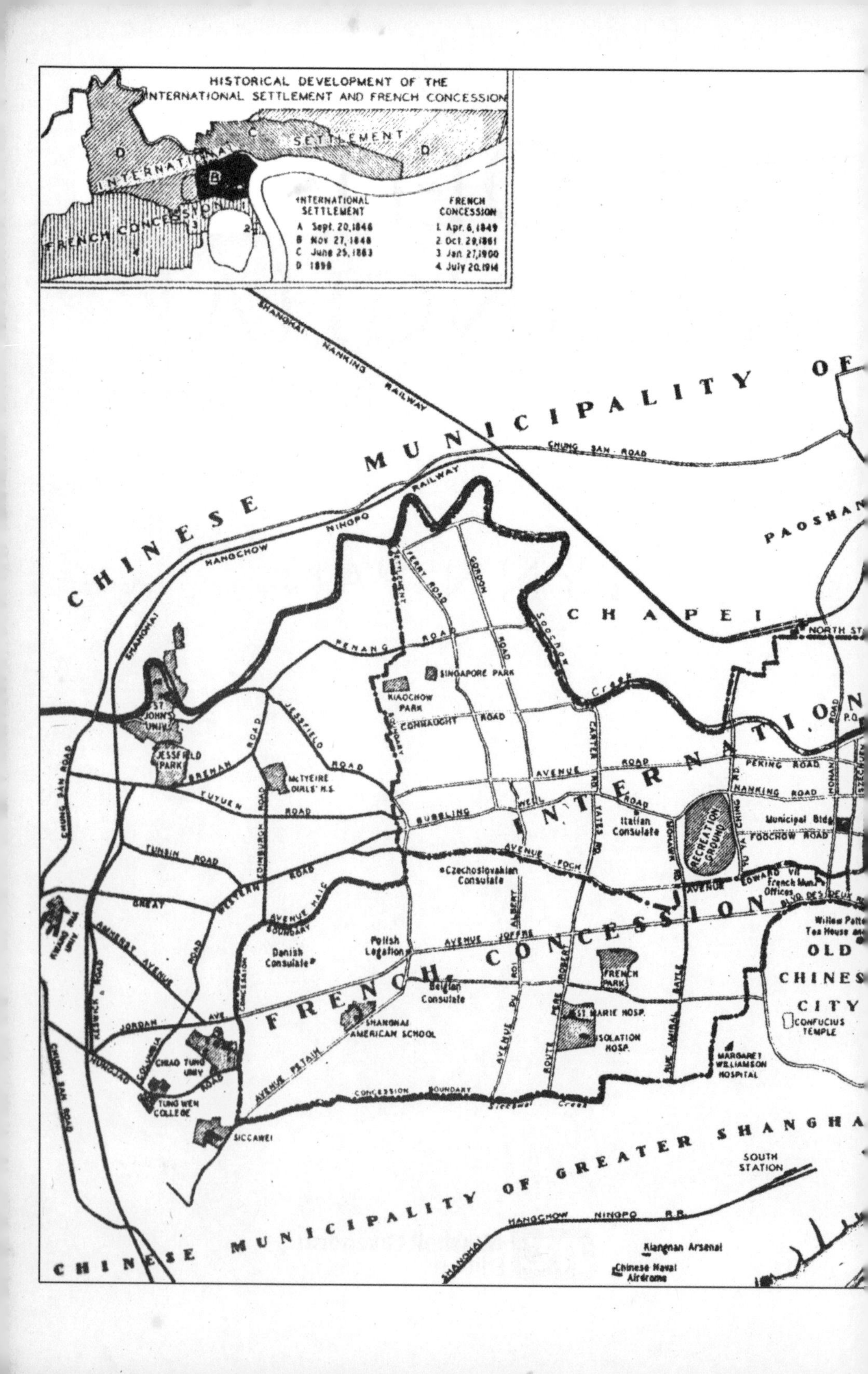

HISTORICAL DEVELOPMENT OF THE
INTERNATIONAL SETTLEMENT AND FRENCH CONCESSION
INTERNATIONAL SETTLEMENT
A Sept. 20, 1846
B Nov. 27, 1848
C June 25, 1863
D 1899
FRENCH CONCESSION
1. Apr. 6, 1849
2. Oct. 29, 1861
3. Jan. 27, 1900
4. July 20, 1914
CHINESE MUNICIPALITY OF
SHANGHAI NANKING RAILWAY
CHUNG SAN ROAD
HANGCHOW NINGPO RAILWAY
CHAPEI
PAOSHAN
NORTH ST
INTERNATION
PENANG ROAD
SINGAPORE PARK
KIAOCHOW PARK
CONNAUGHT ROAD
ST JOHN'S UNIV.
JESSFIELD PARK
JESSFIELD ROAD
BREMAN ROAD
McTYEIRE GIRLS' H.S.
YUYUEN ROAD
BUBBLING WELL ROAD
PEKING ROAD
NANKING ROAD
Municipal Bldg
FOOCHOW ROAD
RECREATION GROUND
Italian Consulate
Czechoslovakian Consulate
AVENUE FOCH
AVENUE EDWARD VII
French Mun. Offices
FRENCH CONCESSION
AVENUE JOFFRE
Polish Legation
Danish Consulate
Belgian Consulate
FRENCH PARK
ST MARIE HOSP.
ISOLATION HOSP.
SHANGHAI AMERICAN SCHOOL
AVENUE PETAIN
CHIAO TUNG UNIV
TUNG WEN COLLEGE
SICCAWEI
CONCESSION BOUNDARY
Siccawei Creek
OLD CHINESE CITY
CONFUCIUS TEMPLE
Willow Pattern Tea House
MARGARET WILLIAMSON HOSPITAL
CHINESE MUNICIPALITY OF GREATER SHANGHAI
SOUTH STATION
HANGCHOW NINGPO R.R.
Kiangnan Arsenal
Chinese Naval Airdrome

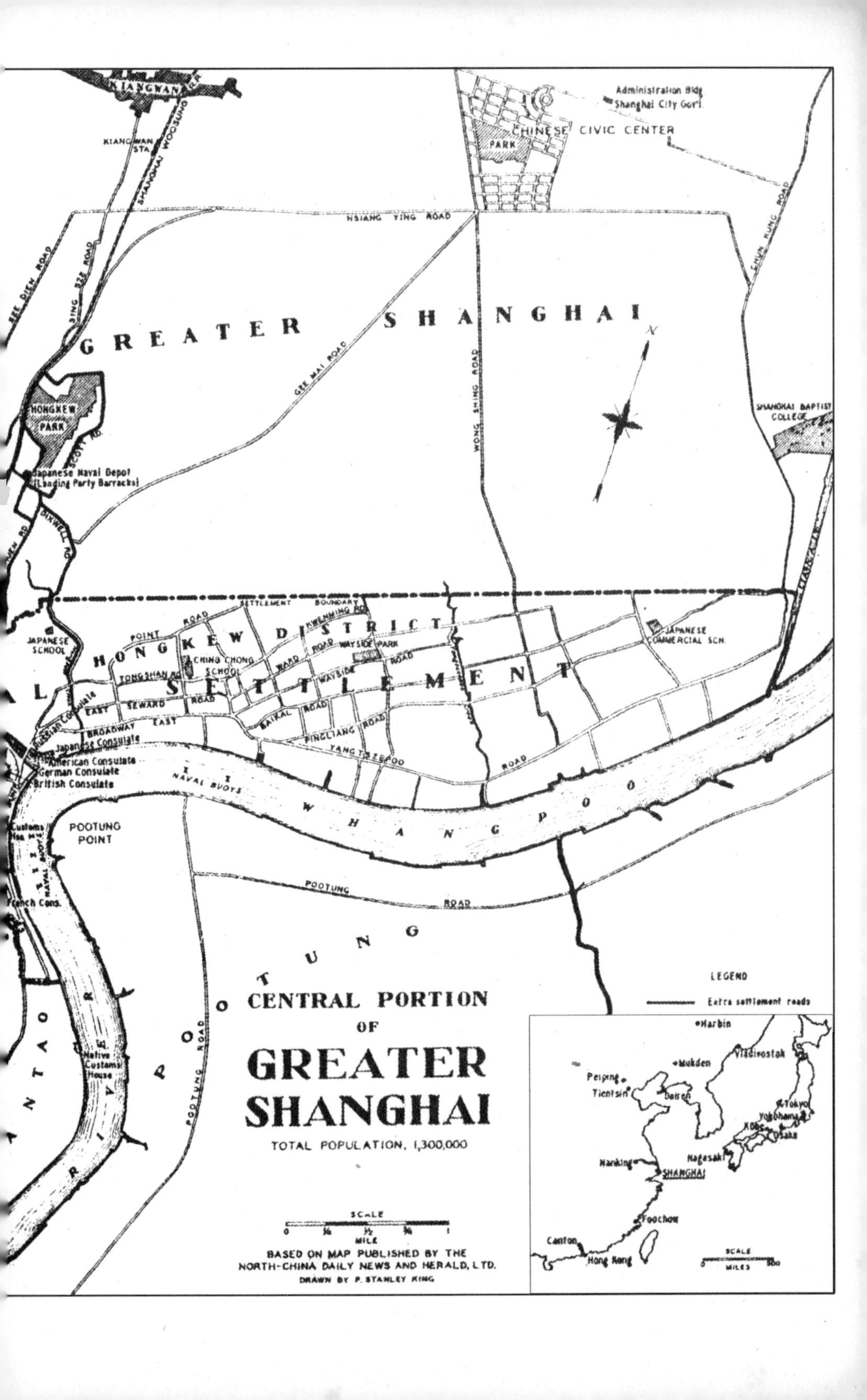
CENTRAL PORTION
OF
GREATER
SHANGHAI
TOTAL POPULATION, 1,300,000
GREATER SHANGHAI
CHINESE CIVIC CENTER
Administration Bldg Shanghai City Gov't.
PARK
KIANGWAN
KIANGWAN STA
SHANGHAI WOOSUNG RR
HSIANG YING ROAD
CHUN KUNG ROAD
SZE DIEN ROAD
SING SZE ROAD
GEE MAI ROAD
WONG SHING ROAD
HONGKEW PARK
SCOTT RD.
Japanese Naval Depot (Landing Party Barracks)
DIXWELL RD
SHANGHAI BAPTIST COLLEGE
SETTLEMENT BOUNDARY
HONGKEW DISTRICT
SETTLEMENT
JAPANESE SCHOOL
POINT ROAD
KWENMING RD
WARD ROAD
WAYSIDE PARK
CHING CHONG SCHOOL
TONGSHAN RD
WAYSIDE ROAD
EAST SEWARD ROAD
BAIKAL ROAD
PINGLIANG ROAD
BROADWAY EAST
YANGTSZEPOO ROAD
JAPANESE COMMERCIAL SCH.
Russian Consulate
Japanese Consulate
American Consulate
German Consulate
British Consulate
NAVAL BUOYS
WHANGPOO
POOTUNG POINT
Customs
NAVAL BUOYS
French Cons.
POOTUNG ROAD
POOTUNG
POOTUNG ROAD
Native Customs House
NANTAO
RIVER
LEGEND
Extra settlement roads
Harbin
Mukden
Vladivostok
Peiping
Tientsin
Dairen
Tokyo
Yokohama
Kobe
Osaka
Nagasaki
Nanking
SHANGHAI
Foochow
Canton
Hong Kong
SCALE
MILES
500
SCALE
0 ¼ ½ ¾ 1
MILE
BASED ON MAP PUBLISHED BY THE
NORTH-CHINA DAILY NEWS AND HERALD, LTD.
DRAWN BY P. STANLEY KING

First published by Heinemann Educational Books

This edition published by Marshall Cavendish Editions
An imprint of Marshall Cavendish International
1 New Industrial Road, Singapore 536196

Other Marshall Cavendish Offices:
Marshall Cavendish International, PO Box 65829, London EC1P 1NY, UK • Marshall Cavendish Corporation, 99 White Plains Road, Tarrytown NY 10591-9001, USA • Marshall Cavendish International (Thailand) Co Ltd, 253 Asoke, 12th Flr, Sukhumvit 21 Road, Klongtoey Nua, Wattana, Bangkok 10110, Thailand • Marshall Cavendish (Malaysia) Sdn Bhd, Times Subang, Lot 46, Subang Hi-Tech Industrial Park, Batu Tiga, 40000 Shah Alam, Selangor Darul Ehsan, Malaysia

National Library Board, Singapore Cataloguing-in-Publication Data
Pan, Lynn.
Old Shanghai : Gangsters in paradise / Lynn Pan. – Singapore : Marshall Cavendish Editions, [2011], c1984.
p. cm.
ISBN : 978-981-4351-42-3
1. Du, Yuesheng, 1888-1951. 2. Shanghai (China) – History – 20th century. 3. Shanghai (China) – History – 20th century – Anecdotes. I. Title.
DS796.S257
951.132 -- dc22 OCN719774673

Printed in Singapore by Fabulous Printers Pte Ltd

CONTENTS

ILLUSTRATIONS

PREFACE

I ATTEMPT THIS historical reconstruction because I want to shed a little light on some unexplored experiences of the Chinese in the half-century before their country burst into a Communist revolution. A complete canvas of the face of society in those tumultuous years can never be painted: even the sketchiest outline would fill volumes. What I try to do instead is to present, through the medium of biography, some concrete illustrations of that singular age. In the lives of men and women who in their different ways embodied the temper of their times, I seek to depict certain features that contribute to the total picture.

The story unfolds through a series of interlocking biographies — of a Shanghai gangster who was also the leader of the city's underground resistance during the war with Japan; of China's pre-eminent traitor and several of his fellow collaborators; of the chief of the most powerful wartime secret police organization in Asia; and of the quite extraordinary women behind the scenes. The unifying thread of the reconstruction is provided by the gangster Du Yuesheng. The choice of Du Yuesheng as the centrepiece of the book requires little justification. In China he is legend, and since we know that in that country it is legend which moulds people, and not the duller facts of formal history, we must concern ourselves with the legend.

All the people and places in this book are real, but the final image which they have in it, drawn from the array of historical facts, biographies, memoirs, quotations and reminiscences which constitute its source, is necessarily coloured by my own interpretation. Although, as a reconstruction of historical figures and their times, the book borders on fiction, I have made an effort to adhere closely to the historical evidence. But where it has been necessary to choose between what history tells me in the way of facts and what it points to in the way of psychological reality, I have often chosen the latter. In all cases, though, I have tried to do so with good reason. If, in some scenes, my reconstruction is not true in every detail of objective reality, I believe it to be true in the atmosphere and feeling.

The book had its germ in a trip I made to Shanghai in 1981. There, as a guest at a banquet, I found myself sitting next to a man addressed by those present as 'Papa Du' and discovered that he was none other than Du Yuesheng's son. It was evident that he was a man with clout, and this despite his father's role in the slaughter of Communists in 1927 and after. Paradox and tactically mobile loyalties, it seems, are ever endemic to life in the Communist State.

I note here the materials that I used for this reconstruction, though to provide a complete bibliography would be beyond the scope of this work. For Du Yuesheng's life I used Zhang Jungu's *Du Yuesheng zhuan* (A Biography of Du Yuesheng, Vols I–IV, 1967–69) and Xu Zhucheng's *Du Yuesheng zheng zhuan* (A True Biography of Du Yuesheng, 1982). For Dai Li I used Liang Xiong's *Dai Li zhuan* (A Biography of Dai Li, Vols I & II, 1980); Shen Zui and Wen Qiang's *Dai Li qi ren* (This Man Dai Li, 1980); Chen Shaoxiao's *Hei wang lu* (The Black Net, 1965) and Milton E. Miles's *A Different Kind of War* (1967). For Wang Jingwei I used *Wang zhengquan de kaichang yu shouchang* (The Beginning and End of the Wang Regime, Vols I–IV, 1961–62) by Zhu Zijia; *China and Japan at War 1937–45*, by John Hunter Boyle (1972) and *The Peace Conspiracy: Wang Jingwei and the China War 1937–41*, by Gerald E. Bunker (1972). For Hu Lancheng and Zhang Ailing I used Hu's *Jin sheng jin shi* (This Life, This Age, 1976) and Zhang's *Liu yan* (Written on Water, 1968). Wan Molin's *Hushang wangshi* (A Shanghai Past, Vols I–IV, 1973) and Tao Juyin's *Gudao jianwen* (Isolated Island Gleanings, 1979) were also consulted. Among Western works that I built upon may be mentioned A. Doak Barnett's *China on the Eve of Communist Takeover* (1963); Robert W. Barnett's *Economic Shanghai: Hostage to Politics 1937–41* (1941); Lucien Bianco's *Origins of the Chinese Revolution 1915–49* (1911), Jean Chesneaux's *The Chinese Labour Movement 1919–27* (1968), and Parks M. Coble Jr.'s *The Shanghai Capitalists and the Nationalist Government 1927–37* (1980).

I have used pinyin romanization except for a few accepted forms such as Chiang Kaishek, Canton, and Swatow.

PART I

Even the hooligan was probably invented in China
centuries before we thought of him.

— H.H. MUNRO

Chapter One

AUSPICIOUS TUESDAY 9 JUNE 1931

AS HE SET OUT from his mansion on Rue Wagner, in Shanghai's French Concession, Du Yuesheng, immaculate in silk gown and mandarin jacket, paused to savour his crowning moment in life. The day was Tuesday, 9 June 1931 — an auspicious one, so the augur had said — and the splendours of an occasion unparalleled in the history of Shanghai were about to begin. Today the memorial temple he had erected to honour his ancestors would be dedicated in Pudong, his humble birthplace on the eastern banks of the Huangpu, Shanghai's famously muddy river. His fingers prickled to think there were crowds outside for whom he himself was the chief attraction, crowds gathering in Pudong, awaiting the moment when, the doors of the clan hall flung open, their eyes could peer into its depths and fall upon the slabs of polished Yunnan marble within.

Throughout May the gifts had poured in: scrolls and paintings, wreaths and bouquets, curios and silk banners embroidered with words of gold and, inevitably, those horizontal tablets with their high-sounding inscriptions, without which no grand Chinese occasion was complete. It pleased Du Yuesheng that the guest list included not only the top dogs of Shanghai's underworld, but also perfectly respectable businessmen and blue-blooded dignitaries from the highest circles. Most gratifying of all, he had been presented with a memorial tablet by Chiang Kaishek himself, with an inscription which said that his filial piety was nothing short of perfect — an observation not wholly accurate, but in tune with the hyperbolical requirements of the genre.

Walking out into the June brightness, Du Yuesheng exulted at the banners arising all over the road, sensed the masses staring at him, shifting and murmuring as he approached. The procession had assembled before daybreak outside his house, and now, on the dot of nine, it began to move. For two and a half hours the pageant rolled through Shanghai, slowly, in one tremendous noisy pulse, converging upon the Source of Golden Profit Quay, where launches awaited to ferry the party across to Pudong.

Was he overdoing it? Many citizens thought so. But for much of Shanghai it was the kind of showiness for which the city had always had a weakness, and even the coolie and the beggar were momentarily beguiled by the let-up in their grey reality. Thousands leaned out of windows; innumerable eyes watched. A cavalcade of British constables rode out, stiffly mounted on Arab horses; behind them a forest of banners emblazoned like heraldic shields with the Chinese character for 'Du'. Then came the Annamese policemen the French Concession's gendarmerie had provided, unmistakable in conical bamboo hats and riding four abreast on brightly polished bicycles. A Chinese Army band played; a regiment of infantrymen marched. The inscribed tablets presented by Chiang Kaishek and two other dignitaries were held aloft, each borne by a row of eight men. Then came more musicians and more displays of gifts, then decorative parasols, floats and guards. The pageant was two miles long, and when the front ranks reached the pier, a burst of firecrackers rang out.

Pudong ('east-of-the Pu'), being on the wrong side of the Huangpu River, was nothing but wharves and open fields, but when the procession landed, the bands playing all the while, it found the place gaily done up in gas lamps and bunting. Du Yuesheng was Pudong's best known and richest son, and to live up to this reputation and to the role, assumed by himself as assigned to him by others, of grand seigneur, he had donated to it its twenty-three stone bridges and the cost of completely facelifting the Temple to the Goddess of Mercy, now crumbling no longer in that corner of his own native village in Gaoqiao. With that thoughtful charity which the Chinese people, more ostentatiously and more unblushingly than any other, trail in the wake of their rapacities, Du Yuesheng would send over a thousand pairs of cotton padded tunics and trousers every winter, and nothing if not thorough, would even provide the coffin if, his largesse unavailing, any of his fellow Gaoqiao villagers should die.

Now the living were jamming the paths to the clan hall, craning their necks to see the celebrities arrive. Already the grounds of the clan hall were festive with marquees and pavilions, rigged up

Du Yuesheng as a young man

here for the serving of meals, there for the performances of opera. The most dazzling gifts were on display; the special counter set up by the Shanghai General Post Office was issuing guests with commemorative writing paper; the famous Hangzhou Restaurant in Shanghai, paid to close for three days so that it could move its entire kitchen to Gaoqiao, was emitting fragrances of wood smoke, spring onions, sesame oil and rice wine. Though there were 200 banqueting tables, each meal had to have several sittings, so unceasing was the flow of guests to the table. And it was later said by more than one Shanghai newspaper that over the three days of festivities no fewer than two thousand meals were served. Day and night the orchestras played. Beijing Opera stars sang, stomping and pattering across the stage, their feathery head-dresses quivering, their rich silks rustling, their fingers flexing, eloquent as eyes. It was all very noisy, just as it should be, the brassy din of gongs clashing with the shrill falsetto of the singers, the hubbub of the spectators rising and swelling against the music. Tea and wine cups flew. Then, the long awaited moment approaching, the audience's inattention turned to awe, for a split second letting in a hush; Mei Lanfang, that heavenly doyen of

Du Yuesheng (front row centre) and Mei Lanfang (on Du's left) and other actors, at a later celebration, probably in 1936

operatic female impersonators, that emperor of them all, swept onto the stage, and the whole place dissolved in adulation.

The memorial service itself was quiet and sombre, with Du Yuesheng going down on his knees before the family altar, flanked by his wife, his concubines and his sons. I am in the full, warm radiance of a summer's day, he thought as he knelt there, his head deeply bowed, my dream a living glory. How fortunate that we can make of our past what we will, and by the alchemy of our memory and the splendour of our means, turn squalor and degradation into gold. These my parents, base and unknown in life, are gilded and honoured in death. And I, Du Yuesheng — destitute orphan, village urchin, waterfront hood, secret society gangster, opium racketeer, underworld boss, enemy of Communism, confidant of Chiang Kaishek, pillar of respectable society — am now in the full prime of my life, my talents and efforts brought at last to this rainbow flowering.

Chapter Two

WATERFRONT URCHIN 1887–1908

UNTIL HE WAS TWO Du Yuesheng lived in the small township of Gaoqiao in Pudong, in a run-down mud house that his parents shared with his uncle. There were some two to three thousand households in Gaoqiao, and only two of these were well off, which by the standards of Pudong meant that they got by without too much of an uphill struggle. The rest were all peasants, artisans and paupers. As a matter of fact, beggars were a Pudong speciality. Periodically, whenever the population of beggars in Shanghai's white enclaves reached the point where it outran the tolerance of the foreign settlers, the police would round them up, herd them together, put them on the ferry, and have them dumped in Pudong. But no sooner had the miserable tramps saved up enough money for the boat fare than they were back on the other side again. This was a standard ritual until about the first decade of the twentieth century, when the arrival of the motor car and the opening up of roads further inland made it possible for the police to spread them out more evenly across the countryside.

Drifting with the tide of migration to the glittering metropolis, Du Yuesheng's father had washed up at Yangshupu, a suburb of Shanghai that was beginning to fill up with tenement workshops and musty rice-and-soya-sauce stores. With a couple of friends, the elder Du had opened a rice shop there. But business was none too good and back in Gaoqiao his wife had to take in washing to augment the family income.

The thing about being poor is that the violences of weather enter more implacably into your lives than they do those of the rich. Living as they did from day to day and from copper cash to copper cash, too much or too little rainfall could mean severe shortages of rice and cotton and therefore empty bellies, while too cold a winter could spell collective death. In the summer of 1889, when Du Yuesheng was two, it rained day after day for a whole month and a half, and the hot air as it blew through the sodden granaries and cotton warehouses reeked of damp and putrescence. The icehouses — barns of mud and straw where the ice collected from the ponds and creeks in winter was stored to be sold off in summer — lay empty, everything that was worth anything having been cleared out. Earlier there had been an epidemic; now the rice was rotting.

At any time in China there were people on the starvation line, and in hundreds of thousands the survivors would make for the cities with their bundles and wheelbarrows and their children on their backs. The same need now propelled Du Yuesheng's mother. Opposite, on the west bank of the river, lay Shanghai, fast getting into its stride as the country's greatest port. She had heard that the foreigners, who had wrung concessions there from the Chinese government after defeating it in the Opium War, had made things very nice there — lively, at any rate, and you could scratch a living, not like in Pudong, where there were only mosquitoes and grave mounds, and some paddy if you were lucky. But she'd also heard that it was every man for himself in Shanghai, and if you didn't make out you were in for it worse than in Pudong.

Well, her husband wasn't making out: she could see this the moment she arrived in Yangshupu and stepped into that dingy rice shop. Business couldn't be worse; no wonder he wasn't sending any money home. That night, after putting her son to bed, she went to sleep amid the debris of her hopes. Earlier in the day, trudging through the streets and jostling among the market stalls down by the waterfront, she had been utterly dazzled by Shanghai. Staring at the tall buildings, the mounds of vegetables and fish and the shop counters heaped high with silks and satins, it was as if the wonder of the world was spread out before her eyes, so palpable was the prosperity. Now her earlier enchantment mocked her, as her hopes lay in tatters. The next morning she got up early, dressed herself in clean clothes and applied to a factory for a job.

In the following summer she gave birth to a baby girl. Shanghai was in the throes of another epidemic and the heat as it throbbed in the air dictated swift burial of the corpses that the fever left in its wake. No one in the Du family was infected, but the mother as she lay in her bed wilted in the heat and felt too tired to live. Life slipped out of her hands and she did nothing to hold it. Her husband put her in a coffin of cheap wood and, lacking the money for a proper burial, lodged it in a temporary shelter not far from their old home in Gaoqiao. Motherless, the baby daughter was quietly given away. In its way this was perfectly sensible: her father could neither look after her nor keep her adequately in food and clothes; and anyway, people gave away their daughters every day in China. Years later Du Yuesheng was to spend a fortune trying to track her down, but the women he managed to dig up all turned out to be impostors and in the end he had to give up the idea of finding his lost sister.

The elder Du did not remarry, but took in a quiet and gentle woman to live with him. They made the best of things, not thinking beyond tomorrow, and were happy in their way. But the good times did not last and when Du Yuesheng turned five another bad year was upon them. There were months and months of summer and autumn drought and the winter when it finally came stunned them by its gripping cold. It was that winter that Du Yuesheng lost his father. Again there was not enough money to adorn the death properly, with catafalque and rites and professional mourners. Instead, the body was taken, nailed into a coffin of the roughest wood, back to Gaoqiao to await permanent committal, the widow stumbling along beside it, pale and crushed with helplessness and grief.

Back in Shanghai again, the rice shop faltered and finally closed down. There was nothing for it but to retreat to Gaoqiao once more, for at least there was a house of sorts there, and one or two relatives who might be touched for a copper in an emergency. So stepmother and child returned, and as the brute chill passed, life lost some of its wretchedness. Du Yuesheng attended the village school while his stepmother took in washing, but the money for his fees ran out before four months were up and he never saw the inside of a classroom again. In 1895 Shanghai was rocked by an earthquake and ravaged by cholera, and in the ensuing devastation and disorder Du Yuesheng's stepmother vanished — abducted, in all likelihood, and sold into slavery or prostitution by the organized desperadoes that lurked in the neighbourhood at that time.

So by the time he was nine, everything of decisive emotional significance in his life had happened to Du Yuesheng: the death of his mother and his father and, to all intents and purposes, that of his stepmother as well. Now he would have to live by his wits. He was already old for his age — the sort of boy who looked as if he'd lived out half his age by early adolescence. Each day became an occasion for toughening up. He drifted into delinquency under the influence of village bullies and layabouts, getting together with them in an old teahouse or in one of those wagering booths rigged up for the local gamesters. At thirteen and with very few coppers jingling in his pocket, Du Yuesheng could go in for only the most pitifully modest speculations, but the seeds of the vice were sown and the addiction was in the blood. At first stealthily, then blatantly, he flogged the family bedding and pawned the furniture to raise the money for his bets. Once, at a table of players twice his age, he staked his all for the miracle of a big win. Everyone was deeply impressed and he made his exit with a respectable profit and a new edge to his confidence. Among his cronies he began to enjoy a certain notoriety, and in the neighbourhood he became something of a heavyweight.

Yet it was not nearly enough. For all his strut and swagger, Du Yuesheng was shaken by the violent contradiction between dream and reality. As he prowled the country lanes of Pudong and saw the wheezing old men and women toiling in the fields in exactly the same back-breaking way as their fathers, and their fathers' fathers, had done before them, his imagination reached out to the infinite possibility of the city across the water. In Shanghai the riches and abundance of life are accruing to everyone else, he thought; I have to make them accrue to me.

To raise the money for the trip across the river he thought of selling his parents' part of the family shack. When he broached the subject with a relative and his uncle got to hear of it, the whole clan was strident with reproof. His uncle proceeded very loudly to recite his sins. Where was his filial piety? Shame on him, he disgraced the memory of his parents. He was a prodigal. Who did he think he was, selling his family home? The nerve of it.

The dressing-down made flight even more imperative. He thought at once of his maternal grandmother, whom he knew to be more indulgent and trusted to be more easily cajoled. And just as he had thought, she did not disappoint him. Wheedled into giving him a contact in Shanghai, she got a literate neighbour to write him a letter of introduction, addressed to a fruiterer on the Shanghai waterfront who might be able to take him on as an apprentice.

Assured at least of a place to head for, Du Yuesheng set out one clear morning in 1902, a change of clothes in his bundle and an expectant spring to his step. The old lady walked part of the way with him, saying little but weeping copiously. They parted at a distance of some three to four miles from Gaoqiao, when the grandmother's bound feet gave out and she could go no further. He broke into a run then, the raw air swishing past his face. He was determined to become — somebody. In the big city he would better himself, he was sure of it, and he would never come back to Pudong except as a very rich man. But then when he stopped to catch his breath the city seemed more remote than ever and the road went on and on.

SHANGHAI! To the gangling fifteen-year-old boy from Pudong it must have offered all that could be imagined of urban abundance, swarming and humming as befits a would-be world capital. Here was Shiliupu, clustering about the Chinese stretch of the waterfront to the south of the French Bund: a market of babbling confusion and plenty, where everything from paddy crabs to cabbage to tinware could be bought at a bargain price, if you could find your money before the pickpocket made off with it. Behind lay the Little East Gate, one of the seven gates piercing the rampart of the city walls that enclosed the dark crowded lanes of the old Chinese city. Amidst it all lay Hongyuansheng, the small but busy fruit shop that would give Du Yuesheng his first job.

To the north lay the French Bund — Quai de France to the French residents who, after the British had prised open the port to opium trade and Western settlement, had raised their flag on a corner of Shanghai too, just along the foreshore from the British zone. The Americans had driven their stakes into the scruffy northern purlieus, in the parts of town which the Chinese called Hongkou and Yangshupu, and from which would presently spring the workshops, cotton mills, electric power stations and wharves that would underlie Shanghai's industrial vigour. The Suzhou Creek, a tributary of the Huangpu and a landmark, waters their southern edges, sliding in-between the British and American concessions, and supporting flotillas of small craft.

The Americans were half-hearted about governing their concession though, and quickly plumped for a merger with the British. The International Settlement thus formed was run by the Municipal Council, a powerful assembly of *taipans* and nabobs, who set up their own police force and defence corps, and ruled the place as though it were an outpost of the British Empire. The French administered through their own municipal council, but the Chinese residents in the foreign enclaves, though they far outnumbered the whites, had no franchise in either. The French had a gendarmerie too, but neither it nor the British force made Shanghai any the less attractive to law-breakers. Shanghai was an outlaw's dream: a few miles could put him beyond the reach of one set of authorities and into the territory of another, with neither knowing or caring much about what had happened over the border.

None of this meant anything to Du Yuesheng at first, uninvolved as yet in the kind of activity into which such things would enter as part of his calculations. As a fruiterer's assistant it was all he could do to stay on his feet, for trade was brisk and the chores unending. For his board and lodging, and just enough money for the odd bath and haircut, he ran errands, emptied spittoons, washed out commodes, and did whatever a dogsbody was supposed to do. He grew adept at carrying baskets of fruit about, hung from the coolie's carrying pole in swinging loads, and as time went by graduated from the purely domestic side of the business to the commercial.

He was three to four years at the fruit shop, but it got him nowhere and he began to feel hemmed in. One day, when he was standing amidst a crowd watching a street juggler perform, a young man who had been a fellow apprentice at the fruiterer's came up to him. Du Yuesheng could tell by the way he dressed that this young man had done well for himself. In fact, since leaving Du's boss he'd opened his own fruit shop and wouldn't mind giving Du a job — one with board and lodging and pay. There was an instant comradeship between them and Du accepted at once. Soon he found himself comfortably settled in his new job; it was much less of a slog, friendlier and altogether more lucrative. And with more money now clinking in his pockets than he'd ever had before, Du Yuesheng could at last sample the many varieties of pleasure that were to be found in the back streets of Shanghai.

The city unveiled itself to him. The 'gateway to China', already on its way to becoming the 'paradise of adventurers' and the 'Paris of the Orient', Shanghai was the conduit through which the bulk of what went in and out of China was funnelled. What the Chinese knew of the West, they mostly knew through the medium of this port and its people, by whose nimble wits and extraordinary receptivity the ideas and techniques of the outside world were distributed across the rest of China. In the thick of the old walled city, it was still all dank dirt and squalor, but once you crossed over to the foreigner's domain, everything was richer, cleaner and smarter. Your eyes skimmed the solid wall of the great commercial houses along the esplanade — the Hongkong and Shanghai Bank, Jardine, Matheson and Company, the Oriental Bank, Russell and Company — and you knew you were in the presence of money, and of the merchant-adventurers who were making it.

Du Yuesheng was all alertness and, as the city unfolded itself to him at closer quarters, he registered the heady mixture: the well-heeled European in his Oldsmobile; the prosperous comprador in his teahouse; the vessels of the international shipping lines in the river mouth; the gracious villas and lawns set back from Bubbling Well Road; the silk shops and tailors clustering around Nanjing Road; the singsong houses on Fuzhou Road, inviting sensual spoliation by men who could pay, and the sailors lurking in the shadowed corners of Blood Alley, roaring drunk, and singing songs in languages Du didn't understand.

Among the social flotsam washed up onto these streets were pedlars, port coolies, costermongers, money-lenders, pimps, pickpockets, hustlers and down-and-outs from the country provinces come in search of pickings. The fringes of the underworld, where you developed sharp wits, a facility for fast reckoning, and an exquisite skill in the arts of cheating, extortion and sharping, became for the next few years Du Yuesheng's home and school. Shiliupu and the tangle of streets behind — the core of Shanghai harlotry and the stamping ground of punters — drew from him the rushing tides of youthful lust and the ancestral instinct for play. Sexual adventure was to alternate with gambling sprees.

Tawdry varieties of sex were easy to come by in Shanghai, a city that catered to all sexual tastes and every gradation of income. Du Yuesheng was unfussy in the one and limited in the other. Having inherited in full measure the immemorial desires of Chinese men — desires of an infinitely old culture which has explored every avenue of sensual delight and dreams no dreams of imperishable love because it knows only too well that such enchantment is transitory — Du Yuesheng sought merely ecstasy. Barred to him were the sumptuously high-class 'salons' at the top end of the scale — geisha houses where the courtesans were cultivated and the atmosphere was refined. The best of the coquettes in these establishments could sing and play musical instruments, and recite stories in the traditional manner from legend and history as well as any skilled artiste. A client paid through the nose just to hold parties there, but he'd have to be wildly free-spending to be allowed to establish his right to the favours of one of these women and to stay the night. They were known as Number Threes, these ladies at the summit of their profession, the numeral being a reference to the amount of silver dollars you paid to have a drink with them. They were almost all from Suzhou, that town further inland where the girls were porcelain of skin and sexy of voice, and where it was customary for men to be idle and for women to toil. Then there were the Two-Threes, on the next rung down, who gave you a drink for two silver dollars and the joys of their body for three. They were mostly home-grown, but even Shanghainese prostitutes liked to assume the Suzhou lilt to beguile their customers (who like all Chinese were intensely provenance-conscious) into thinking that they were getting the genuine article. It was not that the Suzhou whores were necessarily better at their job; it was just that this was the received opinion — that you had a headstart if you were known to hail from Suzhou. And really, there was no harm in a girl arrogating an extra allurement to herself in this highly competitive business, so long as her accent was good enough for her to pass it off.

'Flowers and fume', the whole lush scene was called: the flowers symbolizing the girls, all brightly in bloom for the plucking, and the fume suggesting the opium pipe, a standard fixture of the singsong house. Like tea and wine and melon seeds, opium was always part of the bill of fare. The reasoning behind this was simple: pleasure being the special province of the brothel, if the tastes of the customers should run to opium — as it did among the majority — then there was every incentive for the brothel to provide it.

For Du Yuesheng, all these pleasures still lay ahead. Of bejewelled singsong girls sped through the streets of Shanghai in their twinkling rickshaws (or, if they were pubescent, on the shoulders of their ponces), dashing from teahouse to party in their gold and silk, he had yet only the occasional ringside glimpse. They spelt the lustre of wealth and power in some distant realm of light and alabaster whiteness, infinitely inaccessible. Even the One-Twos, in their cramped quarters off Avenue Edouard VII, would have overstretched his resources if a bawdy-house keeper hadn't taken him under her wing, looked upon him as family, and given him the run of the house. If that hadn't happened, he would have had to make do with masculine resorts of two to three more shades of cheapness and squalor: the Cantonese Salt-water Sisters, seen down by the waterfront plucking at the sleeves of the foreign sailors who, because the girls could speak a little pidgin, were their particular speciality; the Wild Chicks who had been sold into prostitution because they were orphaned and destitute; and right at the bottom of the trade, the street-walkers from the 'naileries', the girls who could be had standing against a mouldy alley wall (or 'nailed' as the trade jargon would have it) for only thirty cents a go.

Those were wild days for Du Yuesheng, flesh assuaging a lingering restlessness and gambling answering a passion. He took to following a roving game operator around — a man who doubled pimping with sharping and was known in the neighbourhood as the Lot Drawer. In Shiliupu and the Little East Gate, the hubs of his regular beat, he was never seen without his basket of peanuts and jujubes and his worn cylinder of bamboo sticks. The comestibles were part of the payoff and the cylinder contained the game. The game was of two sorts: there was either the one where you were dealt a hand from a pack of thirty-two numbered tallies and you compared their face values with those of your opponents; or the other kind where the pack, numbering fifteen sticks each looped with a piece of coloured cotton at the hidden end, was divided by colour into sets of five, four, three, two and one, and the winner (who took the pot) was the player who had correctly guessed which colour would come up at the draw. The game was derived from the better known *huahui*, a variety of lottery with a thirty-six-to-one payoff that was all the rage in Shanghai and Canton. In *huahui* the tickets were the names of thirty-six well known figures, each accompanied by the animal symbolizing the year of his birth; playing was attended by a great deal of noise and flourish, each draw being announced by a report of fireworks and a hasty posting up of the lucky ticket — a magic name in large Chinese characters, boldly inscribed on a cotton sheet hoisted high above the gaming table.

By now Du Yuesheng's life had become a dizzying round of *huahui*, mahjong, craps and cards. The ancestral passion had seized him, and to those who watched him at play among the tables and upon the pavements, moving day and night from game to game, with that restless energy, that undivided lust, it seemed as if he was a man possessed. As indeed he was: whenever, among those eddying back streets, dice were cast or mahjong tiles clattered, there, as if he would never tire, would Du Yuesheng be. The fruit shop was forgotten; on the few occasions that he did manage to turn up for work, he was lazy and light-fingered. His boss was surprisingly forgiving, but Du begrudged every minute of the time he spent away from his gaming, and in the end stopped showing up for work altogether. He turned to nobbling as a means of making a living, becoming one of the 'boats', as these runners were called in the vernacular, that plied between the shops and the teahouses enticing people to drop stakes or lay bets. At the time he couldn't think of a job that suited him better, and only started to have second thoughts when his luck ran out and what he had collected in wins was returned with interest in losses. The only ones to profit in the end, he realized, were the operators who hired him, and when he lost even the money that other betters had deposited with him, and which he had blithely diverted to his own pocket, he decided that it was time to decamp. He lay low for a while, a wanted welsher. It was the year he turned twenty, a year that would become something of a milestone in his life. For in that year the Lot Drawer, who had taken the young Du on as his protégé, let him into the secrets of the Qing Bang, or the Green Gang. Lot Drawer was a member and Du would soon become one too. This was the critical turning point of his life: acceptance into the fold of that brotherhood formed the foundation of all his future action and launched him once and for all into his career.

Chapter Three

SECRET SOCIETIES AND OPIUM 1908–1915

BEYOND LITTLE EAST GATE, some distance from the centre of the city, there stood a small temple in whose inner shrine a line of spirit tablets was propped up, displaying the names of seventeen men. In black calligraphy against a yellow ground, the names were of men of a dynasty or two before, venerated patriarchs around whom the whole initiation rite would now revolve. Here, before the swirling fragrance of incense sticks and candle smoke, the novices of the Green Gang would take their vows, the fraternity's elders would recite their formulas, and the weight of a tradition rooted in centuries of Chinese cabalism would be brought to bear on all.

Outside the night was starless. A dozen figures could be seen hurrying towards the temple. They stopped before the gates in silence, as the Ushering Master stepped forward to announce them. An interchange in rapid Shanghainese dialect with someone from inside the temple followed, the answers, as if rehearsed, coming hard upon the questions. Then the doors creaked open and the light from inside fell upon the group on the steps, dark and ghostly in the still unrisen moon. Du Yuesheng — for he was one of the men in the company — entered, and as he did so his eyes fell upon the ten Masters now ranging themselves about the altar, with Lot Drawer, soon to be deferred to as the initiates' Old Man, taking the central place, and the nine Uncles disposing themselves on each side of him.

Now a basin of water was passed round, each of the dozen or so novices washing his hands in it — a symbolic purification before the rites to come. Then a sacramental vessel followed, and by turns the novices lapped from the libation, not allowing their lips to touch the rim. Ready, finally, for the devotions to the Green Gang's founding fathers, the Incense Master stepped forward, face towards the outer hall, and with a solemnity befitting the occasion invoked their blessings in a stanza of verse, binding the past to the present, the departed to the living. Then with a joss-stick in one hand and a candle in the other, he bowed three times before each spirit tablet, offering up the incense and candle at each obeisance.The other Masters waited in the wings, until, fifty-one kowtows later, it was their turn to kneel before the patriarchs. In a stream the Masters passed: the Sponsoring Master first, the Ushering Master next, then the Preaching Master — and so on until each had made his supplication before the altar. Now the candidates knelt down, but doing so in unison, and together they heard the drone of the Preaching Master's voice, intoning the names of the fraternity's three lodges and nine generations, and reciting its origins and elaborations. Then, still on their knees, the novices made their much-rehearsed pledge and, when the right moment came, proffered their written applications for membership, with the name of their sponsor as well as their own spelt out on one side, and the sixteen-character fraternal oath on the other:

Sprung from one ancestor,
Down the centuries was passed —
As eastward flows the river,
A pledge of no return.

At this point Lot Drawer, as the candidates' sponsor, began to instruct them in the history, catechism, symbolism, passwords, secret signs of recognition and codes of conduct of the Green Gang — information to be faultlessly learnt by the new recruits. 'Within the four seas, all men are brothers' — so an ancient sage had said. The Green Gang and the Red Gang, the Elders and Brothers Society, the Heaven and Earth League, the Triads, the Tongs: all had sprung from the same desperate tensions as had exploded in the popular uprisings of Chinese history, making brothers and comrades of men. The Qing Bang and the Hong Men — alias the Green Gang and the Red Gang, and both of them collaterals of the Elders and Brothers Society — had mingled into them those same elements of mutual help and protection, of opposition, subversion and crime as had been embedded in the Heaven and Earth League and its extensions, the Triads and the Tongs. Once they all had their own territory: while the Green Gang ranged through the rivers and lakes of the lower Yangtze basin and the area immediately below Shanghai, the Red Gang's ties were to provinces much further south. But in Shanghai the borders between the sects' urban offshoots were much less clear, though the Green Gang's supremacy was never in question.

How it all began, what the genealogies were, which rituals were authentic — no two accounts exactly agree. Tradition has it that the Green Gang started life as an organization of boatmen employed in the transportation through the Grand Canal of the grain levies exacted by the court in Beijing from the Yangtze basin. It was a rough business, prone to both internal strife and external mischief by brigands and robbers along the way. So when the three founding fathers proposed to the emperor the creation of a defence society that organized the boatmen gangs into provincial sub-units to escort the grain tributes to the capital, the court had thought it a good idea and agreed, not realizing that the bands thus formed would presently be drawn into the web of intrigue and revolution that would eventually threaten the throne itself. When the grain tribute system was abolished in 1901, and members of these bands found themselves out of a job, they turned to salt-smuggling, piracy and raiding, only occasionally throwing up a bandit-hero with the attributes of a Robin Hood.

This was the tradition into which Du Yuesheng would pass, and whose spirit he would come to embody. His domination of the Green Gang yet lay ahead. Now he was still being initiated into its rules and regulations, Lot Drawer sententiously reciting them. There were ten in all, two requiring deference to elders and two loyalty to the fraternity; one rule forbade the violation of women and another the oppression of the weak. There were strictures against robbery, mischief and law-breaking (regulations which in fact were honoured mostly in the breach). And it would be a member's end if he divulged gang secrets or sold out his brothers. The *bang* was all: your father and your mother; its friends your friends; its foes your foes; where the brotherhood led, there you would follow.

All Lot Drawer's words had already their dim counterpart in Du Yuesheng's mind. It is the secret-society man and not the law-abiding citizen who appreciates most deeply the inviolability of codes, because his punishment is swifter and more unremitting. It was, Du supposed, inevitable that he should become a secret-society man; he was a natural recruit, by instinct as by walk of life. His instinct was for the cabalistic, the scheming behind closed doors, for the swift and ruthless despatch. His walk of life bordered on what is known as the *jianghu*, a society of men that had coalesced over the generations around the vagabond: the itinerant professions, the roving entertainers, the wandering knight-errant of old even, who lived by their wits and took life as it came. Caring little for respectable society and still less for its laws, the *jianghu* yet had its own demanding code of honour. A sense of justice and solidarity was basic to it: this was *yiqi*, the old morality of chivalry, of standing up for the weak and sticking up for your friend, of never breaching a trust and always repaying a favour. All his life Du was to have pretensions to this kind of morality, seeing himself as being neither without conscience nor without principles. If he stood for the worst of the *jianghu* walk of life, by his own lights he also stood for the best.

While such thoughts drifted about his mind, something of a personal character was about to transact itself in the ceremony. He found himself being slotted into the gang's hierarchy and being given the name appropriate to it. There were twenty-four layers to the Green Gang, each designated by a character, just like the successive generations in a family. In the line of seniority Du was placed twenty-third, a 'generation' that carried with it the character *wu*, or 'awakening'—a name he would share from now on with all his fellow novices.

The rites were nearing their end; unlike those of the Red Gang they did not include grotesqueries like the severing of a cock's head, the pricking of fingers and the mingling of blood. Soon Du found himself stepping out of the temple into the streets once more, a fully-fledged member. He heard the doors being bolted behind him. The precincts were empty. Rounding a curve in the lane, he slowed down to a leisurely walk, and as he walked he smiled to himself, his excitement unmuffling itself into a sense of arrival, of kinship with some eternal brotherhood. There was, there continued to be, all the compelling romance of the secret-society tradition; the legendary force of its pantheons of heroes, its evocations of brotherly solidarity, of heroism, patriotism, and mystique were now all heightened by the experience just undergone, and no amount of reality would make them loosen their hold on his imagination. Du knew all the stories that underpinned the ethos. Because they are legendary, to the Chinese they have also always been real, and literal truth never comes into it. Popular literature — that most time-proof of preservatives — has embalmed the heroes. Just as Liu Bei, Guan Yu and Zhang Fei, those greatest of hero-warriors in the *Romance of the Three Kingdoms*, had met in a Peach Garden and enacted in symbolic sacrifice their oaths of blood brotherhood, so Du Yuesheng and his fellow recruits had solemnly united themselves in bonds of lasting fraternity. In the spirit of the occasion, were there not also reminders of the bandit-heroes of the *Water Margin*, sworn brothers in noble outlawry? (So readily did the image of the Chinese secret society evolve in these terms that even now the unobjectionable aspects of its character — the daring, the constantly reiterated pledges of mutual solidarity, the patriotism — tend to come to the forefront in the popular conception. For years afterwards, the *kungfu* movie was endlessly to exploit these classic motifs, and to make the Shaolin Monastery part of the permanent props.)

Shaolin, half-hidden among the trees in the Nine Mountains of Fujian Province, was the very heart of the martial arts tradition. It gave birth to the Heaven and Earth League, but it became something of a fetish among other secret societies too. In the tree-shaded seclusion of this mountain retreat, a group of extraordinary monks had perfected the study and practice of military tactics and defence, attended by the acolytes who had flocked to the monastery from all corners of the empire. It was during the reign of a Manchu emperor that the monks' talents were most dramatically tested. The empire was shaken by an insurrection of a tributary state, the emperor was helpless. To his rescue came the monks of the Shaolin Monastery, and in three months the rebels were quelled. The emperor wanted to deck them with honours, but declining these and other rewards the monks returned to the mountain retreat, only to be attacked by the emperor's forces, which set their lighted torches to the monastery, and burnt it to the ground. The gullible emperor, persuaded by scheming courtiers that the militarily gifted monks posed a threat to the throne, had evidently ordered the place to be annihilated. Only five monks survived, to provide the inspiration for the creation of the Heaven and Earth League. Claiming for itself a sense of justice higher than that of the State itself, the secret society deemed its purpose and destiny to be the toppling of the Manchu dynasty. This vocation, inherited by a spawn of secret societies, was to achieve its fulfilment in the revolution of 1911.

In about a decade from the time Du Yuesheng became a member of the Green Gang, both it and the Hong Men, or Red Gang, would degenerate in Shanghai into little more than an urban underworld, a Mafia of racketeers and kidnappers. By then the revolutionary streak in the secret society had begun to recede into history. But in 1908, the year Du joined, the revolutionist and Triad man were one. Away in Japan, the China Revival Society, a traditional secret society with republicanism as its platform, had been transformed into the Revolutionary Alliance, the precursor of the Chinese Nationalist Party, or Guomindang. At its helm was a Triad man — Dr Sun Yatsen. He had become a member in Canton, and had also, while in Honolulu, officiated in an overseas lodge there. Armed with a hopelessly idealistic vision of a republican China, backed by overseas Chinese money and unimpeded by what Lenin was to describe as his 'inimitable... virginal naivete', Dr Sun plotted to remove the Manchus from the dragon throne. And the secret societies were ready to help.

Meanwhile Shanghai was becoming quite a nerve centre of revolution, where it was accepted, by well-heeled businessmen and hot-headed students alike, that the hopelessly corrupt and impotent monarchy must go. The foreign concessions teemed with revolutionists, being more hospitable to plotting than any Chinese-run place. It was there, too, that the revolutionists could make good use of their connections to the Green and Red Gangs. When, on 10 October 1911, a successful uprising was staged in Wuhan, Shanghai very soon followed. In a matter of months China was relieved of the Manchu dynasty and turned from an empire into a republic. Shanghai, as soon as it fell to the republicans, was a tumult of white flags.

Among the revolutionists who had fought to secure the region for the republic was a twenty-four-year-old regimental commander called Chiang Kaishek. Chiang had been drawn into the cause while studying and finding his vocation as a soldier in Japan. Back in Shanghai, once the fighting was over and Dr Sun Yatsen's plans for ushering in democracy had gone awry, it would not be long (given his inclinations and given the ties between the revolution and the secret societies) before Chiang drifted into the circles of the Green Gang. Once in, it was inevitable that he should come across, and eventually be in association with, Du Yuesheng. But like Du, he first had to meet Inspector Huang Jinrong.

HUANG JINRONG EARNED his reputation not long after he started policing the French Concession. Of course his father had been a policeman before him and the old clout was still there, but Huang Jinrong was not merely his father's son and it wasn't long before people began to seek him out in his own right. He got used to those worried looks and fawning flatteries and, after the polite enquiries after health and kinsmen were out of the way, that inevitable appeal to his gifts as a fixer: 'Can you help us out of this sticky spot?'

There was a period of a few years when he quit the French gendarmerie and betook himself to Suzhou. That was after he had arrived at a party given by his French boss in a reddish-purple brocade robe, all new and classy, and had been ticked off by the police commissioner for dressing above his station. Such attire was too flashy for the likes of Chinese policemen, the Frenchman had implied, and Huang Jinrong had immediately lost his temper, banged his fist on the table, and stalked off, flinging his police officer's card in the Frenchman's face.

The card was Huang's badge of office — an odd office that combined the comprador, contractor and police investigator, and whose bearers, to use the Shanghainese term for them, might be called 'contract-detectives'. The existence of this class had something to do with the unique governance of Shanghai. Over in the International Settlement, an inner circle of mostly British businessmen was in command, calling itself the Municipal Council, declaring its neutrality with respect to China's rebellions and civil wars, and organizing its own militia and police force. The system, for all its lack of legal foundation, worked quite efficiently. The French in their concession insisted on going their own separate way, but the system they evolved proved to be not all that different. In 1900 they imported twenty-nine Annamese gendarmes from their other Asian territory, just as the British had brought over large numbers of Sikh policemen from theirs. But it soon occurred to them that some natives might profitably be brought into the higher ranks of the gendarmerie, since it became obvious that it took a Chinese to catch another Chinese. Though the French were prudently uninterested in Chinese political conspiracies and outlawry, so that their concession very rapidly became the favourite hideout of revolutionaries or fugitives from Chinese law (a condition aggravated by its proximity to the Chinese quarter), still they were often embarrassed by kidnappings and bomb discoveries. The Annamese gendarmes were good and hardworking to a man, but half the time they didn't know what was going on because, like their French masters, they did not speak the local language. Chinese ways were hideously complex — all those provincial rivalries and labyrinthine intrigues, those secret societies and indeterminate loyalties, all that obscurantism and subterfuge; one minute they seem full of perfect good sense, the next minute you wonder if the Chinese are mad. If in the European trading houses East-West relations were being so smoothly bridged by the Chinese comprador, why shouldn't somebody like that be employed in the gendarmerie too?

So ran French reasoning behind the contract-detective arrangements. And it was eminently sound: Shanghai's jumbled underworld was impenetrable to the foreigner. One reason the Chinese detective was so much more successful in getting his man was that he could tap a dense web of runners — small-time sleuths who haunted the teahouses and nosed out the suspects. The Shanghainese, who would never use a formal name if they could use a nickname, called these men the Three-Times-Bare Fellows, seeing that they had neither office, nor salaries, nor rations. Another ingredient of success was the Chinese ability, not merely to run with the hare and hunt with the hounds, but to do so on the basis of a perfect understanding between the two. This was largely a matter of having the right instincts, and of being Chinese: you didn't get a look in unless you spoke the same jargon. For form's sake you made a few arrests a month, but you knew better than to touch the big boys and you agreed on the scapegoat and the size of your rake-off beforehand. Neither of you went back on your word because that would go against the spirit of the *jianghu* way of doing things, the sense of justice and solidarity — *yiqi* — that was so central to the gangster's credo. For their part the French were quite happy to pretend not to notice — provided the level of crime stayed within tolerable limits, and provided they themselves were correspondingly enriched.

At the time Huang Jinrong joined the force there were some thirteen plainclothes Chinese detective inspectors to thirteen European ones, so the kickbacks and tea money amounted to quite a figure. Not that these men were more susceptible to corruption than any other, but those were hard-won seats of power they were sitting on, and they would be thought fools if they didn't exact the spoils — the rights even — that flowed from them. They were only conforming to type, after all: the Chinese have always looked on officialdom as a nest of corruption, and if you said you were an official, they take this to mean you were a grafter, willy-nilly. The city was a free-for-all; if you didn't play the game either somebody else would or else the whole system would collapse.

It was some years after Huang Jinrong had left the gendarmerie in a huff, and gone to live in Suzhou, that what he knew was bound to happen did: he was sent for. Emissaries from the French in Shanghai came, asking if he would go back and help them on a couple of hideously intractable cases. It was too embarrassing, their inability to crack them. At once Huang pounced on the fact of his indispensability and laid down his conditions. The French demurred, but only momentarily. With accustomed ease they agreed to Huang Jinrong's demand for a permit to open a theatre in the French Concession, admitting privately that he did indeed need the proceeds to pay for all his runners, those ears and eyes on which so much depended. He had horse sense, connections and discretion, and the French knew that such a man was not to be had for whistling.

Huang Jinrong, back in Shanghai, cast about for a place to live.

He found a row of houses in a lane off Boulevard des deux Républiques and snapped them all up, he and his wife making their home in one and letting all the others. For he was now married, to a woman he had met in Suzhou, and whom he had rather effortlessly detached from her previous husband. She was more clever than pretty, but she had a way with people.

The life led by the couple was a far cry from what one would expect of a police officer and his wife. He rose at ten, breakfasted, and after a leisurely toilet, sauntered over to the Treasure Teahouse on Rue du Consulat, where he took his usual seat, sipped tea, and in the course of the morning allowed himself to be besieged by callers, runners, supplicants, theatrical people, demi-mondaines, and finks. Information and intelligence darted from runner to listener, and any bystander could see, from the way Huang Jinrong set his people to work, that it was not for nothing that the Treasure Teahouse acquired its reputation for being the place where the best runners cut their teeth. When not at the teahouse, Huang spent the afternoons playing his favourite card game, hovered over by refreshment-bearing servants.

The story of Du Yuesheng's fateful encounter with Inspector Huang is now a matter of Shanghai lore. The crucial introduction was made, it seems, by one of the Uncles of the Green Gang. For only by belonging to that fraternity, at once so ramifying in its connections, and so closely knit in its internal relations, could such a thing have been accomplished. Du had been scraping along, intermittently getting into a hole and being helped out of it by a fellow Green Gang member. He was not, obviously, doing too well for himself. He had no fancy for regular work, but when the Uncle had suggested applying to Huang Jinrong, he had whipped up quite an enthusiasm, for he had heard of the detective inspector, and thought that he'd be on to a good thing if he got taken on by his entourage.

On the day of the interview Uncle led the way, Du following with his belongings, a quilt, a change of clothes, a face flannel. Across Rue du Consulat, into Tongfu Lane, past a group of men in black Canton gauze suits, Du walked in something of a daze. So many people milling about the house, he thought, and wondered who those unsmiling fellows in black were, sitting stiffly in a row before the gates.

'Bodyguards,' Uncle hissed, guessing what was on his mind. 'You should see the way they jump to when the Boss appears at the door; they go everywhere with him.'

The room they entered was quite typical of Shanghai — an uneasy mixture of Chinese and European furnishing. Persian pile and Hunan lace doilies, soft European sofas and unyielding Chinese chairs, oil paintings and silk scrolls, sandalwood and mahogany — it was a room, obviously, that was meant to display wealth, if of a rather tasteless kind. The Boss, sitting at his table, swung round at their approach. He was a squat man, thick-set, and pockmarked in the cheek; his very wide mouth was set in an angular jaw, the lips fleshy. Du Yuesheng thought the whole looked a good deal less unprepossessing than the parts, for he had an unintimidating manner, and was expensively attired. Du grinned at Huang Jinrong and felt, as it often happened to him with strangers, immediate sympathy.

Huang was disarmed. He looked at the young man before him and took in the ill-fitting robe, the lean shoulders and their loose-limbed swing, the face with the faintly simian strain, the unglazed eyes and the startlingly protuberant ears. The fellow is obviously not athletic, he thought, but the physical meagreness was carried in a way that did not suggest mental insufficiency. There was nothing in the fellow's manner he could take exception to, and much in his speech he could find pleasing. He could use a man like that; let him move in, run errands, make himself useful around the house. It was settled; he would move in straightaway; sleep in a room behind the kitchen; become a member of the huge Huang *ménage*.

For Du the next few months were learning days. He observed; he picked up things; he drank it all in; things fell into place. Indeed, almost the first thing that clicked into place was what lay behind the style in which the Huang household lived. He had been trying to work it out, to grope for the final piece in the jigsaw; and now, all of a sudden, it became crystal clear to him. The thing that made it possible for thousands of dollars to change hands at the card tables, for the place to swarm with servants, orderlies and bodyguards, for huge sums of money to be distributed to outstretched hands at regular intervals; the thing which lent the house its shuttered atmosphere, that gave the traffic through its kitchen and backdoor its surprising density, was opium. Du Yuesheng, when he realized this, was seized immediately by a passionate interest.

Opium, that infamous export of British India, was now a staple of Shanghai trade. Not legally, of course, though no one took much notice of niceties like that. It was a complex business, involving regional groupings, secret societies, colossal stakes, and hideous clashes of interest. The pioneer traders in 'earth', as the drug was called in China, were not Shanghainese at all; for well over half a century the trade had been dominated by men from Chaozhou, a place in the far south. Indeed, Shanghai's very first opium retail company, the Hongtai Opium Shop, was a Chaozhou enterprise. This was one strand to the tangled character of the opium business. Another was the secret society connection. The Triads came into the picture in 1853, when Shanghai was besieged by the rebel troops of the Small Swords Society, a Triad offshoot led by an undersized but warlike ex-sugar-broker from Canton. It seems that this man was the head of the Cantonese lodge of the Triads in Shanghai, and an opium smuggler. Shanghai managed to rescue itself in the nick of time from the Small Swords Society insurgents, but it became stuck ever after with a Cantonese-Triad opium racket.

The Huangpu used to bob with opium-carrying vessels — vessels belonging to trading houses like Jardine, Matheson — openly shipping the drug in from India. But then, under international pressure, the British government undertook to reduce the amount of opium exported from India if China concurrently reduced her own domestic production, signing an agreement in 1911 to refrain from importing the drug into a Chinese province that had been declared 'clean' of local poppy. Two places stood outside these restrictions, however, and these were to stay open to opium imports until such time as all cultivation in China had ceased. These two places were Canton and Shanghai; especially Shanghai, opium emporium of China, where the demand for Indian opium, so much stronger, so much more smokable than the native variety (which tended to be an adulteration, of opium dross, pork rinds, dried pig's blood and sesame seed cake), remained unabated. Even after the drug was made illegal by international treaty, the opium run thrived, the smokers relaxed, and in divans all over Shanghai the customers cleaved to their pipes.

But the trade was not without an element of volatility, as Du Yuesheng was quickly to learn. It was a no-holds-barred business: as far as the people engaged in it were concerned, any consignment of opium, no matter who had brought it in in the first place, was fair game, open to being pounced upon and hijacked at any point in its transit from ship to store. Even as the vessel steamed up the river, someone would be waiting in the wings to divest her of her precious cargo. If, to avoid inspection by coast guards further up the Huangpu River, she unloaded her cargo before coming into dock, lowering the oilskin sacks of opium into the water at high tide at night, sampans would be waiting to whisk them away the minute the tide receded, fishing the bobbing bales out with long bamboo poles — a method known in the trade as 'hooking it'. Boulevard des deux Républiques, between the French Concession and the Chinese city, was another vulnerable point. Here were the opium warehouses, and here, where the consignments were divided up and separately shipped out in kerosene drums, hijackers in horse-drawn carriages would lie in ambush. Their particular implement was an empty wooden crate. No sooner had the kerosene drums left the warehouse than they would be clamping these boxes over them, pitching them onto their carriages, and making off with them at top speed. In bandit jargon this tactic was known as 'capping it'. Yet another style of robbery, called 'bagging it' by those who practised it, simply involved darting out when a likely consignment came past, grabbing it and scooting away at breakneck speed down some narrow alley.

Du Yuesheng had realized for some time now that Mrs Huang, the Boss Lady, disposed of a little army of such bandits. Of course her husband was in it as thick as she was, but being the law he had appearances to keep up, whereas she didn't. Du thought he could be useful to her. Already his stock was high; she glimpsed in him a social acuity and a flinty intelligence that matched, or even surpassed, her own. Cultivating her, he had made himself useful in a hundred little thoughtful ways, collecting the interest for her, for example, from the loans she was making out of her housekeeping money behind her husband's back, and not squealing. In a subtle, unspoken way, he was becoming her collaborator and friend. Between them an understanding ran, a tacit agreement that Huang Jinrong needn't know, that it was no more than what all wives did, no matter how devoted they were to their husbands, in an age and country where men were compulsive philanderers, and a woman's security in the home was never unshakeable.

He was to impress her even more. Late one evening, when Inspector Huang was out, one of his men rushed in to report, in a state of considerable agitation, that a consignment of 'earth' had gone astray: he scarcely knew what had happened; the footpad entrusted with bringing it back to the house had simply made off with it in a rickshaw; what a catastrophe, when none of the other footpads were home to give chase. Du Yuesheng, listening to all this by the Boss Lady's side, snapped to attention. Ordinarily, what he was now about to suggest just wouldn't get a hearing: he was untried, and uninvolved actively in the household's business operations. But today there was simply nobody else about. He turned to Mrs Huang, who was more flustered than he had ever seen her, and asked if he might go after the thief. She nodded, after the briefest pause, and asked if she should get anybody to help him.

The answer was a succinct 'No.'

Grabbing a rickshaw, Du Yuesheng set out. It was a night for speed. Signalling the cabbie to hurry, he trained his mind on his mission. Where could the thief have gone? Nowhere in the French Concession, that's for sure, not if you wanted to get out of Huang Jinrong's way. Nor in the Chinese walled city, since the gates would be closing about now. In a flash, Du Yuesheng decided it could only be the International Settlement, lying just across the Yangjingbang, the creek which the French and British enclaves shared.

'Yangjingbang, hurry!' he rapped out, jerking his pistol to the ready. It was none too soon, for as the smelly old creek came into sight Du suddenly spotted his quarry racing towards the safety of the International Settlement ahead. Swiftly he gained on it, and above the thud and clatter of the two speeding rickshaws, he shouted at the other cabbie.

'I'll give you two dollars to turn round and take this passenger to Tongfu Lane! Tongfu Lane, you hear? Don't worry, this has got nothing to do with you.'

The cabbie gaped, then swung round. The thief, a beast at bay, fell to spluttering pleas for his life above the din. Past Rue du Consulat, down a dark alley, into another, and up again into a boulevard the rickshaws jogged. Even before they reached the house a door was flung open and part of Tongfu Lane was flooded in light. Du Yuesheng entered in triumph, mustering the reclaimed opium and penitent hijacker, and delivering the whole to a pleased and impressed Mrs Huang.

For his dashing exploit Du Yuesheng was rewarded, the charmed Mrs Huang urging her not-unwilling husband to bestow upon him a cut in the protection of Gongxing Ji, the Collective Prosperity Club, one of the three largest gambling establishments in the French Concession. But that was only the beginning. One day, Mrs Huang suggested to her husband, 'I think we should make over the whole of Gongxing Ji's protection to Yuesheng; he should have more going for him.'

'That's a big job. Are you sure he can manage?' Inspector Huang was thinking of the host of levers Du would have to grease, the sea of extortionists, hoodlums, touts and loafers he would have to keep at bay.

'Quality talks,' she said. 'Why don't you try him out and see?' And she gave him a look that indicated she knew just what he would see.

The gambling business, itself illegal, was one of the worst sufferers from the ruffianism that clung about such trades. The *habitué*, if he was not careful, was apt to find himself set upon and pillaged by the street thieves who skulked about the casinos, waiting to ambush the first customer that came along. Among locally notorious hazards, 'pig skinning' — the wholesale fleecing, including the disrobing, of a solitary passerby — was what the returning gambler, his winnings perhaps still a new sensation in his pocket, laid himself open to with particular vulnerability.

This was bad for the casino business, and now that Du Yuesheng was the 'protector' in charge, it was up to him to do something about it. What he came up with was that pragmatic solution that would ever be his response to difficult situations — a deal. It sliced right through the many-layered underworld like a knife through bean curd. He sought out the leader of each of the criminal bands that preyed upon the casinos and made him an offer, for his agreement to lay off, of a monthly percentage of the protection. Soon everyone was on his payroll and the precincts of Huang Jinrong's three casinos were the safest places in town.

Du turned next to the other thorn in the casino operator's side: the inconvenient raids by the French police. The risk of being busted dampened business like nothing else, for it subjected the patron to the double humiliation of arrest and public exposure, the latter experience specially galling to the face-conscious Shanghainese, involving as it did a march through the streets with all the culprits herded together by rope. The predicament had all the helplessness of *dazha xie*, those famous freshwater crabs that every gourmet knows (and for which, indeed, the plight was named in the jargon), sold invariably live, the legs and claws, but for the reeds that bind them, flailing.

The first thing he must do, Du saw clearly, was to persuade the police to be more predictable in the timing of their visits. Of course the raid squad had to do their job, to publicize, by body count, the arrests they were making and the success they were having. Since the quantity of arrests made mattered more than the quality, Du Yuesheng figured he could get the police to agree to a scheme whereby both their public image would be upheld and the whimsicality of their timing lessened. Bribes paving the way, the deal was swung. From then on the gendarmes raided the casinos only during the morning sessions. The clientele on these occasions, it was soon discovered, was less squeamish about being busted than the earlier ones. Why was this so? The answer could be sought in these customers' manner and gait, which had to their swagger and coarseness a distinct touch of the thug. And thugs they indeed were; the very ones, in fact, that Du Yuesheng had winkled out of their lurking places by the casinos and coaxed into good behaviour.

In other parts of the world such methods might not have worked, but here in Shanghai they were almost foolproof. For here the politics of the underworld, for all Shanghai's facade of urban modernity, was still largely feudal, turning on the relations of the power brokers and their respective capacity to mobilize their followers, to make alliances and to give patronage. The eye of the authorities did not penetrate too deeply into the undergrowth of the city, and like the weakly controlled, brigand-infested interstices of a peasant society, the streets of Shanghai left plenty of room for banditry to flourish. For this in essence was what criminal activity here was — its reach local, its perpetrators little more than 'bare sticks' or village toughs, its pecking-order elaborate, its obligations binding, its leaders kings.

Accordingly, the methods Du Yuesheng used were instinctive and conventional: instinctive in the sense of a natural intuition, an unconscious skill; conventional in so far as there was always something traditional to the process, something inherited from Chinese experience that gave to his negotiations with his opposite number a tacit common ground, an understanding that whatever might be the differences that divided them, each was still 'one of us' more than he was 'one of them', that there was more to be gained from a private arrangement between individuals than from an appeal to public arbitration. Already, as he went from transaction to transaction, the hallmarks of his later style were beginning to be discernible: he never fumbled; he never bungled; there was nothing niggling either to his thinking or to his action. 'Whatever you do,' his style seemed to suggest, 'you must do the thing handsomely.' Above all he was a man of his word; this was to become the cornerstone of his reputation, that he lived up to everything that he promised, whatever the cost and however seemingly insurmountable the odds — that his word, in short, was his bond.

Chapter Four

GANGLAND AND WARLORDS 1915–1927

GAIETY AND NOISE possessed Tongfu Lane one morning in 1915. A red and gilded sedan chair, the dragon- and phoenix-adorned kind hired for such occasions, brought a bride to Du Yuesheng. Curtained off by the bridal veil, the young lady's high, powdered cheekbones and generous mouth did not show, nor the high and square forehead which, for beauty's sake, she had painfully scraped to a hairless smoothness, interrupted by the long arc of her eyebrows. All these, unveiled, would have been a revelation to the groom had he been from a good family and had had his marriage arranged for him, for he would then not have ever seen the bride before she came to him on the day of the wedding in her sedan chair. But as it happened Du Yuesheng knew this lady, and had indeed chosen her himself.

Sadly she was barren, and they had to adopt a boy. She then languished, Du Yuesheng being often in the bed of another. In the stillness of her room, she pursued the torpor of opium dreams, day by day sinking into deeper and deeper habituation, suffering the vacuity known to many married women of her time. She seldom left her room, so that her spectral face, already white, blanched further in its withdrawal from light, and the only embers of life about her were her dark staring eyes, and the knob of heavy-scented narcotic glowing in her chased silver pipe.

When a man advances in the world, his sexual frontiers are not normally allowed to lag behind. There was never a shortage of trembling virgins thrust forward by the sycophancy of friends for his delectation. Not long after the adoption of his son Du Yuesheng took two concubines, the gifts of friends, one at each end of the year. They were both from Suzhou, that fount of singsong girls and nubile beauty, and they were both aged fifteen, for Chinese men look for beauty only in nymphets. To the gangster whom opportunity had catapulted from obscurity to opulence, women represented the spoils of victory quite as much as money and influence. The second of the concubines was to stay with him all his life, but with the first things had never come right. She was as accustomed as any Chinese girl to the idea of a loveless marriage, but the morning after her wedding she awoke in astonishment: the height of intimacy — the sleeping body in her bed — she looked at with complete detachment.

The three wives were installed one on each floor in a large villa on Rue Wagner. Inside the house servants and minions thronged; outside a fleet of cars awaited. Between them the three ladies had six sons but no daughters. When the boys were old enough Du hired White Russian bodyguards for them all. He himself was surrounded by four: an ex-gardener; an English-speaking ex-waiter at the Shanghai Club; a one-time chauffeur at the American Consulate, after whose Stars and Stripes (or Flowery Flag to the Shanghainese) the man was nicknamed; and a hot-headed blacksmith aptly dubbed Fiery Old Crow. These four toughs went everywhere with him, and could be seen each midday hovering about the teahouse and the steam baths, where beverage and vapour daily lubricated their boss's gut, skin and business dealings.

The business was going very well indeed, but only after Du Yuesheng had put paid to some competition from the International Settlement. Before that time there was mayhem among the opium hijackers, for a new protection racket calling itself the Great Eight-Legged Band had started up and cast a pall upon the business. Headed by a bent policeman, it had bought over the Municipal Police, the anti-smuggling squad and the coast guards, and had gone round the harassed opium enterprises offering to act as their protectors. 'Hijacking's finished,' observed Du Yuesheng to Mrs Huang, 'unless we wage a guerrilla war of the streets.'

And so it came about that the Little Eight-Legged Band was formed. For an army this was small, but it had Du's four bodyguards in its ranks and Du's professionalism in its organization. It had the finest street sense of any gang in Shanghai, and its instincts were uncanny: it could read an alley in a second, and never went down one without knowing right away if it was going to be ambushed. Its timing was superb and its elusiveness unsurpassed. Its transit of the Settlement gen-

Two of the Three Kingpins of Shanghai:
Zhang Xiaolin (centre) and Du Yuesheng (right)

erally included a detour through the funeral parlour of the Chaozhou Guild, one of those mutual aid societies that sojourners from the provinces could never do without in Shanghai. This was to throw off scent and temporarily to cache its plunder. It would not occur to anyone to look into the unoccupied coffins, and so it was without anybody knowing how that Mrs Huang regularly renewed her stocks.

For Du Yuesheng it had all come to pass — money, gangland reputation, unchallenged supremacy. But he was determined to carry it further. To his aid came the man that would become his third partner. This was Zhang Xiaolin, together with whom Du Yuesheng and Huang Jinrong would come to be known as the Three Kingpins of Shanghai. It was hard to say whether Zhang ever worked for a living. He did have a go as a textile worker in his native town of Hangzhou, but he was not accustomed to being ordered about or to a regular job, and most people believed he was better suited to be a huckster. He could always use some easy money and it was not long before he and Du talked business. He had two qualities that the syndicate urgently needed: he could speak the Northern dialect, albeit interspersed with many a universal obscenity, and he had some fringe warlord connections. Du knew that he stood to make more money if he cut in the satraps who were ruling the roost in Shanghai. For such an extension of empire he needed a right-hand man like Zhang, who could chum around and talk to these people in their own dialect.

Du Yuesheng knew these warlords for what they were: men who coveted their neighbours' goods even when they had quite enough of their own. As he had to keep up with whatever the action happened to be, Du had to keep company with these people. It was like that in the years that followed the overthrow of the empire, all grab and self-interest. Those warlords were perhaps inevitable to that time of disintegration. The Republic which Sun Yatsen had dreamed of had become a mockery, a sport of the military, the game of whichever military commander had won the last round of the civil war. Evanescent cabinet had succeeded evanescent cabinet. One faction had conspired against another. The south had fought against the north. A monarchist movement had absurdly tried to put an emperor back on the throne again. The predatory Western powers had been tendering loans in expectation of plunder. There was Dr Sun establishing himself and his Republican Party in the south, in Canton, but for all his declaration of independence from the government in Beijing he remained a fief of the local satrap all the same. The republican cause had become hazy, and Sun was at a loss as to how he could unify the country, to ride the tricky undercurrents of party squabbling and treachery and to recycle the revolution on a new lease of life.

It was a pity one could not have a better class of people taking over from the Manchu dynasty, but being Chinese the populace got on with living and sat out the political disunity. Theirs is a sense of racial oneness, a powerful sentiment of linguistic and cultural unity which they, not demanding logic of themselves the way the white race does, combine effortlessly with a sense of regional otherness, a mixture obviating the political necessity of a nation.

As for Du, he didn't mind doing business with these warlords so long as everybody made out on the deal. They loved coming to Shanghai and foraging through the neon attractions of Frenchtown and beyond, and Du Yuesheng was always around to give them a good time. For them he booked up the high-priced Number Threes four or five at a time, for he knew that this impressed them and was their idea of class. One place he took them to was the Maison of Lush Spring, his favourite singsong girl's salon on Swatow Road, using that house of joy like it was some chamber of commerce to welcome these provincial satraps to town.

It was where he took the notorious warlord of Shandong, deeming it wise to soften this quintessential bandit when he swept into town with his rampaging soldiers at the start of 1925. The man was the one they called the Three Imponderables, after the three unknown quantities in his possession: the amount of money he had, the number of soldiers he commanded, and the number of concubines he kept (one estimate put the last figure at 42, half of whom were said to be White Russians). People also said of him that he was elephantine of build, pig-like of brain, and tigerish of temperament, and he was said to have a sorceress for a mother.

The evening which Du Yuesheng planned was exactly to this warlord's taste. At dinner the girls were all in attendance, one girl going with each course. Du Yuesheng's own favourite came with the chef's *pièce de résistance*, the last but one course. Enter the lady, lustrous as the wings of some splendid exotic imago, the hair sleekly drawn back from the white forehead to gather in a chignon at the neck; and the face itself, all smiles and highlights, was bright with the spontaneity bred of studied art. The Shandong warlord blinked. Seated by his side, she leaned forward from her chair, to confide her message urgently, to press its sweetness into the ductile channels of his hairy ear — the language conventional, even mechanical, the words so consecrated by custom that they could no longer be called calculated and seemed to have been known to women for all eternity. And later, when the banquet had ended and the mahjong tiles were cleared away, it was this sense of participating in some immemorial ritual that benumbed the whore to the horror of the scene of spoliation which he in drunken lurches wreaked upon her.

ONE JULY MORNING in 1921 a twenty-eight-year-old schoolteacher from Hunan Province was walking under the intermittent shade of plane trees down a street not far from where Du Yuesheng lived. At 106 Rue Wantz he paused, then slipped in quickly through the carved portals. Inside, the heat of the summer sun ebbed a little, though the walking man was physically quite unconcerned.

There were perhaps a dozen men in the room. One was a fellow Hunanese, but would not otherwise have been particularly noticeable. Two were not Chinese: a representative of the Trade Unions International named M. Nikolsky, and another Soviet agent called Hendricus Sneevliet, a Dutch Communist assuming the pseudonym G. Maring. The gathering was clandestine, and none of those present was to remember the details very well. But the twenty-eight-year-old delegate, and the resolves he took home with him to Hunan, were presently to change the world.

The man was Mao Zedong, and the meeting was the opening congress of the Chinese Communist Party. Five of the men at the meeting were to lay down their lives for the Party; the fellow Hunanese, Zhou Fohai, was to turn traitor.

Being a man of Hunanese blood, Zhou Fohai was emotional and changeable in a way which Mao untypically was not. Zhou had come to the meeting as the representative of the Chinese students in Japan, where he himself was at university, and to which he would return for another three years after the meeting. You could see why the Japanese called him Buddha; for, minus the horn-rimmed glasses, his face had about its broad, clear forehead, its faintly aquiline nose, and its round cheeks and chin a touch of that sacred figure as executed in religious art. It was perhaps also his name, the characters of which, *fo hai*, spelt Buddhist Sea. Mao Zedong's name, which means something like East of the Pond, has the same watery element if not the grandeur. Seeing the two men together, that day in 1925, you would have said that Zhou would go further, seeming to be the more hurried. In all his life Mao was only impatient of the one discrepancy, between man as he was and man as he might be.

The meeting went on for four days, the delegates putting up at Bo Wen Girls' School, at nearby Rue Auguste Boppe. They had the place to themselves, the girls being on holiday, and their meals were cooked for them by the school janitor. All might have proceeded smoothly if the suspicions of the French gendarmerie had not been aroused, but on the fourth day a strange man appeared at the house asking for an address that was in fact a few doors down the road. The delegates believed him to be a spy, and decamped only just in time to escape a raid by the police. They repaired to a lake some eighty miles to the south of Shanghai, and finished off their meeting amid the floriate fretwork of a hired pleasure boat.

'The salvoes of the October Revolution,' Mao would write, 'brought us Marxism and Leninism.' Not unnaturally, the Russians wanted to keep an eye on what the Chinese did with these faiths. A search for an ally to give the fledgeling Communist Party some solidity came along with this; by itself it could hardly engage in national revolution, or drive out the foreign imperialists. The Kremlin did not rule out the possibility of an alliance with some strong and amenable warlord, but for a bedfellow Maring preferred the Guomindang. Leaving Shanghai after the congress, he travelled south to have a talk with Sun Yatsen. The year before, a Comintern emissary, who had come to China to work for the establishment of the Communist Party, had had an interview with the Guomindang leader, upon whose 'modesty and cleanliness of attire' he had seen fit to remark in an article he wrote for *Pravda*. Maring thought that Sun Yatsen was probably their man.

He did not find him an immediately willing instrument. It took some time to convince him that an alliance between the Guomindang and the Communists was his best hope of achieving national unity. In the end Sun Yatsen did plump for the Soviet plan, perhaps because he despaired of winning the support of the Western powers, who were partial to warlords and forever snubbing him. What he didn't know was that the real intention of the Soviet overtures was to use the Guomindang, as Joseph Stalin was to put it, like a lemon: to squeeze it until dry and then discard it. Not for a moment did the Moscow Bolsheviks envisage the Guomindang absorbing (as Sun Yatsen hoped) the Communist Party; quite the contrary, in fact: they saw the Guomindang as the proper arena for the pursuit of their anti-imperialist mission, and its infiltration by the Chinese Communist Party as the means whereby it might be transformed into the Russian image.

Thus it was that before very long Soviet arms were streaming through the harbour of Canton. Some ten miles to the south, on the site of an old fort by the banks of the Whampoa River, a rough copy of the Red Command school that Leon Trotsky, as the Soviet commissar for war, had forged for training officers for the Red Army, was raised on Chinese soil, producing the famous Whampoa Military Academy. The Guomindang itself took on deeper shades of Leninist anti-imperialism under Russian tutelage. The Communist Party, induced by its Russian mentors to ally itself with Sun Yatsen, became in practice the leftwing appendage of the Guomindang. In the autumn of 1923, a delegate of the Soviet Communist Party's Politbureau, Mikhail Borodin, came to take up his post as political adviser to Sun Yatsen. In that same year Sun sent a thirty-six-year-old clerk with the Shanghai Stock Exchange to Moscow for a six-month course of indoctrination in military techniques. The following year that young man, imbued by the experience with a lasting antipathy towards the Russians and their suffocating Communist faiths, took up his appointment as commandant of the Whampoa Military Academy.

The man was Chiang Kaishek, and the officers he bound to himself by the Whampoa *esprit de corps* were to form the as yet gestating Chinese leadership's most influential cabal. Some years earlier he had been studying to be a soldier in Japan, but in the first years of the Republic he was a nonentity kicking his heels in Shanghai. If his career at the Stock Exchange there was significant, it was so in terms of the opportunity it gave him to meet the right people. It is common knowledge that at about this time he drifted into the circles of the Green Gang, and that Inspector Huang Jinrong took him under his wing. Though the inspector was not then a card-carrying member of the Green Gang — it would not square with his job as police chief — he took on protégés and accorded patronage as though he were. In Shanghai Chiang also learned to enjoy the company of women — Japan had failed him there. Those salad days would someday be slurred over by his official biographers, but Shanghai provided him

Wang Jingwei, 1912

with one of his two launching pads: his underworld ties, coupled with the Whampoa loyalties, would stand him in very good stead in his later career.

Sun Yatsen was now trying to revive his faded dream of national revolution and unification, his party having been invigorated and his army remodelled along Russian lines. In November 1924 he set out on a leisurely journey by sea to Beijing, there to negotiate a conclusion to the quarrels with the warlords. But by the time he reached his destination, on December 31, he was already gravely ill. At the Union Medical College he learnt that he was dying of cancer of the liver.

Dr Sun's closest disciple at the time was, and had been for a long time, a fellow Cantonese called Wang Jingwei. When, on his deathbed, Dr Sun expressed his last thoughts and wish, that his comrades complete the revolutionary journey he had begun, it was to Wang that he confided them. Wang Jingwei wrote down the words of the last testament as they were dictated to him by the dying man. He had to hold back his grief when he saw, each time he raised his eyes from the paper, the slight head sunk, foreshortened in the pillow.

That Sun Yatsen chose to dictate his last testament to him was a tribute to Wang Jingwei's own revolutionary endeavours. The life that led Wang to this moment began, as far as these endeavours went, in 1905 when he was twenty-two, and a student of constitutional law and political theory at the Tokyo College of Law. It was in that year that he published the leading article in the inaugural issue of the *Min Bao*, the vehicle for sowing seeds of anti-Manchu feeling among the expatriate coterie of Chinese students in Japan, and became the dazzling exponent of Sun Yatsen's nationalist ideas.

The doubts which assailed him now about the future of the revolution were unknown to him then; an intellectual radical with a price on his head, he felt himself then to be borne on the tides of history, not tugged back, as now, by their undertow. Believing his revolutionary purpose to be as fixed, his response to its far horizons as unfaltering as that mythological bird which, driven by some compulsion to fill in the sea, bent its lifelong energies to depositing wood and pebbles in its waters, he called himself Jingwei, after the allegorical creature.

And with what intrepidity, with what sense of destiny, did he undertake that act of spectacular hazard in 1910, when he travelled incognito to Beijing and made an attempt on the Manchu Prince Regent's life. Killing the four-year-old emperor's father, he imagined, would turn the spluttering flame of revolution into a brilliant flare. Though there was something gauche, even ludicrous, about the idea of going about Beijing with explosives and copies of the *Min Bao* sown into the lining of his clothes, it cannot be denied that there was heroism in it.

He had two accomplices, one a girl still in her teens. He was later to marry her, releasing himself from a prearranged betrothal to another girl who, in compensation for the dissolution of vows, or perhaps in extension of them, bound herself to another promise and took the veil. The future Madame Wang Jingwei came from a rich overseas Cantonese family hailing from the very same native place as Wang, but settled in Penang. She was strong-willed and showed, in deference to him, a great deal of revolutionary fervour. They had met when Wang was travelling about Malaya with the fugitive Dr Sun, raising funds from the overseas Chinese communities and making speeches. She heard him speak, and he moved her to the heart. He did have great beauty, a beauty beyond gender; he spoke beautifully, and there was beauty to the cause he was so passionately espousing. Always there was a transparent patriotism, a faith that things could be accomplished, so long as you were prepared for sacrifice. Flouting convention and defying her father, she packed her bags and followed him back to Japan. And when he and his other accomplice embarked on their dangerous mission in Beijing, she insisted on coming along too.

The explosives, made from photographic supplies by Russian anarchists who had fled to Japan after the 1905 revolution in their own country, were laid under a bridge that the Prince Regent was known to cross on his way to the imperial palace almost every day. But from the first nothing went right. Barking dogs alerted a posse out looking for an absconded wife, and the bombs were discovered. Wang's accomplice, returning to the bridge to see what had happened to the bomb, was spotted by two police spies disguised as bird-sellers and tailed. Knowing nothing of this, Wang Jingwei went to the railway station the next day to see his fiancée off to Tokyo. As the train pulled out of the station Wang gallantly lifted his hat, a gesture which utterly gave him away, for by it he revealed to the lurking police spies that his queue was artificially plaited to his hair — a sign that he defied the Manchu ruling that all Chinese grew a pigtail, and was a revolutionary.

He was picked up by the police, held in a prison where many an earlier insurrectionist had died, and presently tried for treason. When his captors came upon the revolutionary journals in his clothes and asked for an explanation, he said, 'These articles were written in ink; I want to translate them into blood.' He awaited the martyrdom for which there was already a strain of longing and preparation. He would most certainly have been beheaded if the Court, its authority already shaky, had not feared reprisals; if Japanese diplomats had not interceded; if the eloquence of Wang's own defence had not impressed the judges; and if, so people said, the Empress Dowager had not fallen victim to his physical charm.

With decapitation commuted to life imprisonment, he was clapped in iron chains, padlocks manacling his hands, feet and neck, and consigned to a gaol this side of desolation. There he pondered the unlikelihood of his survival and the probability of his country dying. Out of rashness or selflessness he had endeavoured to change things. Though his exploit was to make a national hero of him (when the collapse of the dynasty unfettered him his chains were saved for a museum), he did not see that he had really done it for his own reasons, to test or even to glorify himself perhaps. It would not have occurred to him to ponder whether the condition of mankind was more effectively changed by men of unspectacular action, correct analysers and careful strategists, than by the dramatic gestures of charismatic men.

Like many a man of action Wang had a strong streak of the sentimental, and while in prison he indulged himself in versifying (much later, the English publishers George Allen and Unwin brought out an anthology of his poetry in translation). His fiancée came back to Beijing and found a way to smuggle a letter to him; touched, he wrote back to her of his despair and sorrow, using classical verse as the forms for his feelings. His impulse to hold on to her letter was checked by the certain knowledge that to do so would imperil them both, but having neither the nerve to keep it, nor the heart to discard it, he put it into his mouth and swallowed it.

They married in Canton five months after the dynasty fell. Then Wang travelled to Malaya and Singapore with his bride and, doubling his popularity by declining office, withdrew beyond the reach of the new Republic's multiple political rivalries to France, where he and his wife remained for the next five years. Returning to China late in 1917, he re-attached himself to Sun Yatsen's personal entourage, acting as his leader's confidential secretary on that final journey to Beijing in 1925. No disciple could be closer to the dying progenitor of the first Republic of China.

WITHIN A COUPLE of months of Sun's death a violent event occurred in Shanghai, providing one of those anchorages in history by which Chinese revolutionary currents can best be followed. It happened on May 30, at a police station off Nanjing Road, right in the heart of the International Settlement. A Chinese striker at the Nagai Wata Mills had died at the hands of the Japanese foreman, and students were staging protest demonstrations all over the city. Outside the police station there was an appalling development: the students were fired at, and a British officer had given the order. In the mêlée that broke out a dozen people were killed, and another twenty lay wounded. The city was inflamed, and that night a labour organizer summoned a meeting of students, workers, merchants and businessmen, to call for a general strike. It was in a building in Rue Vallon, and Du Yuesheng was there in person. He was all for the strike that was being discussed. Next morning the city awoke to find the schools empty, the shops shuttered, the foreign textile mills deserted. As the week wore on the walkout spread to tramcar and bus operators, seamen, longshoremen, the crews of British and Japanese ships, and even to the Chinese members of the Municipal Police. By mid-month a hundred and fifty thousand workers had struck, and were it not for the armed guards posted at the waterworks and the power plant, most likely more people would have walked off their jobs.

It was a crisis all right, and the first nail in Western imperialism's coffin. Shanghai's militancy was copied by workers all the way down to southern China. In Canton the cadets of the Whampoa Military Academy paraded in front of the British and French marines to demonstrate their solidarity with the Shanghai strikers, and walked into a smack of fire. When reports of the casualties reached Hong Kong — fifty-two killed and a hundred wounded — the working population there left the British island colony *en masse*. For fifteen months the boycott of the British lasted; machines stopped working, shopkeepers stopped serving, sprinklers stopped twirling on green English lawns.

A powerful stream of propaganda called for an end to foreign aggressors. With them were lumped the warlords, who were said to connive with the foreigner and were the 'running dogs of imperialists', besides being cowards and 'thieves who sold their country'. Seriously challenging warlord power at last, the Guomindang proclaimed itself the Nationalist government of China in July, with Wang Jingwei as its chairman.

The current of nationalist feeling was fierce, and the united front of the Guomindang and the Communist Party was swimming with it. In the spring of 1926 the revolutionary forces of the Guomindang set off on the famous Northern Expedition from Canton. A flurry of

Russian advisers and Soviet-trained publicists went ahead, and the Nationalist army, with its secondhand weapons, surged into the green and moist Yangtze valley and was received by smiling people rushing forward to shake thc soldiers by the hand. Seventy per cent of the war, the commander-in-chief Chiang Kaishek was to reflect, was won by propaganda. As it advanced agitprop trains carrying large portraits of Sun Yatsen and slogans hailing the new China made vivid for the country people the notion and intensity of nationalism. The warlords fell back. All south China went over to the Guomindang. Then Wuhan, that strategic conurbation on the Yangtze, was captured, and the Guomindang government transferred there from Canton, to begin its operations to advance down the river to Nanjing and Shanghai.

But what had begun as a war of a revolutionary kind, a march of mass sweep and patriotic movement, was becoming an enterprise from which the revolutionary element was presently to be excoriated. Within the Guomindang, sectarian rivalries for succession to Sun Yatsen, with Wang Jingwei to the Left and Chiang Kaishek to the Right, culminated in an attack by Chiang on the Soviet advisers and Communists, which ended in the Russians being sent home and Wang Jingwei resigning as chairman and going into exile in France. As 1927 began, the rift irrevocably widened, with the group in Wuhan cleaving to the alliance with the Communists and the group in Nanjing clustering about Chiang Kaishek and unequivocally showing its anti-Red colours.

For the moment the ins and outs of the split in the party were not generally known, and were not the concern of the foreign concessions in Shanghai. The foreigners believed a Red revolution to be coming, and pictured to themselves the triumphal march as a Red wave on the Yangtze. They hardly knew what to make of the rumours that were reaching them from out of town, of strikes and butchery, of Chinese men raping white women, and of a European lady dying of fright in Jiujiang. In a letter to friends abroad an American resident described it as more than a civil war. 'It was,' he wrote, 'the French Revolution, the industrial revolution and the Renaissance all taking place at one and the same time.' He said that one would need to reread Dickens'

A Tale of Two Cities and Thomas Carlyle's *French Revolution* if one would really sense the situation in China then.

The foreigners were already panicky. The British, American and Japanese members of the Municipal Council steeled themselves to fight to the last ditch. Twenty thousand British troops were on their way from England. The Shanghai Volunteer Corps and the Marines stood to their arms. A contingent of North Indian Punjabis arrived from Hong Kong, and stomped through the streets to the strains of brass band and bagpipe.

Yet when the Guomindang forces did come in on March 22, not a drop of foreign blood was shed. Instead the streets of Shanghai ran with native Chinese blood. In a coup as unexpected as it was ferocious, Chiang Kaishek struck at his leftwing allies, crushed the Communist movement, and provided its annals with a page of the bloodiest betrayal it would ever know. The blame for the Communists' defeat lay with Joseph Stalin, the key to the success of Chiang Kaishek's coup with Du Yuesheng.

Chapter Five

SHANGHAI TAKEOVER 1927–1931

ON 9 APRIL 1927, Du Yuesheng sent a sidekick to the premises of the Huzhou Guild, where the Shanghai General Union had its office, to invite the chairman, Wang Shouhua, to dinner that evening at Rue Wagner. It would just be the three of them: Wang, Du and his confederate Zhang Xiaolin.

Elected chairman of the union only two weeks before, Wang Shouhua was an experienced Marxist cadre, a member of the Communist Party since he was a student, and politically indoctrinated in Vladivostok. He accepted the invitation at once, though it baffled him a little, but it was not until he was well on his way to the party that he felt any real reservations. Du Yuesheng would probably want to talk, he thought, about the bitter struggle for the control of Shanghai; but hadn't that been resolved by the union militia's unqualified victory over the local warlords the month before? Shanghai had quite definitely moved leftwards, only waiting for the advancing Guomindang armies to take up the reins of control. It is true that the city was prostrate with strike action, but that was the necessary prelude to its rejuvenation by Socialism and the Northern Expedition armies. Yet Wang Shouhua had doubts about Du Yuesheng's real sympathies, though he had come out in favour of the strikes with the rest of the city's bourgeoisie after the killings of the students in May 1925. Wang was a reluctant victim of the delusion that an alliance between Communists and capitalists was a workable proposition.

As his car sped past the wide boulevards of the French Concession, the evening traffic hooted out of the way, the momentous events of the past month again became vivid to him. When his comrades in the General Union started an all-out strike in February to demonstrate their solidarity with the approaching Guomindang armies, they never imagined that the forces of the local warlord would break it with such ruthless barbarity — twenty of their comrades decapitated, their severed heads hoisted up in public display at the main crossroads; the executioner impassively riding out, looking neither left nor right; the mass arrests; the savage crushing of the pickets. The uprising was an appalling blunder, premature and badly organized, but it did pave the way for the insurrection, the one they staged on March 21. That was an undeniable success. Work stoppage was total and simultaneous, some 800,000 strikers downing tools. Within forty-eight hours of the union militia's taking up their positions in different parts of the city, the electricity supply and telecommunications lines were cut, the police stations taken, the arsenal and Chinese law courts occupied, the prisoners in the adjoining gaol released, the Southern Railway Station seized.

It was in a mood of triumph mixed with regret that Wang Shouhua now looked back on the fighting in the suburb of Zhabei, where in clashes with the crack battalions of the warlord army, forbidding with their burly Shandong men and devil-may-care White Russian mercenaries, two hundred of his finest comrades were killed and thousands of others wounded. But in the end those troops were no match for the union militia, who fell upon the enemy strongholds one by one (first the Commercial Press building, then the police stations and the Huzhou Guild, and finally the North Railway Station) and sent the warlord forces fleeing from the city. The uprising had given the Communist cadres the chance to display their organizational talents at their most brilliant. Shanghai was now in their grasp, and the scene was set for the appearance on the revolutionary stage of the Nationalist forces.

With such hopeful prospects playing through his mind, the chairman of the Shanghai General Union approached the entrance to Du Yuesheng's mansion on Rue Wagner. He did not notice that the sentries were doubled at the door, nor see the extra cars that were parked round the corner. The house was seemingly quiet. But when the iron gates swung open at Wang Shouhua's approach, precisely at that moment one of the limousines parked at the corner drew up. A moment after Wang had alighted and stepped into the courtyard two shadowy figures jumped out of it and into the union leader's car. Before the driver could raise an alarm he heard the rasp of a whispered command in his ear and felt an icy muzzle against his temple. As the unsuspecting Wang Shouhua entered the mansion the car moved off into the shadows with headlamps unlit. An impeccably planned and seemingly inexplicable disappearance of vehicle and driver would follow.

Inside, the bright interior of the living room suddenly opened up, revealing Zhang Xiaolin framed in his chair and two henchmen standing, one on each side. Without anyone speaking the guest felt a premonitory chill. In instant reflex he made for the door. From in front and behind four men suddenly reared and ringed him, blocking the exit and escape. For some moments his mind sought refuge in incredulity: it was too bizarre; this couldn't be happening. But the men were pressing forward, and their hands were all around him, and when he cried out in pain and fear, they tightened their grip, and kicked him.

Upstairs in his room Du Yuesheng heard the cry. He stirred from the depths of his drug-induced numbness and broke surface, his head instantly clear. 'Don't do him in here. Not in my house!' he rasped out, his voice thick with opium fumes and urgency. In the narcotic, that congenital form of a Shanghai gangster's self-indulgence, he had sought to blot out his jangled nerves, the distant anxiety of having ordained a person's death. The first of many deaths: it was in the days before he'd been anaesthetized to killing.

Du Yuesheng laid aside his pipe and his disquiet, but not his preoccupation with the evening's proceedings. It was the only way the game could be played, and he wished it to progress exactly as Chiang Kaishek would wish it. Downstairs Fiery Old Crow and Flowery Flag were enacting what he, the mastermind behind the operation, knew in finer detail. They would be bundling the labour leader into the car now, and driving towards the border between Frenchtown and the Chinese quarter. The map of the journey, one he himself had travelled, unravelled in city scenes in his mind. Through the captors' eyes he watched boulevards flash by, the encroaching outskirts, the black mass of squat dwellings in which a few small lights, pricking the darkness at intervals, weakly flickered. No squeamishness interrupted Du's imaginings now, of Fiery Old Crow's iron hand grip encircling Wang Shouhua's throat, of the victim's eyes, in the instant when the thread of life snapped, suddenly dilating at the terrifying vision of death, the body jerking backward, as the lungs surrendered their breath.

When Du Yuesheng's mind was conjuring these images, the car carrying Wang Shouhua's body was wheeling out of the suburbs to the west, completing its journey at a dirt road which disappeared into the fields. The car braked to a stop. Out in the open, as the beam of a torch light darted in reconnaissance across the earth and the trees and the graves, the inert body, encased in a hessian sack, was unloaded. The men started to dig. Grey stones thrust up through the hard surface; insects sent up a steady hum. Suddenly a muffled groan arose from the folds of the hessian sack. Fiery Old Crow stopped talking in mid-sentence. The colour drained from Flowery Flag's face.

'Isn't the bastard dead?' Had Fiery Old Crow, for all his deadly blacksmith's stranglehold, been off his stroke?

'He must be!' snapped the strangler, but fearing loss of face. Sharply whirring round, he raised his shovel above the body to finish the fellow off.

Flowery Flag stopped him, cocking his head at the long hole in the ground. Extinction awaits the man right here — why waste your strength? — here under the sod, in the pit no wider than his body, down which he will be flung while the faces above recede, while shovels hurl dirt into his face. There he will lie forever, his innards rotting, the night persisting where once there was the break of dawn.

Twenty-three years later, when China had achieved the Socialist revolution for which men like Wang Shouhua had died, an exhibition to commemorate the martyr was held in the Workers' Cultural Palace in Shanghai. Du Yuesheng, who was living in Hong Kong then, read about it in the papers. When he came to the paragraph about the public display of Wang Shouhua's 'bloodstained clothes' he snorted to himself. The thing's a fake, he thought, for it had been immediately reported to him the instant Fiery Old Crow and Flowery Flag returned to Rue Wagner that at half-past nine that April night, Wang Shouhua was buried several feet underground alive.

Doing away with the labour organizer was but one component

Chiang Kaishek in the 1930s

in the plan; the rest, already perfected in Du Yuesheng's capacious brain, would go into operation on April 12. Remote from the scene of Wang Shouhua's death, nestled back in his couch and loosely reconnected to his opium pipe, Du was thinking that there would be no Red revolution in Shanghai. Those past few months had seen some dramatic struggles, an alarming turn to the nationalist movement. It might have culminated in a workers' revolution spreading to all of China, but for his timely intervention. I'll make them bite the dust, he thought, these Communist agitators and their Russian bosses.

However much they supported the struggle against the foreign powers, businessmen instinctively hated the idea of a people's government. The Shanghainese were chafing under Western control, it is true, but they had certainly not forgotten that their fortunes were built upon the profits of commerce, the sort best conducted under the protection of the foreign flag. A cursory acquaintance with Shanghai would be enough to tell you that free enterprise and money were what the place was all about. It was because he knew this that Chiang Kaishek slipped into town the previous month, and applied himself to tapping the city's resources. To make a revolution you need money, so you look for someone with an interest in giving it to you. Chiang knew how to go about it, which channels to use. Before he went back to military life, driven back perhaps by the losses he had incurred on his excessive speculations, he himself had been a broker on the Shanghai Chartered Stock and Produce Exchange. He soon got the bankers to cough up; for his pledge to right the relationship between capital and labour they advanced him three million dollars straight off, with the promise of another seven million to follow. The money would finance his break with the left wing of his party, and the coup scheduled for April 12; for their money the bankers would see the labour movement broken, and the Red revolution rolled back. It was a business arrangement between interested parties, the sort that prevails throughout the world.

In all this Du Yuesheng's role was crucial. Chiang had sought him out from the start, sending two intermediaries — the commander of the Shanghai garrison and the Guomindang's political security chief — to discuss the details with him beforehand. It was not that Du and his confrères were three of the biggest financial magnates in Shanghai, it was that the newly forged alliance of nationalists and capitalists could go forward only with the help of a third partner, the secret society. Chiang knew that his forces would be barred from the foreign concessions, whose neutrality was pointedly defended by 20,000 troops and forty-two warships. If he wanted to fall on the Communists he'd have to force a passage through the concessions, and to do that he would have to use, instead of his regular troops, those familiars of street warfare and decoy in the Green Gang. Du Yuesheng wholeheartedly agreed. From Shanghai's dark underbelly he would conjure them all; it was plainly a war for the gangster, to be conducted through and through in the gangland manner.

The scale of the operation was so large that Red Gang members had to be recruited to the ranks. Willing, even fervent, Du Yuesheng set about laying the plans. First, he set up a front organization he called the Mutual Progress Society; next, he acquired arms through the agency of comprador friends; finally, because the acquiescence of the International Settlement's governing body was essential to the operation's success, he went to see Stirling Fessenden, the chairman of the Municipal Council.

Stirling Fessenden, with whom Du had had dealings before, was an American, one of those 'feeble creatures', as a member of the U.S. State Department put it, 'who had gone to pieces in the Far East and conspicuously unfit for his position.' In fact Fessy, as he was generally known by most foreign residents, was a perfectly amiable fellow who so liked the lifestyle Shanghai offered him that he never went back to America. He and his White Russian lady friend were often to be seen at hotel dances and in the nightclubs, he very short, and she very tall and blonde. In 1943 he was to die a lonely death in a house belonging to Shell in the French Concession.

During Du Yuesheng's interview with him, Fessenden walked about his office while Du's interpreter did the talking. After his initial doubts he began to see the situation more clearly: the gangsters, being civilians, were perfectly within their rights to move across the Settlement; as long as his police turned a blind eye there would be no trouble. Tacit agreement recommended itself as a response which does not entail responsibility; he said yes to Du Yuesheng.

The fusillade of machine-gun fire that shattered the peace of the hour before dawn on April 12 thus came as no surprise to the foreign authorities. The only people to be taken aback were the victims, the workers and the pickets. Everyone else seemed to have been alerted. At the blast of a bugle sounded from Chiang Kaishek's headquarters on Route Ghisi, swarming hordes poured out of the concessions and the surrounding neighbourhoods; and from Zhabei, from Wusong, from Pudong, from Jessfield, from every corner of Shanghai from east to west, rifle fire rang out in sharp explosions. Clad in blue and wearing armbands bearing the Chinese character for 'labour', the mobsters were easily taken for what they were not; some believed them to be 'armed Guomindang labourers', others thought them 'merchants' volunteers', and yet others lumped them with the Nationalist troops. Up close, they turned out to be Du Yuesheng and

Huang Jinrong's hijackers, pensioners, bodyguards, masseurs, manicurists, hawkers and waiters owing allegiance to the Green Gang, and an assortment of bouncers from the sleazier bars and restaurants.

By the faint light of dawn the length of Garden Bridge could be seen in stealthy movement. The sound of shuffling feet and whispered commands was swallowed up in the rumble of heavy vehicles. Their destination was the Commercial Press buildings, the worker militia's stronghold to the north of Garden Bridge. As they loomed up the buildings looked impregnable, but there was no sign of special vigilance, and inside the pickets peered out in curiosity rather than alarm, moving unsuspectingly across the squares of lighted windows to expose their bodies to the fire. From all around them came the burst of artillery fire and machine-guns. The four hundred pickets inside the buildings fought back desperately, but soon the mobsters were joined by regular soldiers and their position was completely surrounded. From dawn to noon the two sides fought, and all the time the pickets were wondering why they were being attacked.

At about the same time their comrades in the Chinese Tramways Company in the native quarter were falling back exhausted. The assault had begun at 3 a.m., the twenty-sixth division of the Guomindang army providing artillery support. The workers had leapt out of their beds in bewilderment and terror, and rushed about blindly while bullets were whizzing above.

The General Union, with its premises at the Huzhou Guild, was captured by a ruse. At a distance the attackers came into view. The unionists called out to ask which union they belonged to. 'To the Northern Expeditionary Army,' said the officer approaching with his battalion. He had come to help the union disarm their attackers, he added, and both sides should hand over their arms. Up to that point the mobsters had been shooting at the Guild building and the unionists had been shooting back. But now the officer walked up to the mobsters, and as the pickets from their windows looked on, began to take their guns from them. The mobsters were handing them over without a murmur, and some of them even allowed themselves to be tied up with rope. Then the officer came right into the building and was greeted with tea and cigarettes. The officer thanked his

Communist hosts, and said that they should accompany him back to headquarters to sort things out. Presently the Communist commander and six of his comrades were seen leaving the building with the officer. But as they walked down the street the officer turned to the Communists and said that he was going to disarm them. The Communists looked at him in incomprehension. And it was then that the mobsters closed in, three hundred of them appearing all of a sudden from nowhere, and shooting their way into the building as the soldiers watched and stood by. Like sitting ducks the targets were unmistakable; by the time they woke up to the feint the attack was almost over. In the confusion which broke out the Communist commander managed to escape (with him was the future premier of the People's Republic, Zhou Enlai).

Seven hundred unionists were to die before the coup was over, a blood debt never forgotten, and one the Communists would want to collect when they returned in triumph to Shanghai twenty-two years later.

The day after the assault the General Union still hadn't thought it out. 'We shall fight to the death... with national revolution as our banner!' They were still rallying workers and staging demonstrations. The waterfront was silent, the trams had come to a stop, all over the industrial districts the cotton mills were lying idle. But in pouring rain a ragged procession of a hundred thousand workers marched out, heading for the Guomindang headquarters to present their petitions. They wanted their arms returned and their attackers punished, and they wanted an undertaking that the General Union would go unharmed. Some of them were women, some of them children. They did not know that they were about to rehearse by sacrifice the final shattering of the workers' movement.

Riflemen were waiting for them and, as the parade came in sight of its destination, raised their weapons and shot at point-blank range into the crowd. There was no escape from the encircling fire, and everywhere the marchers turned they were caught in the bullets, the rain, the dust, the blood. The bayonets, the broad swords, the rifle butts. Some of the fleeing marchers were shot in the back; some were dragged out of their hiding places and killed on the spot. It took eight truckloads and several hours to cart away the dead and the litter.

With them went the last shreds of the goodwill between the Communists and the Nationalists, and the idea, assiduously fostered by Joseph Stalin for his own interests through the agents of the Comintern, that the alliance must go forward under the leadership of the Guomindang. If it hadn't been for the power struggle in the Kremlin, with Trotsky calling Stalin the gravedigger of the Chinese revolution and Stalin unyielding in his China Policy, the proceedings might not have unfolded to such a bloody climax. It would have helped if China and the Chinese Communist Party hadn't been turned into an arena for the Kremlin quarrel. But, with Trotsky lashing out at the 'bloody lessons of Shanghai' and the transformation of the Communists into 'cattle herders for the party of the bourgeois executioners', Stalin must have felt he had to maintain his position. By late April Trotsky was exiled, but Stalin's China Policy had reached that precarious condition when a belief, to counteract the proof of its fallibility, is clung to with even fiercer tenacity than before.

Meanwhile White Terror gripped Shanghai. At the same time as the Chamber of Commerce was acclaiming Du Yuesheng and the other two kingpins as 'national saviours' who led their 'dare-to-die comrades in the destruction of the General Union and the worker pickets', leftists were being rooted out all over Shanghai and being put to death in their thousands. A whirlwind of house searches, police raids and massacre swept through the city, and at the centre of the turbulence, providing manpower (Flowery Flag and others were seconded to the witch-hunt) and underwriting expenses, sat Du Yuesheng. The British and Japanese defence corps helped too, providing reinforcements and delivering prisoners to the Guomindang garrison by the armoured truckload.

For the Chinese moneyed classes, the bankers and the comprador merchants, the euphoria of April 1927 was soon to dissolve. At first the full meaning of Chiang Kaishek's takeover did not dawn. Labour had been dealt with and a Nationalist government sympathetic to capitalism had been set up under Chiang Kaishek in Nanjing. The bankers were not to know that Chiang would use Shanghai as though it were a cornucopia from which all sustenance flowed:

loans, donations, the wherewithal to feed his growing army and stock up on military supplies. Holding the businessmen to ransom, he made their lives and security depend on massive contributions to government expenditure. As the *New York Times* reported on May 4, 'At the mercy of General Chiang Kaishek's dictatorship, the merchants do not know what the next day will bring, confiscations, compulsory loans, exile, or possible executions....' By such means did the soldier and sometime stockbroker grasp the destiny of Shanghai and China in his hands.

Du Yuesheng was shielded from all this though; for him the horizons widened. In recognition of their services to the *coup d'état*, Chiang Kaishek awarded him and his two confederates with honorifics — Counselor with the rank of major-general. Du Yuesheng travelled to the capital to have the decoration bestowed on him by Chiang in person. The ceremony flattered Du, who had a photograph of himself taken, one hand on his hip, to remember the occasion by. He had a soldier's uniform made specially for the portrait, but it did not really become him, and in all his life he never again wore anything other than the long Chinese gown, even when more and more of his cohorts were adopting the Western suit.

The political patronage was of course a boost to business. Although the Nanjing government was outwardly opposed to opium smoking, and announced a plan to withdraw the drug from circulation within three years in the interest of eradicating the habit, what it had in mind was a government monopoly on the trade. The power to enforce the new regulations was mandated to the Bureau for Opium Suppression, and in Shanghai this organization was headed by Zhang Xiaolin at its inception, and by Du Yuesheng a little later. Hijacking as a way of procuring the drug was superseded by legal impounding, and splitting the profits on the sale with the government kept the business going. Du Yuesheng and his two partners were dealing in quality Persian dope in consistently high volume now, as well as commanding the largest slice of the market for the homegrown product. The threesome had set up their own marketing company, but it was never clear how one distinguished its business from that of the Bureau for Opium Suppression. Contraband seized by the one was always reappearing as merchandise sold by the other, and the annual registration fees paid by addicts never seemed to come up in the bureau's ledgers. But the Ministry of Finance, under whose eye all this went on, did not believe in enquiring too deeply into matters from which it greatly profited.

It was during this time that, profits spawning more profits, Zhang Xiaolin opened his casino at 180 Avenue Foch, the city's biggest and flashiest. It catered to a polite clientele, and was housed in a mansion surrounded by green English lawns. There were tables for roulette, baccarat, poker, mahjong, and any number of Chinese and European games. The patrons, many of them celebrities, were invariably loaded and played for high stakes. The place offered a choice of cuisine in both Chinese and Western styles as well as a variety of opium for afters.

The threesome lived the sort of life commonly thought of as critical to public acknowledgement of their success, and they went nowhere without an entourage, mostly of bodyguards. As with all parvenus, Du Yuesheng liked to be surrounded by glamour, and could often be seen arriving at nightclubs with three or four over-embellished singsong girls. If there were already enough women in his life this was not something anyone commented upon; if all the highest-priced Number Threes were retained by him, this was no more than what tradition ordained. In fact by the standards of his class, Du's attitude to women was enlightened: he exploited women no more than most men and he never in all his life took a belt to one.

At the same time as the mahjong sessions were being played for higher and higher stakes, Du Yuesheng drew closer to the Nationalist government and to politics, that most exhilarating game devised by ambition and the hunger for power. That he had been indispensable to Chiang Kaishek's bid for supremacy put him on a special level and made him aspire to more than the absolute command of the underworld. He wanted a position in the upper-world and saw that money was not only a means of self-realization but could be a means of social upgrading as well. In the following years his public persona was raised to that of a banker and financier. In 1929 he founded his own (Chung Wai) bank; later he became a director of the Shanghai Stock

Exchange, several commodity exchanges, and a string of worthy banks. Later still he sat on the board of the Shanghai Bankers Association, the Shanghai Chamber of Commerce, the Bank of China, the French Municipal Council, and the Chinese branch of the Red Cross.

It is hard to know what he had more of: money, position or sycophants. Even the French looked up to him. In the summer of 1930, he received a call from the Consul-General, who had a strike of transport workers on his hands and didn't know how to break it up. It paralysed the French Concession and looked as if it might be interminable. In desperation he turned to Du Yuesheng. He had no sooner spoken to Du than the strike was dramatically called off. Du's stock with the French soared, and they elected him to their Municipal Council. Had they enquired into the circumstances (which they did not), they might have found him even more extraordinary, for Du Yuesheng had got the strikers to go back to work by agreeing to all their demands across the board, and without consulting any of the employers. As for the money needed to meet those demands, he had simply delved into his own pocket.

Interceding became a speciality. There was a queue for his good offices. He was someone you could always count on in a crisis or an emergency: an arbiter, sponsor, paymaster, fixer, public relations virtuoso all rolled into one. Through the infiltration of the press by Green Gang members many a momentary indiscretion could be prevented from being turned into a front-page sensation. Through his control of the black market of scandal revelations he rescued many a dignitary from being cast up on the wracks of a ruined reputation. He was particularly good at disembarrassing you of paternity and breach-of-promise suits: it was the way he put it to the aggrieved parties, making offers which they couldn't, as it were, refuse.

It was somehow fitting that at about this time he took as his fourth wife a famous Beijing opera singer. It was not only that he had become a passionate fan of opera, even a connoisseur; it was also that in his circles an admired opera singer meant class. Not that he didn't like the lady for herself; indeed, for a time he was almost besotted. But he would be the first to admit that, having come this far in his life, he could settle for nothing short of a star. He installed her in a separate home at Rue Lafayette. The following year she bore him his first daughter (she would give him another girl and yet more sons, though only one of them survived). When his daughter was one year old Du Yuesheng reached the apogee of his career, demanding everyone's recognition of his social arrival by a display of that most lauded of Chinese virtues, filial piety. On that hot August day in 1931, eighty thousand people came to attend the opening of the Du ancestral temple and clan hall. No career built on iniquity ever managed so respectable a veneer.

Chapter Six

THE OPPORTUNIST AS PATRIOT 1931–1937

WANG JINGWEI, his mood lifted by his recent reconciliation with former adversaries in the Guomindang, composed an essay in Du Yuesheng's honour, to mark the dedication of the Du clan hall. Tribute was paid to Du Yuesheng's filial piety, in whose demonstration lay the truism, the essay noted, that the family was the source of all fellow feeling, whose extension was charity. Wang spoke of the exemplariness of Du's beneficence, especially mentioning the endowment of the village library, and remarked how the seeds of the ceremony lay in the ancient rites of thanksgiving. 'A veritable champion,' said the essay about Du Yuesheng, 'a knight-errant' who honoured his word and made light of his philanthropy.

Attaching ennobling epithets to people has never been out of fashion in China, and Wang Jingwei, who credited himself with special sensibilities with words, indulged freely in the fancy. Looked upon as diversion or solace, he could think of nothing better than to write and versify. The words came easily, in parallel lines of language, like paths trodden to smoothness. For anyone who writes in Chinese must write straight into the eye of the cliché, it being his bane and privilege never to use a metaphor that has not been used before, never to overturn the literary precedents of millennia. Tradition, from which all else takes its bearings, so works on the writer that it is almost as though he has to be careful that the ability to write is not acquired along with the abilities to see, to smell, to hear and to feel at first hand. That Wang Jingwei was apt to feel in emotional clichés need not, therefore, be held against him. Nor the touch of soulfulness that came into his expression, the glint of tears that lit up his eye, for these derived as much from the pose that commands attention by seducing it, as from the sentimentalism with which the Chinese people have been over-endowed in the first place, and which accounts for the lachrymose tradition of some of their art forms.

It was this ability to play on inherited emotions that made Wang Jingwei so compelling a speaker. Even if it was often devoid of content his rhetoric was capable of so arousing his audience that if girl students were present, he would be showered with flowers. The impression he made on those he met was generally stunning: it was not only the gently persuasive voice, the special, individualized word and mode of address for everybody, it was also the elegance and the perpetual youthfulness of his looks. (When he was fifty the writer John Gunther met him. Gunther gasped to see how 'extraordinarily handsome, slight and supple' he was. 'Here', wrote the reporter, 'was one of the fathers of the Chinese revolution. He might have been a schoolboy.')

Yet his achievements were falling short of his promise. Though he believed himself to be the natural successor to Sun Yatsen, time and again he found himself in the position of being a second best to Chiang Kaishek. Perhaps it was because he was without the resources that political doggedness might have given him; indeed, he never seemed to have settled once and for all the fundamental question of where his political sympathies exactly lay. While one could not say that Chiang Kaishek's political course was all that steady, ultimately he had chosen his position and lived up to it, whereas Wang Jingwei moved his politics in side-steps, and his stances lacked a sense of solidity.

When he returned to China on 1 April 1927, from his second sojourn in France, he travelled via Moscow to confer with Kremlin leaders, including probably Stalin. He was then the leader of the Guomindang's left wing, and an advocate of the partnership with the Chinese Communist Party. But by May he was half way to a rejection of the entente, and in another month Communism would be renounced altogether. It was a secret telegram, mistakenly disclosed to him by the Indian Comintern agent M. N. Roy, that finally did it; for it revealed the designs which Moscow had for China and the Guomindang. Yet his readiness, by nature, to change his politics was also inextricable from all these moves towards the Right. In July he expelled the Communists from the Guomindang and sent the Soviet advisers packing. The Wuhan government he led was left in tatters, and for the next few years he passed from one political blind alley to another. First he headed an anti-Chiang camp within the party, then joined a separatist coalition with northern warlords to challenge Chiang's power in Nanjing, and finally returned south to Canton where, in the early months of 1931, he got together with some of Chiang's adversaries to set up another short-lived dissident regime. It was when that too aborted that Wang Jingwei decided to give up outdoing Chiang Kaishek.

If not altogether at a loss, he was in a state of abeyance. It occurred to him that it might be better simply to trim his sails to the wind, to capitulate quietly, and seek to make his peace with Chiang Kaishek. Distracted by the exigencies of civil war against the still to be subjugated warlords and the feuding within his party, and now also menaced by a Japanese incursion into Manchuria, Chiang struck a compromise with the secessionist southerners and welcomed Wang Jingwei back into the fold, even naming him president of the Executive Yuan, or Prime Minister. Yet Chiang Kaishek's trust in Wang was hardly absolute, and beneath the surface of official collaboration, the Prime Minister's dissatisfaction rankled. Kept always beneath the eye of Chiang Kaishek, Wang Jingwei found that for all his superiority of rank he really had not much power at all.

ON 28 JANUARY 1932, the night Wang Jingwei was installed as Prime Minister, Japan struck a lightning blow at Shanghai and found, to her surprise, that the Chinese were not as easily cowed as she had supposed.

On the surface the Japanese attackers were sending in troops to protect the thirty-thousand Japanese nationals living in Zhabei, the northwestern neighbourhood of the city's Little Tokyo, from the great surge of anti-Japanese feeling with which the Chinese citizens had reacted to the invasion of northern China. This hatred manifested itself in that habitual weapon of passive protest, the boycott of everything Japanese. Chinese citizens would not buy Japanese products. Chinese agents would not handle Japanese shipping. Chinese banks would not honour Japanese bills of lading. Chinese passengers would not board Japanese steamers. The boycott was total, and those who violated it were fined and denounced and made to stand at street corners in clothes branded with the word 'traitor'. The Japanese residents were understandably hysterical, and hundreds of them tried to get on the first boat leaving Shanghai for home.

On a deeper level, though, Japan was working out her plan, grounded in reasoning employed by the Nazis in Europe, of *Lebensraum*, of expansion. In that scheme the attack on Shanghai was really only a beginning, a foretaste of the time when the whole of China would be turned into an arena of Japanese intrigue and ambition.

So, on January 18, at less than an hour before midnight, Japanese marines crossed into the streets of Zhabei. But far from achieving their objectives within a few hours, which they believed was all it would take, the troops found themselves bogged down in an unexpectedly spirited counter-attack by the Nineteenth Route Army, a Cantonese force that happened to be quartered nearby. The war was to drag on for thirty-four days in a stalemate, and lay waste large sections of densely-populated Zhabei, with the tenement houses and cotton mills in ruins, and the streets a trail of craters. Writing for the *China Weekly Review*, a reporter spoke of his mind running with 'a panorama sharp with images of horror and carnage'. The Chinese soldiers were anything but their chicken-hearted stereotype, and the courage of their commander in particular was to impress itself upon the imagination of China and, as his heroic defence caught the attention of the international press, even of the world.

Yet it could scarcely have ended in deeper national humiliation. The truce, signed on May 5, brought peace, but not much else and not for long. That the Prime Minister, Wang Jingwei, was forced to resign and leave for France was a measure of the unpopularity of the terms; that he had to return the following March was an indication of how brief was the military hiatus. This time the Japanese occupied Jehol.

It must have seemed so easy: the Japanese had struck just when they would be least resisted, with Chiang Kaishek preoccupied with crushing the Communists, who were drawing a certain strength from the countryside, and not up to fighting an external war on top of an internal one. What resistance he offered Japan, and that was hardly any at all, was kept within the limits of the peaceful negotiations in the tricky and humiliating business of diplomatic give and take (on China's part it was mostly give) which he had largely left to Wang Jingwei, to whose re-appointment as Prime Minister was now added the office of Foreign Minister. In a subtle way Wang became his passive collaborator, complementing Chiang's ostensibly hard line with his own deliberately soft one, working in strange tandem with his arch-rival in propitiating the Japanese and taking upon himself, with his lonely sense of duty, the opprobrium of his countrymen for bowing to the enemy.

He himself thought China would do better not to grasp the nettle, but somehow work to avoid the worst stings. He thought he could best exert his influence on events as a conciliator, emerging, because the times required it, beside Chiang Kaishek as the one on whose squarer shoulders had been shifted the almost unbearable burden of dealing with the Japanese. If there was one thing Chiang disliked, it was to show his hand. This being so, he, Wang Jingwei, would take the rap for yielding to the Japanese. Though, to the public, his advocacy of conciliation made anything but a hero of him, he himself believed the matter to require heroism, of the sort he was uniquely capable of evincing.

It was even left to Wang to bear the brunt of a physical attack meant for Chiang Kaishek. The incident occurred on 1 November 1935, at the close of a Guomindang meeting at Nanjing. The delegates were lining up for the official group portrait, and the usual gathering of press reporters and photographers was milling about. For some reason Chiang Kaishek had decided to remain indoors, but Wang was highly visible, and as usual his appearance was arresting. As he took his place in the front row, and presented his celebrated face to the camera, a man, ostensibly a photographer, stepped briskly out of the crowd and just as briskly fired several shots at him with a revolver concealed in his camera.

Security guards fell upon the assassin at once, and there and then put him to death. Wang Jingwei was severely wounded, but miraculously survived the shooting. Though he was rushed to a hospital in Shanghai and surgery immediately performed, it proved impossible to remove all the bullets; one, irretrievably lodged in his back, would add to his afflictions in later life. At the time of the shooting Chiang Kaishek, hearing the commotion, hastened to Wang Jingwei's side. But, as he tried to find some words of comfort, Madame Wang rounded on him and, though she did not accuse him directly of having ordered the assassination, implied as much. Acidly she said, 'There's no need to go to such lengths, you know. If things need sorting out we could very easily have tried talking first.'

Chiang denied he had anything to do with the affair, but was not believed by either Madame Wang or the public when it got to hear of the incident. Relinquishing office, the Prime Minister left to seek medical care in Europe. The newspaper reports, incorporating a large element of conjecture, but quick to offer explanations, said that Wang was the victim of anti-Japanese patriots incensed by his policy of appeasement. Shanghai's *Nippo*, the unofficial organ of the Japanese Consulate-General, said with unwarranted conviction that it was the work of the CC (Central Club) clique in the Guomindang, a party corps which flirted with Fascist ideas. As an explanation, party factionalism suited the Japanese better than the unpopularity of appeasement.

The case was to remain shrouded in mystery for at least four decades but, though no newspaper published the fact, Chiang did prove himself innocent, to Wang's satisfaction, not long after the event. Years and years later, when interest had all but subsided, it came out in some other connection that the plot had been hatched by the seditious Guangxi satrapy, a provincial clique which challenged Chiang's power. The bullets had of course been meant for Chiang Kaishek, and pumping them into Wang Jingwei had been a mistake. The hit-man had been sent by a notorious hoodlum, as part of the services rendered by the 'Murder, Inc.' he ran in Shanghai. The head of this sinister organization was a gangster who owed allegiance neither to the Green Gang nor to the Red, and whose adventurism included an attempt on the life of Chiang Kaishek's brother-in-law, the Finance Minister T.V. Soong.

All this was revealed after Chiang put the head of his secret services, General Dai Li, onto the case. Dai had an instinct for the way in which he could best be of service to Chiang Kaishek, and very soon rounded up all the suspects, including even the hit-man's poor wife, who probably had nothing to do with the affair, but who was dragged out of the hotel where she happened to be staying in Shanghai, and mercilessly flogged and tortured all the same. Dai, who was prepared to discover treachery in any woman, was not disappointed by the hoodlum's mistress, who turned informer for a consideration, and provided just such clues as would enable him to track her lover down and kill him.

What finally convinced Madame Wang that the bullets were intended for Chiang Kaishek and not for her husband, and dispelled her suspicion of Chiang's complicity, was the discovery that one of the conspirators was a member of the political clique loyal to Wang Jingwei in the Guomindang. It mattered whether Madame Wang was satisfied or not, as she was so easily roused to vocal scorn and could so effectively discompose everybody. Now in her forty-fourth year, this one-time revolutionary had become a very plump woman in harsh spectacles and hairdo, to whom the reaction of most was one of awe and a certain amount of distaste. She never bent to flattery, and seldom to humour. She had a head for men's affairs, and she felt secure in this, as also in the fact that she was Wang Jingwei's wife. From ignorance she had an unclouded view of what was right, which she saw always as what her husband had espoused. It could not be said that hers was a harmless vanity, that it was like any human wish to be thought superior, for it had in it a large contempt for human flaws. It is inconceivable that this unbending creature, this rock from whom few could strike a smile, should have been aroused by romantic love, that most fallible of human passions. And yet she clearly had been: she worshipped her husband with an almost adolescent blindness, though she was at odds with almost everybody else.

Wang Jingwei himself was unshakeably loyal to her, possibly understanding that his attachment to her was an intensification of the strongest strains of his careerism; or perhaps prolonged awe is a ground of love. He would later explain to an associate, 'She is my wife, but she is also my old revolutionary comrade, and for that reason I find it hard to make important decisions without consulting her.' He lacked one of her most serviceable qualities — the indifference to what people thought of her; he strove always to be agreeable. 'She can command people,' he thought, 'by her barbed manners; I do so only by my charm.' And he recognized that her way saw one through better.

When he left for Europe that winter following his wounding, and he reflected upon his fortunes during the last five years, he saw that though in the course of three decades he had been involved in almost everything important that had been going on in China, he had never held all the cards. Tracing his departure from the political scene back to its origins, he realized with some horror that all this time his disadvantages had been growing, like an iceberg, for the ship of his political career to founder upon. Rumours were rife — had Chiang perhaps leaked them himself? — that while Wang was selling out China to the Japanese Chiang Kaishek was secretly organizing patriotic resistance. By such falsehoods was Chiang's stock with the public kept high. Wang could not now help wondering if he had played into Chiang's hands, accepting to be the man out in front making his country's peace with Japan while, from behind, Chiang loosed his series of Extermination Campaigns against his fellow countrymen, the Communists.

Towards the end of the year, when Wang Jingwei had been ten months in Europe, what came to be known as the Xi'an Incident occurred. Arriving in that city to launch the sixth of his Communist Extermination Campaigns, Chiang Kaishek was kidnapped by the man he had appointed to command the campaign. The exploit was patriotic in its intention, which was to pressurize Chiang into accepting a truce in the civil war, and joining with the Communists in a united front against the Japanese invader. Bereft of a leader, the government turned to Wang Jingwei. Sent for in urgent appeals received a couple of days before Christmas from China's delegation to the League of Nations in Geneva, Wang sailed for Shanghai on 14 January 1937.

Several times during the journey he addressed himself seriously to the possibilities of a political stage vacated by Chiang Kaishek. Had his hour come at last? At Shanghai there was the usual flow of coolies and handcarts, the honking approach of the city and the clang of tram bells. At Hong Kong, where his ship had called, a Guomindang cadre had travelled ahead to meet him. He was Zhou Fohai, or 'Buddha', the one-time Communist glimpsed at the founding of the Chinese Communist Party some fifteen years before. Wang Jingwei did not know the close association he would presently have with this man; he only knew that Chiang Kaishek had been released by his captors to national rejoicing on Christmas Day.

THE SHANGHAI stock exchanges, which suspended trading when Sino-Japanese tensions flared up, remained closed throughout the fighting. All over the city, business came to a halt. The dealing stopped. Houses were unlit, prices were unquoted. The government, bankrolled all along by Shanghai big business, found itself in something of a crisis. The Minister of Finance, who was Chiang Kaishek's brother-in-law, T.V. Soong, clapped an extreme austerity program on State spending and summoned a meeting of Shanghai's top fifty bankers to discuss ways of palliating national economic distress.

T.V. Soong was all facts and figures, laying before the bankers his plan to modify the terms of government bonds, on the one hand halving payments to bond holders and on the other lowering the interest rate on government securities and extending the period of repayment of the principal.

'Nothing else,' he said, his tone becoming more urgent at the murmur of protest in his audience, 'offers us better hopes of financial rescue.' His eyes met Du Yuesheng's across the audience, and he was reassured by the lack of opposition in them. He recognized an ally.

Soong's success in engaging the bankers once more in the government's dwindling fortunes depended on Du. Between Du and his partner, Zhang Xiaolin, they had the Domestic Bondholders Association where they wanted it. Once Du had given the green light, the other bankers would swing into line behind him. This would spare Soong the trouble of having to resort to a measure that he deplored, the strong-arm tactics which brother-in-law Chiang had found so useful when it came to prying money out of the Shanghai plutocrats.

Chiang was really not much interested in these burgeoning

T.V. Soong, Minister of Finance

capitalists as a class, except as a source of plunder to finance his armies and his anti-Communist campaigns. This hardly endeared him to the Shanghainese, but he didn't much care about that. Soong was different: he genuinely wanted the financiers on his side, not only in the matter of bailing out the government but in maintaining in continuous vigour the entrepreneurial activity by which the interests of both Nanjing and Shanghai, the political and economic capitals of China, could not but be greatly promoted. Soong looked at the paymasters in his own special way, for he had Harvard, Columbia and the International Banking Corporation (New York) behind him. He was a technocrat with a touch of the comprador, that quintessentially Shanghainese breed of businessmen that knew East-West dealings from both sides, and from which most of these bankers were descended. Soong moved amongst them with ease. They knew where they stood with him. With their support and his adroit management, a booming market in government bonds had been created to everyone's enrichment a couple of years before in Shanghai. The banks did well out of these bonds, and now held something like between half to two-thirds of the issues launched. For the rest, a lively private bond market had developed on the stock exchanges, offering investors and speculators high yields and quick profits. The volume of trading had been colossal, and in the last year had surpassed the three-billion mark.

But of late the market had slumped, and now this new proposal to cut the interest rate and prolong the period of amortization would cost the bankers very dearly, and they were profoundly and legitimately disturbed.

They looked to see what Du Yuesheng would do, a man whose interests were scarcely less threatened than theirs: banker, bondholder, heavy speculator on the stock exchange, he had as much to lose, if not more, as they did by T.V. Soong's drastic plan.

He surprised them all. 'Gentlemen,' he said, 'I suggest we stand by Mr Soong's proposals.' As simple as that. And within an hour, what resistance the other bankers were preparing to offer collapsed. It took another hour for conditions and compensatory assurances to be thrashed out, and then Du Yuesheng was making an amiable speech on behalf of the Domestic Bondholders Association, thanking the participants for their goodwill, and commending everyone on their willingness to make personal sacrifices for the greater good. And somehow, in the course of the proceedings, everyone even agreed to word the proposals to make it seem as though the idea had been volunteered by the bondholders in the first place, thereby saving the government's face.

Du Yuesheng seldom turned his back on an appeal to his generosity, and never to one which came from Nanjing. Even a hoodlum could have his patriotic side. If he were asked why he stood so staunchly by Chiang Kaishek, he would probably say, 'Out of loyalty.' The politic loyalty of one who stood to gain by its demonstration. Yet if anyone should suggest that opportunism had a great deal to do with it, he would be doing an injustice to the sincerity of Du's allegiance. The fact that Du profited from the relationship was incidental, not intrinsic. As with the acceptance of the proposed alterations to the bond conditions there was always a price to be paid, though his coffers would hardly go empty with the subtraction of one less dividend. To him there was nothing worse than this niggling over arithmetic: distinctions in the size of profits had no compelling priority in a world where they could be easily and unendingly recouped.

He knew how it could be done. The Seven Star Company, for instance, that instrument for manipulating the bond and commodity markets set up by Soong's eldest sister, the redoubtable Madame H.H. Kung, with whose advance information on market trends Du was pleased to traffic. Du Yuesheng was closely associated with the Seven Star Company, for it had excellent inside information on government moves that were likely to affect the market, the job of Finance Minister being kept always in Madame Kung's family, going as it did to either her brother or her husband.

Madame Kung was not exquisite like her sister, Madame Chiang Kaishek, but she was kept soignée by the lubrications of cash and she could afford beautiful clothes. (When Martha Gellhorn met her she looked to the American journalist like one of those 'stout rich vulgar matrons in Miami Beach hotels'; yet she was elegantly dressed in black velvet, in the traditional Chinese style, the lappet of her gown fastened not by the normal frogs of braided silk, but by button-sized diamonds.) It is certain that she adored being rich, and that she was lucky in her marriage, for she and her husband had more than their American education in common (she Wesleyan, he Oberlin and Yale). They shared at least two other things: they both wanted a fortune banked in an American account against the uncertain future, and they were both good at getting it.

Unlike T.V. Soong, from whom he took over as Finance Minister on 29 October 1933, Dr H.H. Kung (called Duke Kung because he could trace his ancestry to Confucius, who was of noble descent) chose to see things the Chiang Kaishek way. For one thing he would not offend the Japanese. T.V. Soong did wonders with government finance but he *would* go about making anti-Japanese statements to the press. It is not without reason that the Japanese government considered him persona non grata. On his European and American tour that summer he did his best to secure Western investment in China to counteract Japanese economic power. When he resigned, Japan took his removal to be a victory for her diplomatic campaign, though he himself said in private that 'being Minister of Finance is no different from being Chiang Kaishek's dog; from now on I'm going to be a man and not a dog.'

Duke Kung, on the other hand, had no wish to court diplomatic unpopularity. To find the money for Chiang's anti-Communist campaigns, to float bond issues and command Shanghai banking assets, to appear to the world as the amiable and cultivated gentleman he assuredly was — all this he wished for, but not to risk confrontation with Japan or to be identified with any pro-Anglo-American policy.

He had his work cut out. Through the summer months of 1934, the deepening depression in China was beginning to be felt in Shanghai. Rises in world silver prices had badly damaged exports from China, a country whose currency was still on a silver standard. The local papers were tirelessly devoted to matters concerning silver: the passing of the Silver Purchase Act by the U.S. Congress, a law authorizing the American government to buy the metal at home and abroad; the silver quotations in New York soaring as a result; the flow of silver out of China for sale at inflated prices in London and New York; the smuggling set in motion by the imposition of a heavy government tax on silver export; the jacking up of interest rates by the silver outflows and the tightening up of the money market.

All this boded ill for Duke Kung's government bonds, the key instrument of his deficit financing policy. Money no longer came quite so readily from the banks; his hold on the bankers was slipping. Most ruinously of all, the general manager of the ruling Bank of China was dumping millions of dollars in securities and urging stockbrokers to channel their money into the inland economy and away from government bonds. This meant taking money away from Shanghai, the source of sustenance for Chiang Kaishek's armies. After some months of this, Duke Kung and Chiang Kaishek decided that the manager must go, and that the Nanjing government must take over the Bank of China. How he pulled off that spectacularly brazen coup remains obscure to this day. It is certain that Du Yuesheng was an accessory, and was the one who cleared the decks for

A Shanghai street in the 1930s — an East-West hybrid with money as its raison d'être

the action. The takeover had to proceed with caution, with enough violence to unmake the bankers once and for all, but not enough to damage the confidence of the investors and send them running with their money to British and American banks. The scene was carefully laid; Du saw to the practical arrangements, calling meetings between Kung and the business community under the auspices of the Shanghai Civic Association which he headed. On these occasions Duke Kung and Du Yuesheng pleaded for the city's distressed businessmen: let loans be made available, economic relief be provided. The big banks could not know that when they demurred, this was exactly the cue the government had been waiting for: if the banks could not help, then Nanjing must step in. To the bankers' impotent consternation Duke Kung put forward a bold proposition, that the Bank of China and the Bank of Communications should increase their stock and exchange the additionally created shares for government bonds, surrendering majority control to Nanjing. This would enhance their credit capacity, Kung claimed, and make it easier for the business community to fight the depression.

The bankers saw that there was no question of their resisting; it was clear that Kung already saw himself in the driver's seat. That he had Du Yuesheng behind him meant that the matter was as good as decided. When Kung filled all the top jobs with his own people, and named Du Yuesheng a director of the Bank of China, Nanjing's take-over was complete. The seizure flew in the face of the law, and Prime Minister Wang Jingwei came out in opposition to it. But Duke Kung went ahead anyway, and with an audacity that was a foretaste of Nanjing browbeating to come, brought the two banks firmly under government control.

Du Yuesheng was soon sitting on many boards. That autumn, when Nanjing removed China from the silver standard and made government-issued bank notes the legal tender, Du was invited to join other bankers on the Currency Reserve Board, set up to oversee the currency reform. The board had as its adviser one Sir Frederick Leith Ross, a distinguished expert sent by the British government to assist China in her economic rehabilitation. Sir Frederick, knowing something of Du Yuesheng's reputation, had objected to his appointment, but Kung had assured him that Du was a reformed character. 'Of course he is a blackmailer or worse,' Kung agreed, 'but one hundred thousand men in Shanghai obey his orders; he could create a disturbance at any moment....' Sir Frederick was to relate in his memoirs a much-quoted and probably apocryphal story about Du that he had heard in Shanghai. Once, Madame Kung tipped Du off on an impending government move on foreign exchange. Du misinterpreted the information, speculated misguidedly, was caught short, and lost a large sum of money. He went to the husband and said it might be a good idea if the Central Bank made good his losses. When Duke Kung jibbed at this, 'a No. 1 style coffin', ran the story, 'was deposited on Dr Kung's doorstep by half a dozen funeral attendants' that evening. The next day Kung summoned a special meeting of the Central Bank board and got the directors to agree to reimburse Du — 'a patriotic citizen' — for his recent losses in the foreign exchange market in full.

To the end of his life, however hard he tried to throw off his past, the suggestion of thuggery would cling to Du's name. His philanthropy and welfare work, while publicly acknowledged, were never accepted on their own merits, and respectability was a frail construction continually threatened by reminders of a shadier reality.

Yet if his reputation remained unsavoury, it was not for want of whitewashing. Having never learnt to read and write himself, he founded a school for Chinese boys in the French Concession. Yet it could not be said that this was entirely a bid for social acceptance. Like any human aspiration towards distinction it could easily be mocked or disparaged, but as vanities go it was by no means the most reprehensible. Nor was it a place of dilettantism and privilege. The monastic atmosphere was well known and intentional. Inspired by Japanese example, the headmaster insisted on shaven heads. Du placed his own sons in the school, and saw to it that they were subjected to the discipline and rigours the same as everybody else. When it was time for his adolescent eldest son to marry, as a special concession he was allowed to grow back his hair, but so as not to lower the tone of the place he was removed from the school for the duration.

It was not enough for Du that he was the king of the Shanghai underworld; he wanted to command the upper-world as well. While he honoured the customs of the Green Gang, it became daily more obvious that he needed something more — more, that is, than the leadership of an old secret society. What he wanted, he realized, was his own fraternity, and a socially respectable one at that. In 1933 he founded the Constancy Society, to unite by a common allegiance to himself the many clients and protégés that had gathered about him over the years. 'Pupils', he would call his disciples, and they in their turn would address him as 'teacher'. Avenue Edouard VII was where the society had its first headquarters. The membership included many men of fashion, rank and money, including the comprador of that lordly British institution, the Hongkong and Shanghai Bank.

It was the distillation of his secret society career. Under it, protection as a growth industry thrived unsurpassed. Tycoons in many a flashy villa in Shanghai owed their security to the society's guardianship. But it was not all high-level corruption and sentiment. When war proper finally broke out, on the night of 7 July 1937, the comradeship and secrecy of the Constancy Society were easily translated into the qualities necessary for underground resistance work. And it was by its struggles with the enemy, the Japanese and their collaborators, that the secret society most arrestingly distinguished itself.

PART II

Patriotism is the last refuge of a scoundrel.

— SAMUEL JOHNSON

Chapter Seven

BLOODY SATURDAY
14 AUGUST 1937

BOMBS EXPLODED in two of Shanghai's busiest intersections on 14 August 1937. At a distance, British cricketers at the Race Club were annoyed that the stray pieces of falling shrapnel interrupted their game. But at the junctions where the bombs fell — one was in the International Settlement, at the point where Nanjing Road met the Bund, and the other was in Frenchtown, at Avenue Edouard VII — people were dead before they knew what had hit them.

The day was remembered later as Bloody Saturday, the start of a battle said to be the bloodiest since Verdun. Five weeks before, on July 7, an obscure encounter between Japanese and Chinese troops at a place called Marco Polo Bridge, to the south of Beijing, had given Japan, long spoiling for a fight, the chance to launch a full-scale invasion of China. This was something different from the running aggression she had been showing for half a decade or more. It was, as one Chinese writer put it, 'the most terrible, the most inhuman, the most brutal, the most devastating war in all Asia's history'; a war which left ten million dead, forty million Chinese homeless, and spurred a revolution that would turn Communist the most populous nation on earth.

In Shanghai, Bloody Saturday was the climax of a sequence of events that had begun unfolding a few weeks before. There had first occurred what the Chinese press was to ridicule as the episode of the Thin Man. A Japanese seaman had mysteriously disappeared, abducted, according to a bogus witness that official Japanese statements would describe as a 'thin man', by some Chinese kidnappers in a motor car. The Japanese marines proceeded to make a great issue of this, and began sandbagging street corners and mounting machine-guns. But if the alleged kidnap was an excuse for yet another display of Japanese aggression, the ruse sadly misfired, for the seaman turned up a few days later, and confessed that he hadn't been abducted at all.

It seemed that, on leaving a brothel one evening, he had been surprised by some Chinese thugs and got into a fight with them. When they demanded hush money from him, he had thrown away his cap and badges and lain low as a stowaway on a British steamer for a couple of days, hoping by doing so to avoid the consequences of his unfortunate indiscretion.

The Japanese were embarrassed, but went on to play their trump card. The second episode, the so-called Aerodrome Murders, did bring matters to a head. One early evening in August, two uniformed Japanese men were seen driving in a Japanese Naval Landing Party patrol car towards the Chinese military airfield on the outskirts of the city. The Chinese sentries ordered them to stop, but they pushed on regardless through the military fortifications. Not altogether surprisingly, they were fired at until they were dead. It seemed fruitless for the Chinese to suggest that their deaths were perhaps sacrificial, that the whole thing was engineered, or to reason that there was no cause for war. Within three days the Japanese Third Fleet had steamed up the Huangpu River, and Japanese marines had dug in in the zones beyond Western control.

After the two incidents came the four bombs, all of them exploding in nerve-centres of the town. The first three landed on Bloody Saturday, the fourth was dropped nine days later.

Until it happened on Saturday afternoon no one could have foretold the catastrophe. It was blazing hot, and apart from the threat of a typhoon passing up the coast, the day had begun calmly enough. You could see the lighters and sampans going about their normal business on the Huangpu River, the full panoply of British destroyers, sloops and gunboats in front, and the U.S. Fleet's *Augusta* behind. Downstream to the east lay the French cruiser *Lamotte Picquet*, and way up to the north the Japanese flagship *Idzumo* was moored. It was shortly before 4.30 p.m. when the sky was shaken by a sudden roar, and five twin-engined Chinese bombers shot out five thousand feet up from under the clouds, making straight for the *Idzumo*. Every Japanese man-of-war erupted with anti-aircraft fire. There was no fighter cover, and as the bombers ran smack into the barrage of Japanese flak one of them broke formation and peeled off in a dive. Four stray

Death trucks taking away corpses from Avenue Edouard VII

bombs, jettisoned in desperation, came tumbling from it towards the Bund. To those watching it was not immediately clear that the plane had been damaged and that the bombs had had to be abandoned. All they saw were the fountains of mud and water sent up by the two that fell into the river. The other two veered, caught in the wind, and in full view of the horrified spectators one came hurtling down towards the mass of buildings on the Bund.

In a moment the roof of the Palace Hotel exploded in a sheet of flames, and a shower of fragments fell in a cloud of glass and plaster dust. Below, Nanjing Road was ripped apart. In one corner sprawled the body of a decapitated policeman, in another the corpse of a tall European in white flannels. About them lay another seven hundred dead, some of their heads, arms and legs severed from their bodies. For a moment there was complete silence. Then barely half an hour later, the busiest square in Frenchtown was shaken by a tremendous explosion: another stricken bomber had had to shed its load.

Inspector Huang Jinrong, in recounting the incident, would wave his arms to demonstrate how the two shrapnel bombs sliced off the roof of his Great World Amusement Palace. The bombs could not have chosen a more crowded spot. The three thousand they killed were a part of the daily swirl and mingle in front of that house of multiple joys, the fun palace which the inspector owned along with many other places of divertissement in Frenchtown. Now it was charred and war-blackened, and gone were the gambling tables it held, and the restaurants and massage parlours, the peep shows and shooting galleries, the earwax extractors and the singsong girls — all that titillation and juju. Now there was only the squalor of war. The heavy rain of the typhoon added its own tang to the stench. The death carts kept sloshing up and down Avenue Edouard VII, taking the corpses away, but the dank and heavy reek of the bodies lingered; the blood had soaked into the gutters. Inspector Huang supposed he would have to get the contractors in; the place would soon be repaired, but he groaned to think of the dent that the suspension of business would make in his annual profits.

He was not alone in his dismay. Two Cantonese gentlemen, owners of Sincere and Wing On, Shanghai's biggest and smartest department stores, had had their shops wrecked that summer by a bomb, the fourth to land in the city. At the height of the lunchtime jostle, one side of Sincere simply caved in, and a moment later Wing On's windows flew apart in a haze of smashed glass. But no one had heard the plane fly past, and for a time it was supposed that the shell had been lobbed at a long range from across the Huangpu River. Rumours persistently suggested that it was another case of a Chinese bomber shedding its load in distress, but though responsibility for the disaster was never placed, many people believed the culprits to be the Japanese Air Force.

The foreign community, in whose territory every one of these explosions had occurred, rose not a minute too soon to the occasion. The British arranged for battalions of the Royal Ulster Rifles and Royal Welch Fusiliers to come immediately from Hong Kong; the French sent for their troops in Indo-China; and these were joined by the Sixth U.S. Marines and a battalion of Savoia Grenadiers summoned all the way from Abyssinia.

Chapter Eight

THE RISING SUN OVER SHANGHAI 1937–1938

TWO DAYS INTO the Shanghai battle, Du Yuesheng received a visiting-card announcing the arrival at Rue Wagner of General Dai Li, the head of intelligence services last seen rooting out suspects from Murder Inc. following the attempt on Wang Jingwei's life. The two men greeted each other warmly, Dai Li thrusting out a strangely slender and soft hand. His smile was wide and genial. It was only the eyes, beneath the high but not receding hairline, that hinted at the nature of his profession — its horrendous risks, its concern with survival, and its exhilarating glimpses of evil. His most unprepossessing feature was also his most vulnerable spot. It was his nose. He suffered badly from naso-sinusitis and was never without a kit, imported from America, for treating it.

Dai Li was rising in the world, and with an acceleration that made him believe in destiny. There was nothing in his small-town background to suggest that he would go far, except perhaps his birthplace in Zhejiang Province, the same as his patron Chiang Kaishek's. To show how far he'd come Dai Li liked to tell others of the time he had only one suit of clothes to his name, and whenever he washed them, in the West Lake in Hangzhou, he had to sit around naked waiting for them to dry. Another memory from that time was putting up at his cousin's place in Shanghai, sleeping on the floor and, poor relation that he was, suffering the insults of his cousin's wife. He got his own back when he'd risen high enough to give his cousin a job in the service. Dai Li goaded him to take a concubine and rob the wife of her superiority.

It wasn't until he enrolled at the Whampoa Military Academy, where he attended, but did not finish, a cavalry course and found his métier as Chiang Kaishek's watchdog, that he really got into his stride. As commandant of the academy, Chiang was a stickler for ideological straightness and hygiene, by which practice he meant not only the cleanliness of the barracks but also the incorruptibility of soul and body. It was Dai Li who, putting the finger on the backsliders, kept Chiang informed of lapses in the cadets' discipline. In 1932, when a Whampoa clique calling itself the Regenerative Society set up an intelligence unit, it was Dai Li who became its head.

The Regenerative Society spawned what the Communists, following the Japanese, were to call the Blueshirts, an organization pledged to advance the interests of the national leader, Chiang Kaishek. The spread of the Blueshirts movement coincided with the appearance in China of a spate of books on Fascism, Hitler and Mussolini, including the Chinese translation of *Mein Kampf*. Chiang drew on the examples offered by contemporary Nazi Germany, as he did the deep-rooted and to him thoroughly familiar traditions of the Chinese secret society, and came up with an intelligence apparatus that best suited his purpose. Seeing nothing but treachery and intrigue around him, he not only abetted organizations like the Blueshirts, but duplicated them, playing one off against another and, if the need ever arose, betraying them all. Not long before the outbreak of war he further increased the complexity of his intelligence network by combining the existing services into one, dividing that into three (the second headed by Dai Li), and finally setting up the first and the second on their own. Calling these units by different names but keeping their jurisdiction intentionally vague and their functions inextricably involved, he succeeded in making one the rival, and therefore the watchdog, of the other.

It was in Dai Li that the control of the second Special Branch, the Military Affairs Commission Bureau of Central Investigation and Statistics, almost entirely rested. Chiang needed someone absolutely loyal to himself to run this bureau, and Dai Li was just such a man. Chiang saw him for what he was, a straightforward, hearty adventurer, a man more impetuous than calculating, bluff in speech and irrepressible in action, and entirely uncomplicated by inner doubts and contradictions. Dai did not bother much with discretion, but if this seems a grievous fault in a secret agent, it was not one that Chiang held against him.

With Dai Li in charge, a pattern was formed, a routine of arrests, murders and kidnappings which would cause him to be dubbed (by an American historian) 'China's combination of Himmler and J. Edgar Hoover'. Under him the organization expanded, its tentacles stretching from Nanjing to all the coastal ports and beyond. Presently it became the largest spy ring in all Asia, its overseas web enmeshing Delhi, Bombay, Burma, Bangkok, Singapore, the Philippines, Hong Kong, Saigon, the United States, London and Paris. His men were recruited from the Whampoa Academy, and from police stations and garrisons throughout the country. Dai Li himself made it a policy to be accessible to the rank and file, frequently giving them pep talks, in which the importance of shunning corruption, and what he liked to call 'skirts', was continually brought home to them. Family life was something unknown to the secret agent, Dai Li preferring his men to remain single. Though General Dai himself was scarcely the model of rectitude, it was understood that the constant exhortations to moral austerity was by no means disingenuous, or to be taken merely at its face-value. The road to iniquity is after all paved with good intentions, and a concomitant of authority is the privilege of a double standard. Like all public figures General Dai Li lived by a dual morality: one code for his private behaviour, and another for his public behaviour and for his subordinates. This he applied without conceding that doubleness of standard, in its very duplicity, paves the way for treachery.

The concerns of the organization were chiefly two: Communists and traitors. In one way the Communists were more troublesome than the traitors: all the tricks that the Bureau had up its sleeve were built into the Cheka programmes they themselves had learnt from Russia, and could more or less be anticipated. But the misgivings which Dai Li voiced that day, as he sat across the table from Du Yuesheng, had to do with the defence of Shanghai against a more immediate threat, the Japanese. He had in his head the text of a telegram, just received from Chiang Kaishek in Nanjing, which said that he and Du Yuesheng were to muster a ten-thousand-strong guerilla force at once, to augment the regular armies in the defence of Shanghai. As he relayed this to his host, he also mentioned the difficulties which the city peculiarly presented. In Shanghai, the Bureau could not do exactly as it liked, for the International Settlement and French Concession were rendered inhospitable to its agents by their foreign jurisdiction, police force and press, and by their supposed neutrality. In what corners and by what hands the Bureau's victims were seized must remain mysterious; murder, once the victims had been abducted, must take place elsewhere.

Chiang Kaishek had obviously foreseen this, and had not failed to recall how such difficulties were overcome on an earlier occasion. Ten years before, it had been Du Yuesheng who helped to deliver Shanghai from the grip of Communism, and into Chiang Kaishek's hands. Chiang had not forgotten Du's efficiency in crushing that Communist uprising. Of course the foreign powers were helpful then, and could not be expected to be as obliging now; indeed, the British *taipans* wanted nothing better than the reconciliation of British and Japanese interests and believed there was room enough for both in China. Only a few days before, the *North China Daily News*, Shanghai's leading English-language paper, had urged the Chinese to make peace: 'However bitterly Japanese aggression may be resented,' it said, 'it can hardly be denied that its extension would be encouraged rather than stayed by physical resistance from the Central Government and would be accompanied by such complete destruction of China's resources that all hopes of national reconstruction might have to be indefinitely postponed.' But Chiang knew Du to be a man of uncommon flexibility, and when he sent that telegram, was confident that the recipient could instantly see what should be done.

Knowing this, knowing how much Du wanted to contribute to the war effort, General Dai Li proceeded to confide his plan to his host: a secret force was to be assembled, arms and ammunition to be bought and commandeered, troops to be trained, techniques of sabotage, assault and counter-espionage to be perfected. Du got the picture at once. 'Leave it to me,' he said (he used here an expression referring to the sealing of a transaction, and for which the modern equivalent might be 'It's a deal'). He assumed, correctly, that he would be footing most of the bill, but he did not jib at the expense, colossal though it would be.

He always had a touch of the prodigious. When the commander of the famous Ironsides Army arrived in Shanghai to defend his native Pudong on the other side of the Huangpu River, Du presented him with a bulletproof limousine for his private use, and offered for good measure to sink his own ships so as to seal off the Japanese vessels in the Yangtze River. Within a couple of months of Dai Li's visit he had assembled an eighteen-thousand-strong commando force, and set up a body, the Jiangsu-Zhejiang Action Commission, to oversee it. Of course it was scarcely an army, and when it assembled to receive its arms, the gathering was more like a guild or a fraternity, with some of the recruits coming from shops and factories, and others from the ranks of the Green Gang and Red Gang. But it was a do-or-die shock force, and there was, one felt, almost nothing it would not do. (When the battle of Shanghai was over, and the unit was disbanded, one of its detachments was transformed into the nucleus of the Loyal Patriotic Army, a guerilla force which General Dai Li brought under his own command, and whose exploits were to harass the Japanese army of occupation for the next eight years.)

The Japanese did not need much prompting to discover how formidable an opponent Du Yuesheng could be, or how useful an ally. Du was no less adept at reading the signs, and the extent of Japanese designs on him quickly became as apparent to him as if he had been informed of it in detail. At first the Japanese committed themselves to winning him over, and he to declining their offers. This was followed by a stepping up of the pressure, with the Japanese sending General Doihara, that prince of intrigue, to see him. Otherwise known as Lawrence of Asia, General Doihara, of the Japanese Imperial Army, ran a Special Service dedicated to the production of puppet regimes and the recruitment of collaborators. Because he rebuffed Doihara's overtures, Du thought it likely that the Japanese would resort to more drastic methods. And he was confirmed in his fears when one day a Japanese plane began to circle slowly and continuously over his house, with a drone that sounded like a cantor chanting a body to its grave.

With what means more fearful than intimidation the Japanese planned to secure his submission or, for that matter, his extinction, Du Yuesheng did not care to find out. Offered the anonymity of a flat in an apartment block in Rue Bourgeat by a friend, Du Yuesheng and his fourth wife moved out of their respective houses at once.

But they did not enjoy their security for long. Towards the end of October, the Chinese began to evacuate Shanghai's northern suburbs. For two desperate months their troops had made their stand, but it was a death stand, untenable from the start. When the Chinese defence finally crumbled, 90,000 Japanese pursued the retreating army up the Yangtze River, to make the blood spilt lead to more blood, the sacrifices made to more terrible sacrifice, the heroism shown to more wasted heroism. The northern suburbs were put to the torch, and eight miles of blazing fire covered the Chinese retreat. Sixteen days earlier, Du Yuesheng's commandos had evacuated the old Chinese city, the guerillas streaming northwards towards the safety of the French Concession, where Du and patrols by courtesy of the French Consul-General were waiting to wave them in. In deference to the concession's neutrality the men disarmed as soon as they crossed the frontier, handing over their weapons and ammunition to the French patrols as they came in. The surviving detachments then disbanded, the men fanning out across the whole of Shanghai, to surface one day as underground resistance fighters.

Black smoke cast a pall over the northern purlieus. Around the perimeter of the International Settlement, flags of the Rising Sun flew. News of the withdrawal, spreading rapidly through the city, plunged Shanghai into bewilderment and despair. People felt the fight emptying out of them.

Then, when all seemed lost, word flew round Shanghai that a Chinese flag had been hoisted above the big Joint Savings Godown on the northern bank of the Suzhou Creek! Eight hundred men from the 88th Division had stayed behind to defend it to the death. The doomed unit came to be called the Lone Battalion, a name that has gone into history as a synonym for Chinese heroism. The flag had been smuggled to the soldiers the night before; a Chinese Girl Guide had done it at the risk of her life, slipping through the British-guarded defence sector with the flag concealed in her clothes. Later, having delivered her message of solidarity to the Lone Battalion, she was let out by a door on the side of the building nearest the creek, the side that was only a street's width from a bridge patrolled by British soldiers. In abandonment to the rushing of blood and patriotism in her, she plunged into the black depths of the Suzhou Creek and swam across, overswept by a fusillade of Japanese rifle fire. Ashore, on the Settlement side of the creek, and finding herself in a great mingle of people, Chinese and British, she was dazed, but exultant. It was reckless, her going across like that, but as the flag flapped triumphantly across the water, Shanghai took heart.

The cause was still doomed, and at the press conference the next day, the Japanese still spoke as though victory was in the bag, but among Chinese men and women there was a new defiance.

The British and American authorities in the International Settlement, into which fall-out from Japanese artillery fire was landing, urged surrender, sending word to the commander of the Lone Battalion that he and his men would be given sanctuary if they laid down their arms. The commander did not doubt that he would die, yet at the same time as he evoked his own death, stretched out there athwart the sacks of wheat and soybean in the godown, he declined the offer, as if to prove that true victories are not won by armies, but are wrested out of helplessness by men who refuse to be broken. The building was completely surrounded, and Japanese rifle fire spattered the walls. Militarily speaking there was nothing to be gained from its occupation, and none of the soldiers expected to come out of it alive; the Lone Battalion was there simply to sustain an illusion, and holding out with courage was an end in itself.

On the fourth day of the siege the Japanese Commander-in-Chief gave an ultimatum: he would give the battalion until midnight to surrender, and if it didn't he would blast it out with gunfire. The site of the godown being extremely close to the International Settlement, the foreigners minded this even more than the intended victims of the threatened action, and Telfer-Smollett, the British General, appealed to Chiang Kaishek at once to order the battalion's withdrawal. The Chinese leader, or rather Madame Chiang Kaishek, had only one remark to make to Telfer-Smollett: 'No, they must die that China may live.'

But Chiang in the end relented, and a time was set for the

evacuation. At midnight the Japanese fired a warning shot. A few Chinese soldiers began to emerge from the godown, and then a few more. Outside, Japanese fire trained on the road leading to the godown exploded like gushers and then poured across the building. It was in the space between the volleys, when the Japanese were reloading their guns, that the Chinese soldiers made their dash for the bridge to safety. Of the wives and relatives waiting on the other side of the creek, all were tense, proud, each one's heart pounding. The autumn night, the shelling, the British guards at the receiving end, all increased the urgency of the hour, the sense of speed managed against huge and impossible odds. Then the last of the battalion had run the infernal gauntlet to the bridge, and was shedding his arms and flopping forward in exhaustion. To the British guards, the Chinese soldiers, now that they were seen in the flesh, looked too puny for the scale of the epic. Yet for these small, thin men, the word, they decided, was not yellow. Descriptions they had always thought apt — cowardly, faint-hearted — no longer applied where people had demonstrated such heights of courage and endurance.

Of the eight hundred that had moved into the godown four days before, only three hundred had survived. Next morning they were marched to their internment camp. Passersby turned their heads to stare at the men in their tattered uniforms. Some were carrying oiled-paper umbrellas, others walked hand in hand; one man carried a birdcage with a canary. Six girls in uniform, part of the women's comfort corps who had stayed with the soldiers to nurse them during the siege, walked behind. Seeing them, people were whipped to a new whirl of hatred for the Japanese.

After that the city's resistance guttered out. In Rue Bourgeat, Du Yuesheng faced what there was to face, and saw that if he did not leave Shanghai he would be in grave danger. If one could not save Shanghai, one could at least save one's own skin. The matter did not induce panic, and he told his fourth wife not to worry. He left quietly on a late November night, slipping out of his apartment in the company of a valet, and boarding a French vessel bound for Hong Kong.

When it sailed he was lying in bed in his cabin, in the lull before the sleep that his valet's skilful massaging would conjure from his insomnia. His burdens, threatening to roll over him a moment before, receded, and his bed ceased to be felt beneath him. He knew, without looking, that everything familiar was spinning by, yet he had no sense of a permanent departure. There entered his mind a remark that somebody had once made: 'The Japs slap the Chinese and shake hands afterwards'; and he dwelt on it, for its comforting suggestion that things would mend in the end. He told himself that this was the natural sequence in such affairs, and that it would not be long before he could return to Shanghai. In any case, he thought, there were his followers in the Constancy Society to see to things during his absence.

He could not know the havoc his departure would cause. Its effects rippled down through all the tiers of Shanghai society — from the Red Gang, which promptly quarrelled with the Green Gang, to the nightsoil gatherers in the French Concession, who found their monopoly challenged the moment their protector was gone. There being no beggars' fraternity, no undertakers' guild, no union of touts or pedlars that did not owe its constituency to Du Yuesheng's blessing, his exit from town affected the power relations of every street corner and every line of business in Frenchtown.

Meanwhile, in the British colony of Hong Kong, Du Yuesheng was settling into a suite in the Peninsula Hotel. The rendezvous of polite society, the Peninsula is luxurious, the evidence of its exclusiveness tastefully displayed in the boutiques, the jewellers, the gift shops. Du Yuesheng felt quite comfortable there and in due course sent for his family. Of the wives, only the newest came. The third Mrs Du was in England, where her two sons were studying; the second never did get on with him; and the first, dreaming her opium dreams, would not think of leaving her room, let alone Shanghai.

The following month news reached Du that the Chinese capital was lost. Nanjing was sacked, and with so bestial an orgy of rape, murder and plunder that elsewhere, Japanese officers wept for shame at the barbarity of their fellow countrymen, and the world when it read of the atrocities in the press more than ever believed the Japanese to be brutes of a lower animal order. Retreating, Chiang Kai-shek moved his armies and the seat of Chinese government upriver, to Wuhan.

Some time after this Du Yuesheng began to make short trips to Wuhan. Mostly it was to keep up his connections with government circles, for he was anxious that his removal to Hong Kong should not cut him off from State affairs. It was during one of these visits that he was interviewed by the English writers W.H. Auden and Christopher Isherwood, who had been commissioned by their publishers to write a book about the East. In the way of such audiences, Du gave the interview with a score of his own men in attendance. They talked entirely of the Red Cross, on whose board Du was a director. Anyone standing by the window on the top floor of the Broadway Mansions, a huge brown pile on the northern side of the Suzhou Creek, would have had a good view of the refugees pouring into the International Settlement that summer. Below, the creek is packed with life, the sampans sidling by alongside the barges. Opposite, the iron girders of Garden Bridge arch metallically against the sky. To the left the creek broadens towards the Huangpu River, sweeping away to the mighty Yangtze beyond. In front is the Bund, seen end-on, so that the British Consulate, its grounds edging the Creek, is the most distinct of the sweep of buildings lining the waterfront. Beyond it lies the Public Gardens, a park in the English style.

The scene is bathed in sunshine, but for as far as the eye can see the view is blotched by humanity. Refugees — ants carrying their morsels of bundled possessions — clog up the bridge and the waterfront, making the approach to the Settlement seem like some backwash of scum and bobbing rubbish. All around the Public Gardens, up past the Banque de l'lndochine, the Glen Line Building, Jardine, Matheson and Company, the Cathay Hotel, past the bronze lions of the Hongkong and Shanghai Banking Corporation and the Shanghai Club, the ten-mile phalanx of humanity shambles. The August sun beats down. Already, temporary shelters are springing up by the sandbag barricades thrown up in front of the public buildings. The contrast is cruel, between the evidence of comfort and well-being glimpsed through the windows of these buildings, and the squalor of the homeless huddling in the recesses outside.

The refugees had come upon Shanghai like a flood-tide, engulfing its streets and bridges, some coming from the suburbs, others

After the Japanese attacks, Chinese refugees pouring across Suzhou Creek and onto the Bund

from villages further afield. In the Chinese quarter abutting the French Concession, the lucky ones found a home in the famous Refugee Zone, set up by the Catholic priest Father Jacquinot, a gaunt missionary who had lost an arm in the Great War, and sported a gun in the folds of his cassock. Those less lucky put up makeshift shelters in the streets.

At the same time as the Chinese poured in, the European inhabitants of the foreign enclaves poured out. The Shanghai Club, whose cloistered auras of pink gin and cigar smoke could be savoured by the ladies only one night in the year, on the occasion of the annual ball, now filled with wives and mothers making ready to evacuate to Hong Kong: the Americans on the *President Taft* and the *President Jefferson*, the Britons on the *Rajputana*, the Germans on the *Oldenburg*, the Dutch on the *Tasman*. Down by the wharves they embarked to the strains of each ship's orchestra, leaving bachelors and grass-widowers behind.

They, unattached, took their consolations in the clubs and the cabarets. In the evenings it seemed that there was no end or limit to the pleasures that Shanghai could provide. Restaurants and nightclubs, recreating the decor, moods and and cuisines of their European originals, allowed ersatz nights to be spent in Paris, Prague, Berlin, Vienna, Moscow, Tokyo, and New York. In those few square miles of European settlement, Shanghai seemed less like the commercial centre of China than an extension of some vast universal metropolis. A gentleman could have a beautiful hostess, of any of five or six nationalities, sit at his table and wipe his brow, tease him to a bottle of champagne or a caviar canape, waltz with him on the dance floor and then, if he wished, stay with him all through the curfew, on one of those beds the nightclub proprietors provided for just such eventualities. In the afternoon there was always tennis or squash at the Country Club, or a garden party at some consul's private villa — with drinks and cold buffet, and silk-clad Chinese servants bowing from the waist. There might be heard the rattle of machine-guns in the distance, but for the moment life would go on almost exactly as before.

Won by so many generations of administration and investment, such a life could not be easily relinquished. Would the British or American settler stick it out to the end, and put up a fight to safeguard his interests? The Chinese government certainly hoped so. Chiang Kaishek, by flinging the best German-trained units of his army

A Chinese cabaret in the 1930s

into the Shanghai battle, had shifted the action, against all Japanese calculations, to that part of China in which the foreigner's money and heart were most deeply embedded. The whole drift of the war had been north; now, unexpectedly, it had moved south. He clearly wanted the Western powers to be drawn into the fighting — the British and Americans most of all; the Russians next; or, failing the intervention of these powers, the Germans and Italians as a last resort.

But neither the British nor the Americans would engage themselves in China's sad fortunes. The machine-gunning by the Japanese of a car travelling between Nanjing and Shanghai, seriously wounding Sir Hughe Knatchbull-Hugessen, the British representative in China, produced consternation, high tension and an exchange of face-saving notes, but did not precipitate British involvement in the war. Nor could the United States be roused, not even when the Japanese, either in ill temper or provocation, or perhaps even by mistake, bombed and sank the U.S.S. *Panay*, an American gunboat on the Yangtze.

In Brussels, Chinese emissaries did their best to enlist Western support. In Rome, a goodwill mission sent by Wang Jingwei and led by the Minister of Propaganda tried to win the sympathy of the Axis countries for the Chinese cause. It saw Benito Mussolini and his son-in-law, the Foreign Minister Galeazzo Ciano, but though the Chinese minister and Count Ciano had been close friends when the latter was Consul-General in Shanghai, and had shared many a pleasurable evening at the nightclub and singsong house, yet when it came to an alliance between their two countries Ciano was unsympathetic. What the Chinese envoy particularly minded was that, knowing Count Ciano's taste, he had gone to the trouble of asking for a large sum of money for the mission in order to include in it a certain lady from Shanghai. However much the Italian might appreciate the gift, he did not see this as a good reason for pledging his country's support. Indeed, he made no bones about the fact that he thought the Chinese cause hopeless, and that China should make peace while she can; it was better, he said, 'to lose a leg, even if the operation is a painful one, than the more vital parts of the body.'

Back in Shanghai, though the foreigner was on thin ice and he was never safe from Japanese outrages upon his rights and person, the international zones remained neutral, and Japan on the Municipal Council was still acknowledged as a partner. Like an infirm man, that civic body discovered it could turn in only one or two positions; to attempt more was to tip itself down a collision course, to hasten the end that awaited the white man in the Far East. The international town was an island, three sides of it surrounded by occupied territory, and all the streets crossing its borders patrolled by Japanese guards.

Japanese sentries, with their antiseptic masks and bayonets, were all over the Chinese sectors. They stood in the centre of Garden Bridge, the conduit to the occupied area, and demanded bows of everyone that crossed it on foot. The Chinese would perform these obeisances, but would be inwardly convulsed with rage. Under his breath he continued to call his new masters 'bandy-legged dwarves'; he could not bring himself to corroborate the fancy ideas that they had about themselves. One thing particularly rankled. It was the victory parade the conquerors staged in December. When the Japanese Army marched through the International Settlement, and scores of Japanese civilians crowded in from the far side of the Creek to watch and cheer, each carrying a little paper flag of the Rising Sun, a Chinese merchant flung himself from a rooftop, shouting 'Long live China!' as he fell. The column quickly regained its composure, but as it filed past the hotels and department stores of Nanjing Road, right in the heart of the British enclave, a bomb was hurled at it from somewhere in the throng, and four of the marching soldiers were brought down. That was how deep it went with the Chinese.

The Japanese were like that, arrogant, insensitive, unconscious of the hatred they were arousing. 'We have nothing against the Chinese,' some of them would say; 'we're only trying to save China from herself, from internal disorder and decay. If only she would negotiate, she could save herself all this trouble.' As the Japanese military envisaged it the matter was a straightforward one: a settlement between the two sides, the acceptance by China of Japanese tutelage and indirect rule. They saw their imperial ambitions as reasonable, were convinced of their necessity — the backward condition of the Chinese justified almost anything that might be done to them — and they cast about for Chinese statesmen with whom they could negotiate the practical details. Indeed, they were tireless in their search for puppets and collaborators, and resorted to every kind of intrigue to convert them.

Their Chinese clients went over to them for reasons opportunistic and usual: to save their skins, to seek personal aggrandizement, to see if brighter vistas opened up for them. Some succumbed to bribery, others bent to blackmail. Inevitably, they were unremarkable men, for those of a higher calibre kept out of the way. In their clients the Japanese sought high political and social standing, business success, and a sympathy with Japan's wishes, but they never found these qualities united in one person. Indeed, when they set up the Great Way Municipal Government, a puppet regime in the part of Shanghai beyond foreign control, the only kind of people they could find to run it were small-time racketeers.

Many were warned off by the fact that those who went over to the enemy stood in danger of being eliminated by General Dai Li's agents. These were everywhere in Shanghai, and though you didn't know who they were, it was chilling, the way their acts of terrorism homed in on the collaborators. Once a man had agreed to be recruited, he could hope for no quarter. A retired foreign minister of advanced age, one of those Grand Old Men of Chinese politics, was found axed to death that summer in his house in the French Concession, no doubt for having accepted the Japanese offer to set him up as the head of their prospective puppet government in Nanjing. Earlier in the day, he had been visited by a door-to-door antique dealer who, it quickly became clear, was one of General Dai Li's operatives in disguise.

Of course the Japanese were not going to take this lying down, and their Special Service instantly retaliated by rounding up a gang of Chinese ruffians, and set them to work as secret agents and terrorists. In Shanghai the Sino-Japanese War was turned into something like a contest of gangland personalities, thugs employed by the Japanese military versus hoodlums hired by the Chinese Secret Service. One morning in February, policemen arriving for work at the gendarmerie on Rue Chevalier found a severed head hanging from the telegraph pole standing opposite the station. Its features were fudged by curdled blood, but a strip of white cloth tacked to it explained that it signified the end that awaited every resistance fighter. Police investigation identified the victim as the editor of a small daily newspaper, lured three days before to the Japanese dirty tricks department in the New Asia Hotel. However, the police sergeants did not press their enquiries any further, for three anonymous letters arrived for them, each with a chopped-off finger in it.

Some months later a Chinese businessman friendly to the Japanese was shot at as he was leaving the Cathay Hotel. He was seriously wounded, but not killed. His White Russian bodyguard fired back. There was a flurry by the entrance, and a pool of blood; in the scuffle several people were shot. Incidents of this kind took place again and again, so that people became inured to them, and if anything felt a relief each time something happened, as at the rupturing of a seemingly continuous state of suspense.

ON 16 JANUARY 1938, Japanese Prime Minister Konoye issued his famous statement ruling out Chiang Kaishek as the sort of person with whom his country would like to negotiate. Up to that moment it had been Chiang that Japan had most wanted to enlist, but there had followed the realization that he would not so easily become their man.

The Japanese-sponsored municipal government of Shanghai. Troops parade before the Civic Centre.

This search for a friendly negotiator was a preparation for the working out of a wider, more ambitious plan. To Japan, China was best governed through a federation of local friendly regimes that would somehow become united in a central government offering allegiance and useful services to Japan.

The winter before, the Japanese military had implanted a client government in Beijing, and in another two months one was set up in Nanjing (working out of Shanghai's New Asia Hotel to begin with, its officials believing that city to be safer). Long before these there was the venture in Manchuria, and just a month earlier they had sponsored the Great Way Municipal Government in Shanghai. In this way did the Japanese Army impose itself, for the regimes were nothing more than the cat's-paws of different regional commands, each vying with the other to beget the ultimate, central government.

Lacking a strong leader, one who could make everyone fall into line, such a government would have no validity. This the Japanese officers knew, and so far as they were concerned, no one was more eligible than Chiang. Secretly they began to send him peace terms to consider. The German ambassador Oskar Trautmann, whose country had a good reason for wanting peace and stability in China — it would free the Japanese armies for diversion to the Soviet Union — acted as mediator between the two. Chiang's willingness to enter into negotiations created no scandal at the time, since he never thought to communicate this information to the public. His enemies later exposed him, and claimed that it was a close thing, his near capitulation to Japanese terms. Yet for all the equivocations the exchanges led to nothing, Chiang remained aloof, and the Japanese officers found that they had to look elsewhere.

It was then, when the door to the peace route had silently closed, snapping the web of intrigue so assiduously spun, that Prime Minister Konoye made his announcement. Henceforth, he said, Japan would cease to deal with the Chinese National government, but would instead 'look forward to the establishment of a new Chinese regime, harmonious coordination with which can really be counted upon.' With such a regime, he added, his country would warmly cooperate to work for the adjustment of Sino-Japanese relations and the building of a rejuvenated China.

But who would head such a regime? If China's top man would not, it was at least essential to find a good second best. It was not unreasonable that Wang Jingwei's name should crop up at this juncture, for he was, at least in name, second in command to Chiang Kaishek and the first to admit that fighting Japan was useless.

The possibility of Wang Jingwei coming forward to lead a peace movement came up in conversations which Gao Zongwu, the Chinese Foreign Ministry's Asian affairs chief, had with certain Japanese officials in Tokyo. Gao was a gifted thirty-year-old confidential agent who represented neither Chiang Kaishek nor Wang Jingwei but who seemed, inexplicably, to have the trust of both. Chiang, wishing to forestall any suggestion of capitulation on his part, had been happy about the ambiguities of Gao Zongwu's role: never was it entirely clear whether, in his talks for a ceasefire in Tokyo, Gao was speaking on behalf of Chiang, himself, or any other member of the Chinese government. Nonetheless everyone probably knew, pretending not to know it, that if the peace talks led to a satisfactory settlement Chiang Kaishek would recognize Gao Zongwu for one of his own.

But Gao was now set on a tangential course. The turn that the talks were taking covered yet another Japanese plot, Chiang now concluded, to deepen the fissure in the Guomindang and thus to sap Chinese strength.

To Wang Jingwei however, there was in the new tone of the negotiations an idea which assuredly appealed, and that was the idea that Japan made peace on condition that Chiang resigned from the leadership in Wang's favour. It would have struck anyone else as ludicrous, this idea that Chiang would resign, especially now that, in the new national mood of patriotic resistance, his apparent refusal to surrender had turned him into an object of public adulation. But it was part of Wang's misfortune that he was always so ready to credit such fancies, in spite of having spent well over twenty years in Chiang's shadow, and in his heart he must have known that any new bid for the Chinese leadership would merely lead to a re-run of the earlier political setbacks, the failures that brought him back again and again to the position of being, at best, a deputy to his competitor. Nor did those in Tokyo who proposed to trade peace for Chiang's resignation see the idea for what it was, a conceit of the first order: they were far too Japanese for that. For in this as in much else, only the Japanese within the bounds of his own curious culture and abstruseness could be so out of tune with the Chinese mind.

As for Wang Jingwei, he thought he had every reason to work for appeasement. For years he had advocated it in the Guomindang; there was no doubt in his mind that China's defeat was unavoidable, that Chiang Kaishek's wait-and-see stand was senselessly suicidal. It was tragic, the way Chinese cities were falling one after another to the Japanese armies. His own Canton was captured; all the coast was lost, all the North China plain, the middle Yangtze valley. To slow the Japanese advance, Chiang Kaishek had ordered the breaching of the dykes of the Yellow River, an action which destroyed a vast region, killed thousands, and wiped out whole towns and villages at a single stroke. And then, in October 1938, Wuhan itself was lost, so that the government had to fall back on remote Sichuan Province, and take refuge in Chongqing. It was appalling, this destruction, and it seemed to Wang that if his government was not to forfeit more territory, his people to bear greater suffering, then China must sue for peace. Now that a door had been opened to the office of the Prime Minister in Tokyo (and better still to the Japanese General Staff) he was prepared to take the lead, even at the price of a breach with his government and party — of treachery, in fact. He was not entirely without supporters in government circles, and he felt sure that once he got his peace movement going, more would throw in their lot with him.

Japan's formula for peace was couched in such terms as 'anti-Communist cooperation', 'economic aid', and 'neighbourly friendship'. What it actually envisaged was the creation of a Japanized China. Behind it were notions long tossed about at home, of Japan's divine mission and the hierarchy of race, of Pan-Asianism and the New Order in East Asia. There were Japanese who truly believed the struggle to be 'a method of making the Chinese undergo self-reflection', as in a family where, 'an elder brother having taken all he can stand from his badly behaved younger brother, has to chastise him to make him behave properly.'

Though, with the benefit of hindsight, apologists of Wang Jingwei's defection were later to make much of the anti-Comintern element in his compact with the Japanese, and his prognostication that a prolonged war would serve to stimulate the Chinese Communist movement, he never really did know, deep down, what Chinese Communism was all about, or how irresistible was its ultimate triumph. He utterly lacked Chiang Kaishek's obsession with the Communist bugbear, the thing which gave Chiang his singleness of purpose, that extra dimension whereby a national leader's stature swells up from the uncertainties of its real underpinnings and captures the awe of a people.

It mattered to Wang Jingwei that his befriending the Japanese had a precedent: Dr Sun Yatsen himself had said, 'The relationship between China and Japan is one of common existence or extinction. *Without Japan there would be no China; without China there would be no Japan*.' It was one of the things that relieved Wang's feelings, and he turned to it again and again, as a sop to his own conscience. He would not admit its falsity or the fact that this view, given at least twenty years before, was an anachronism by the time he invoked it. For all his life, woven like any other of illusions and self-exonerations, Wang Jingwei made those words survive into the present, in order that he himself might live. In this he was doing no more than what most people do, which is to take a belief, a faith, and make it fit the facts, so to speak, backwards.

In the long secret negotiations for his defection, two men proved indispensable. One was Gao Zongwu, the freelance confidential agent who, with his flair for such things, saw to the political juggling inevitable in dealings with the Japanese. Gao spoke fluent Japanese, a language he had acquired as a student of law at Kyushu Imperial University and as a *habitué* of geisha houses. Sino-Japanese diplomacy was the very game he was trained for, having written a doctoral dissertation on the subject. On top of this he was all for an armistice himself.

The other person was Zhou Fohai ('Buddha'). A man like Wang, between whose dignity and the crudity of political horse-trading there lay a certain distance, could do with a man like Zhou, especially when it came to dealing with the Japanese. For Zhou Fohai was a born intriguer, and conducting politics through plots and cabals was exactly his style.

He needed little prompting to share Wang Jingwei's fortunes: his political sympathies were chiefly distinguished by their inconstancy. He had begun his career on the revolutionary side, had begun as a Bolshevik in fact, a founding member of the Chinese Communist Party. At the time of his last appearance in these pages, meeting Wang Jingwei off his boat from Europe in January 1937, he was one of Chiang Kaishek's backroom boys in the Guomindang propaganda department, and staying completely clear of the Left. Indeed, he became a cadre of the CC (Central Club) clique, the extreme righ-twing corps of the party, and a leading figure in the Blueshirts movement, to whose pro-Fascist views he must certainly have subscribed. The habit of joining cliques was strong in him, and was perhaps the only consistent thing about his career. Before he deserted the Guomindang in favour of Wang Jingwei's cause he was a core member

Zhou Fohai and his wife

of the Low Key Club, an intellectual circle which met to deplore resistance.

Like Gao, Zhou had gone to university in Japan, but had not taken to the people there, claiming that in all his seven years in that country he never made a single Japanese friend.

Both men were present at a secret meeting with officers of the Imperial Army that November to work out a plan for Wang Jingwei's defection. The meeting was at a house in Shanghai, but the style of it was Japanese, and all the delegates, the Chinese included, padded about in bare feet and kimono, for all the world as if they were at some Japanese hot-spring resort. The talks went on for eight days, and the plan that took shape was this: on December 8, Wang Jingwei would leave Chongqing for a place where he could enjoy freedom of speech; on December 12, Premier Konoye would announce the conditions for an armistice; to this Wang Jingwei would publicly respond — favourably, it was understood.

Wang himself did not participate in these talks and he had no idea whether the Japanese were sincere; when it came to making the final decision he was appallingly at sea. If only he could talk his party round to appeasement; yet when he raised the matter, far from eliciting support, he was greeted with any number of objections. His colleagues evidently did not foresee, the way he did, the course and conclusion of the war, the wanton destruction of China.

If he deserted the party, as he would have to do to respond to Konoye's overtures, this was only so as to make another bid for his country's salvation, the same as what Generalissimo Chiang Kaishek purported to be doing. He knew his way to be the more unpopular — much more — but he thought that in some ultimate, historical perspective he would be vindicated.

The days passed quickly. Madame Wang Jingwei, in whom the idea of a peace movement had perhaps taken root more firmly than it had in Wang himself, saw to the practical details of the impending journey. It having been decided that Wang would proceed to Hanoi via Kunming, the capital of Yunnan Province, Madame Wang paid a secret visit to the warlord of that province to get him to promise a safe conduct for her husband.

In Tokyo, the head of the General Staffs China Office and architect of the project mentally prepared himself for *hara-kiri* if the plan should fail. On December 5 Zhou Fohai flew to Kunming on the pretext of Guomindang business. The 8th, the date set for Wang Jingwei's departure, came and went. Then the 10th came, and there was a cable from Wang Jingwei to say that his flight would have to be postponed for another few days: Generalissimo Chiang Kaishek, who had been out of town, had unexpectedly returned to Chongqing on the 6th. Tokyo wondered if it was being let down. 'I don't think,' said Premier Konoye, 'we are being deceived by them, but since the other party is Chinese, perhaps we might have been deceived all along. I am quite concerned about this and have reported it to the Emperor... I don't think we were cheated and strung along by the Chinese. And yet, if we are to think the worst, we could have been....'

His public announcement, scheduled for the 12th, was postponed to the 14th, then cancelled altogether. On the 16th Wang Jingwei saw the Generalissimo for the last time, but no two accounts agree on what they said to each other. On the 18th the thing was done. At 9 a.m. that morning, Wang Jingwei with his wife and personal secretary boarded a plane for Kunming. (The reservations had been made, without the names being revealed, through the deputy Minister of

Transport, one of Wang's protégés.) Nearly everyone in Wang's household — all the relatives and retainers — had chosen to follow Wang into exile and set off on their overland journey in four cars, taking the bulk of the luggage. In Kunming Wang's nephew chartered a plane from Eurasian Airlines and on the 19th Wang Jingwei and his party arrived in Hanoi.

For Chiang, Wang had left behind a note. It read: 'Henceforth you shall bear the lighter burden and I the heavier one.'

Chapter Nine

APPEASEMENT AND TERROR 1938–1939

WHEN THE NEWS BROKE in Chongqing's highest government circles, everyone's day stopped. Before the Generalissimo two imperatives immediately loomed. One was to assure the foreign ambassadors (the British and American ones especially), who might be wondering if their confidence in his regime was not misplaced, that whatever Wang Jingwei might do or say had nothing to do with the Nationalist government, that his own resolve to resist remained unflagging, and that the Guomindang was not about to split and collapse. The second necessity was to let Wang know that he might still recant if he wished. To that end he ordered the gears of the Guomindang machine to grind. Public statements which he had personally phrased went out in praise of Wang Jingwei's 'sincerity' and 'unselfish devotion'. Local newspapers were prohibited from reviling Wang, and secret agents to entice him back were flown to Hanoi.

Few outside the highest circles guessed at the truth. What exploded in print in the morning and evening editions at home and abroad were mostly wild speculations: gone to negotiate with the Japanese with Chiang's blessing, said one; gone to recuperate from a sudden illness, said another; Chiang's resolve to resist was a sham, believed a third. Rumours had it that Chiang and Wang were somehow in it together—joint impresarios of a double act, put on to obfuscate the fact that the Generalissimo was selling out to the Japanese, or deviously hedging his bets. A crack ran through the fundamental premise of Western support, which was that the Chinese government was genuinely determined to resist. Great Britain's intelligence system reported that Wang was merely Chiang's emissary, and in conversation with an American official, her ambassador to China let drop as much.

Meanwhile, in Hanoi, the first few days were taken up with finding a place to stay. The responsibility devolved on Wang's personal secretary and loyal disciple, Zeng Zhongming, for this young man spoke French very well, having studied for a doctorate in literature at Lyon University. During his sojourns in France there was no one on whom Wang had relied more; and down the years, Wang came to love him quite as much as his own son.

Installed in a house giving on to a small garden in a quiet street in the suburbs of Hanoi, Wang Jingwei and his party waited for what they knew was bound to come. On December 22 the Japanese Premier issued his promised statement. A part of the text ran much as Wang had envisaged it: 'The Japanese government are resolved,' it said, 'to carry on the military operations for the complete extermination of the anti-Japanese Guomindang government, and at the same time to proceed with the work of establishing a new order in East Asia together with those far-sighted Chinese who share in our ideals and aspirations.' But on the most critical point the statement departed from the version agreed upon between the Japanese and Chinese negotiators at the November meeting in Shanghai! The Chinese had believed that Japan would agree to the withdrawal of troops within two years of the restoration of peace and order, and Wang could scarcely credit that on this point Konoye's statement would say nothing — not a line, not a word, nothing.

It was an appalling, stinging omission. When Zeng Zhongming brought the news to his master on the morning of the next day, Wang Jingwei just stood there, not speaking, not even facing him.

Zeng made a movement, gave his master a chair. The room, on the second floor, was Zeng Zhongming's bedroom but it doubled as an office and living room in the day. Wang turned, and looked at the press statement again, as though he could not take in the fact of its being different from what he had expected. When he looked up Zeng thought his face was white and haggard, and his eyes were fixed. You couldn't say he looked terrible — one could never say that of Wang Jingwei — but you could see that he'd been struck a mighty blow.

At lunch the food lacked taste; Wang ate too fast, swallowing greedily. Yet by afternoon the focus of his indignation had shifted from the possibility that the Japanese had betrayed him to the possibility that the Japanese negotiators themselves had been overruled by some higher authority. It made things more bearable, seeing the matter in this light. He began to emerge from the depths of his shame and anger. And the more he thought, the less he suffered, with his wife and privately. Whereas earlier he could only think they were trying to make him look a fool, now it struck him that he would have to take account of something more, the competing factions in Tokyo's political life. It could very well be that while one group wanted those peace terms, another group wanted something else.

As he was pondering his next move, the confidential agent Gao Zongwu came to visit, and Wang Jingwei sought his counsel. Should he, as promised, respond to the Japanese peace offer? Gao thought not, and said so; unless they reverted to the earlier terms, Gao advised that Wang should bow out and go into exile in Europe.

Wang's closest friends were of the same opinion; yet when, a little later, Wang Jingwei arrived at his decision, it was the reverse of what they had advised. On December 29 he drafted a telegram responding to the Japanese statement and sent it to the Guomindang and the Supreme National Defence Council, reiterating his argument for conciliation. Two days later the text appeared in the *Nanhua Ribao* (*South China Daily*), a paper he himself sponsored in Hong Kong.

As he had more or less expected, the Guomindang reacted by calling an emergency meeting and expelling him from the party. That day, it was all over Chongqing that Wang Jingwei had turned traitor — a marionette whose strings were pulled by Japanese fingers; and though this too was what he had envisaged, when it actually happened his having foreseen it did not lessen the sting.

To make matters worse the new year brought the bad news from Tokyo that Prime Minister Konoye and his Cabinet had resigned. The vicissitudes of politics which sometimes work against a person were seldom so consistently prejudicial as in the case of Wang Jingwei. Had Konoye's resignation come about through the failure of the peace manoeuvre he championed, this at least would have suggested to Wang that his cause was taken in earnest. As it was, the affair had little to do with him, and Konoye had been embroiled in issues more pressing at home.

Wang Jingwei was at a loss. Holed up in this country not his own, he had never wished so intensely to be home. His quandary was the more desperate for the spotlight of universal scorn which he felt was cruelly trained on him, and he wondered if exile might not deliver him. Madame Wang, more of a careerist than her husband and less of a quitter, thought that he should hold on. Nevertheless she busied herself getting visas for France, England and Germany, in case they had to fall back on them. The British embassy in Chongqing, on receiving her applications, checked discreetly with Chiang that it was all right to grant them. Chiang was all for it, and saw to it that Wang was issued with a passport and a generous government subsidy to cover travelling expenses.

It was now February. Wang took to the mountains, where he had rented a house, to write and give himself to waiting. Madame Wang was away a lot, spending days in Hong Kong to drum up support for their cause. During those trips she stayed at 49 Hollywood Road, and it was from there that Wang Jingwei's mouthpiece, the *South China Daily*, was published. Indeed, it might be said that the place was the peace movement's launching pad. But nothing was yet moving: Wang Jingwei and his companions neither submitted to their apparent drift towards futility nor moved very decisively against it. Agents kept coming from Chongqing, sent by a still-hopeful Chiang Kaishek, but to the Generalissimo's invitations to return to the fold, Wang said no with all the elaborateness of his customary courtesy.

He wished he knew how Tokyo felt about it all. He would send Gao Zongwu there to talk to the Japanese once more. He hoped there was still an honourable way out, some trigger that might release him from this dead end, this inutility. He hoped something might happen.

And something did. Seven men were sent from Chongqing to kill him.

Some weeks before, a house near the one occupied by Wang Jingwei and his entourage was quietly let to a group of Chinese, so quietly that the other Chinese household didn't even know that it had new neighbours. It was General Dai Li, it turned out, who had posted these men to Hanoi. Dai had planned everything in great detail, down to the inclusion of a French-speaking operative in the group. Installed in the house down the road from Wang's, the men had little trouble keeping him under observation.

They noticed that, Wang having turned down a French offer to post sentries outside his house, the entrance was completely unguarded at night. They also noticed that during the day, he spent almost all his time in the bigger of the two upstairs rooms; indeed it was where he worked, saw friends and received callers. They naturally assumed that it was where he slept.

So it was towards that room that the seven men made their way, the night they stole into the house. When they got near enough, they rammed their weapons against the door. The central pane of frosted glass shattered, and through the jagged gash they could see the room inside and the sleeping couple on the bed. They fired at the taller of the two figures, and immediately afterwards they heard the other cry. They thought at first that it might be Madame Wang Jingwei cowering there behind the bed, and they could not take in the fact that it was the secretary's wife, Mrs Zeng Zhongming. They had not expected this at all, and it took a second or two for the idea to sink in that they had got the wrong man. It was Zeng's bedroom, and not Wang Jingwei's, that they had forced their way into. They turned their backs and ran, and almost at once, people were thudding upstairs from their rooms.

In the afternoon of the next day Zeng Zhongming died in the French military hospital of fatal wounds in the intestines and the heart. His last words were: 'My mind's at rest — there's Mr Wang Jingwei to see to China and my wife to see to the family.' His voice then halted, as his soul wandered on. Wang Jingwei by his bedside sat still. He was numb, and being numb is an armour against grief. But soon he would have to get up and confront his loss, of one who was dearer to him than even his own son. Down the years, Zeng had so rarely left his side that people dubbed him 'Wang Jingwei's handbag' in jest.

And not the least troubling consequence of this loss was that it put paid to all hopes of going to France. Without Zeng's knowledge of that country and its language daily life there would be intolerable. Just then exile seemed unimaginable to Wang, and this, together with his sense of having narrowly escaped death, compelled him to a more determined position on the war.

He was full of fight. In a public statement he made on March 27, he divulged the secret negotiations which Chiang Kaishek had had with Japan through Trautmann, the German ambassador. The exposure naturally embarrassed Chiang, but if Wang had hoped to show that the Generalissimo was at least as capable of treason as he, the result fell far short of intention, for the pendulum had quite swung the other way, and Chiang's popularity was beyond the reach of any such attempts to harm it.

With the disclosures of public secrets went the avowals of private emotions, the declarations by which men show themselves smug or insecure: 'Nobody can question my loyalty and love for the Republic founded by the late Dr Sun Yatsen,' he was to assert. 'My heart bleeds to see China perish at the hands of ignorant people. It was for this reason that I made my proposals, disregarding all difficulties and dangers. My only desire is to see that the peace terms will not lead to the extinction of China, and that China may regain her vitality and retrace the path to prosperity. These views I will maintain to the last, even if I were to sacrifice my life. Neither threat nor slander will make me falter.'

His situation was in fact untenable, and continued sojourn in Hanoi both meaningless and dangerous. He was hamstrung by the restrictions which the French authorities had placed on his political activity, and disconcerted by the discovery that an apartment on the third floor of a building adjacent to his house had recently been let to the European Asian Airlines, a company belonging to Chiang Kaishek's brother-in-law T.V. Soong. Nobody doubted that the airline was a cover for Chongqing's agents, and its appearance not only suggested surveillance but portended a renewal of violence.

Far away in Tokyo the Japanese sensed the danger. Even though they had not been in Hanoi, the precariousness of Wang Jingwei's life there was not unimaginable to them. Thinking about Zeng Zhongming's murder, and about what might yet befall Wang Jingwei, they wondered what they could do to save him.

We shall have to rescue him, one of them said — in a freighter.

It was as good a solution as anyone could think of just then. The president of the Yamashita Steamship Company was prepared to lend a vessel, and on April 6, the *Hokkōmaru* left Japan bound for Haiphong, the port for Hanoi. There were, apart from the rescuers, who posed as employees of the Taiwan Colonization Company to allay suspicion, a German sheep-dog that they thought might come in useful. The journey took ten days, and in the meantime a Colonel Kasega and two other Japanese were to proceed by a different route to make contact with Wang.

Wang's representative and Kasega's party had agreed to meet at a race-track in the suburbs, the latter to be standing in the ticket queue, and Wang's man to greet them like they were long lost friends; specifically, he was to say 'How are you?' to them in English. This all happened exactly as planned, and immediately afterwards the Chinese whisked Colonel Kasega and his companions away in a car. The car took, as caution required, a circuitous route, and the party arrived at Wang Jingwei's house without being followed.

As the iron gates swung open at their approach, Wang Jingwei came out to greet them. It was a surprise to have him appear like that, in the flesh, after all that had been said about him. He was then fifty-six years old, though he looked considerably younger. While his gestures of courtesy were not quite made for his guests' benefit, it was apparent that he was good at *politesse*.

Inside, once seated, the callers were to learn something of the way in which the man saw himself, a man who, for what he was about to do, insisted on his love of country (as if this were an absolution). It must be understood, he said, that it was because Chiang Kaishek had been prevented from seeking peace by his compact with the Communists that he, Wang, had had to come forward. He could not thank his visitors enough, he added, for coming all this way to rescue him. But it was not really necessary; he had made arrangements to go to Shanghai, in whose foreign zone he could yet maintain a measure of independence. For himself, he would like nothing better than to return to Canton, wherein lay his roots and his constituency, but the place was now under Japanese military rule, and to pitch his tent there would savour too much of truckling to the enemy. There was no doubt that in going to Shanghai he was risking his life, for by now political assassination had become integral to the city, like the night-life and the money-making, but in that risk was his chance to display the very heroism that captured people's hearts. China in that moment of implacable patriotism was especially receptive to the persuasion of great gestures.

To the astonishment of his callers Wang Jingwei went on to reveal that he had already chartered a boat, a French-registered freighter of only 760 tons, to take him to Shanghai. Since the *Von Hohenhoffer* (as the boat was called) was very small, and the probability of an attack by Chongqing great, it might be as well for the *Hokkōmaru* to follow. He aimed to get to the French Concession, where he owned a house, and where he might fall back on French protection.

It was apparent to the Japanese that Wang wished to keep them at arm's length, choosing not a Japanese ship but a French one, not Japanese-controlled Canton but European Shanghai, not Japanese security but French protection. The quiet manner in which he spoke made it impossible for his guests to protest. There was nothing now for them to discuss, the matter having been decided even before their arrival. Apologizing, Wang got up and retired, leaving his subordinates to work out the practical details of the journey with the Japanese. When, two hours later, he came in to bid them goodbye, they all stood to their feet in his honour. The last thing he did was to lead his callers upstairs, to take a look at the murdered secretary's bed. It had, as though it were a museum piece, a black ribbon tied around it; and that, at that moment, seemed more poignant than even the death. Colonel Kasega cried, and looked away as from an open grave.

The Japanese completed the day's tasks with drafting telegrams to Tokyo, suggesting that maximum security hideouts be lined up in the parts of Shanghai that were under Japanese control. They passed the next two days nervously, a dozen spectres of possible assassinations raised in their imaginations. (To understand their uneasiness in Hanoi, one must remember that as a nation the Japanese are always a little thrown by being abroad.) One of them went so far as to take the precaution of going about disguised as a Vietnamese fisherman.

One of the things they awaited was the French authorities' permission. The matter had to be referred to Paris, and it was not until instructions had been received from the French Foreign Office that the ships could set off. At last Paris gave its consent, at the same time offering to assign a police guard to escort Wang Jingwei to the boat. The two vessels cast off the next morning, having agreed to meet up in four days' time at Nightingale Island, five miles from the port of Haiphong.

The Japanese ship arrived at the rendezvous first. Before her was the island, but there was no other vessel to be seen. The *Hokkōmaru* sailed round and round the island in gathering fog, but neither her careful search nor her signalling in the agreed radio code turned up any signs of the *Von Hohenhoffer*. Three days dragged by. The leader of the mission lay in his cabin sick with stomach trouble and worrying that he might have caused Wang Jingwei's death, that the Emperor would get to hear. There appeared to be nothing he could do, except submit to the loss and resume the journey.

It was when the Japanese had waited for four days that a message suddenly crackled on the radio: Wang Jingwei's party was safe, and would meet up with them at a harbour in Swatow the following day. Immediately, the worries of the last few days resolved themselves into practical concerns, and the Japanese crew made ready to sail for Swatow, a town spreading over a peninsula along the south China coast. It was dark when the ship came to anchor, and all the crew had a restful night. But when they woke up the following morning, there came a crowd of Chinese fishermen who, the Japanese quickly realized, were pirates at the same time. The Japanese reached for one of the two rifles they had on board. This seemed to intimidate the pirates, who just stood and watched. One of the Japanese soldiers began to give a demonstration of marksmanship, somewhat in the way of the samurai, and this seemed to elicit awe, and eventually indulgence, in his spectators. At any rate the Japanese were left unharmed.

It was a night and the better part of a day before the Chinese party arrived. A man Wang Jingwei sent over to the Japanese ship gave a recital of the troubles his boat had had on her journey out of Haiphong — some problem with a dock strike, the outworn facilities on board, the smallness of the vessel and the miscalculation of her speed. So great was the relief at the missing boat turning up that it did not occur to anyone that the *Von Hohenhoffer* might have been delayed because she had stopped in Hong Kong, as Japanese intelligence later suggested. When it was learned that Wang had approached the British authorities for permission to reside in Hong Kong, the Japanese would wonder if, at the time his boat went missing, he wasn't stopping at the port to await the reply. The British had very politely said no; had they said yes there was no knowing what Wang Jingwei might have done — gone into exile in Hong Kong probably, and given up the whole enterprise awaiting him in Shanghai. Why is it, the Japanese would wonder, that at the very moment you begin to trust the Chinese, they go and do something to make you think twice? More than their duplicity probably: something to do with their feeling that the Japanese were barbarians, and *ipso facto* not worthy of honour.

Of the two nations, it was the Japanese who turned out to be the more two-faced. During the remainder of the journey, the question of setting up a 'peace government' under Japan's wing to rival the Nationalist government in Chongqing came up. How it emerged is hard to put down in any way, because so much was dissimulation — on Wang's side, conjuring up popular support which he did not, and could not, have; on the Japanese side, playing up to misconceptions and raising false hopes. Later Wang Jingwei would go to Japan to negotiate the terms in earnest, but it is a measure of the ambivalence with which the Japanese viewed the whole project that whether Wang considered them cooperative or unyielding, as giving him his due or as palming him off on less, each impression seemed equally possible yet utterly false.

In fact to the Japanese it made no odds whether he formed a government or not; while it would be bad for Chongqing it would do Tokyo no harm. It is true that Japan wished to see a sympathetic central government knitting together the existing puppet regimes in China, but it was impossible just now to say that the one Wang Jingwei proposed to set up was what she had in mind. It was so sudden too, this motion to form a government. The Japanese found that when it came to the point they were less sure about what they exactly wanted than they had supposed. They didn't intend to take their hand off Wang, but neither would they engage in any deep commitment. They would let him walk his chosen path, but they would keep him on a tight leash.

Yet when they talked things over, Wang and Kasega, sitting on the deck of the *Hokkōmaru* (to which the Chinese had transferred), it was not doubts or misgivings, but an optimistic excitement that hung about the two men. Wang's mood moved to the momentum of his thoughts — of inaugurating a new government, of returning it in full panoply to its proper seat in Nanjing. He lounged back in his chair. That was it, he thought — it wouldn't be a new government, more a regeneration of the one Dr Sun Yatsen created for the Guomindang. Whereas he might have been exercised over the peace terms he would be offered on his impending trip to Tokyo, Wang Jingwei at this moment thought largely in terms of cosmetics — of the Blue-Sky-and-White-Sun of the Guomindang flag going up on all the roofs and flagstaffs in Nanjing.

The ship docked at the mouth of the Huangpu River on the afternoon of May 7. Though the arrival was supposed to be top-secret the news had leaked from Tokyo and the Shanghai correspondents of the Japanese newspaper *Asahi Shimbun* turned up in full force to see Wang disembark. Colonel Kasega thought that for safety reasons Wang Jingwei and his wife should remain on board until nightfall, while he and the others went ashore to check all the arrangements. The day before he left Hanoi he had got in touch with Tokyo and had asked the War Ministry to line up a few houses for Wang in Shanghai.

He drove towards one now. Late afternoon light touched the clouds above the city roofs as he approached the northeastern suburbs. The battle-scarred walls of a large villa in European style loomed up as the car passed the Civic Centre. By prearrangement Gao Zongwu and Zhou Fohai were at the villa to await his arrival.

Later on, when dinner was served, the three men took stock of the situation. There appeared to be a divergence of views: Gao was for a negotiated settlement and Zhou was for setting up a government in occupied territory — for out-and-out collaboration, in other words. Gao was uneasy about the new turn of events, and thought he saw where it would lead them — to enslavement and failure; but already his view was being superseded, and it looked as though it was Zhou's judgement that would finally prevail.

It was while they were sitting at dinner that the telephone rang; it was Madame Wang, who was very cross at being cooped up on the boat. Her indignation poured out in the form of imperatives: let me spend the night in my own house in the French Concession — I'll swim there if I have to; arrange for my disembarkation at once. Unable to pacify her, Kasega agreed. This ended the harangue, but did not restore her good humour. The crew helped her disembark, and a chauffeur was sent to fetch her; but if she had meant to be agreeable to these people, she could not rise to it when the moment came.

DU YUESHENG'S HOUSE in Hong Kong, enclosed on four sides by a high wall, was filling with people — family, guests and hirelings. Two large round tables were set in the dining room, the lunch laid out on them; through the window there was a view of trees and sky. There was ham and chicken and a generous variety of very fresh seafood. The fare was Shanghainese, for though Du Yuesheng was getting used to the principally Cantonese flavour of Hong Kong, food was the one area where he found it difficult to compromise. Indeed, entertained to dinner one evening by an unusually generous Cantonese host, he had been horrified to find snake, turtle and civet on the table, the *pièces de résistance* of Cantonese cuisine, but unfamiliar and distasteful to most Shanghainese palates.

Living in Hong Kong had not cut Du Yuesheng off from the mainland, and many of the people gathered here were exiles from Shanghai like himself. In fact, it was owing to Du Yuesheng that they were here, and not in occupied China or Chongqing, working for the Japanese under duress or running away from them. Had Du Yuesheng not contrived their escape to Hong Kong they would most likely, from either coercion or temptation, have gone over to the enemy; for they were certainly rich and important enough for the Japanese to want to use them for their own purposes. From such a fate Du Yuesheng had snatched them, while leaving the others, the irredeemable traitors, to die by the necessary accident.

In the case of many a potential defector, what Du did to procure their loyalty was, very simply, to bribe them. He would so subsidize their income as to make them resistant to Japanese enticements. At first the money came from his own pocket, but as from this year, he would receive half a million dollars a month from the Nationalist government in Chongqing to carry out this task.

No one was better equipped for it. Du had numerous followers in Shanghai; his sources of information were excellent; he knew people in the commercial shipping lines who could act as couriers for his personal messages. His house was open to all, and as though this were not enough he had taken a suite at the Gloucester Hotel to provide extra room and hospitality. Above all his heart was with the Chongqing government, and no one could be as trusted with that sort of job as he.

It might be said, as he leaned back in his chair and looked across the table at his guests, that he was surveying the fruits of his labour. If the conversation, much of which was taken up with describing the fate of those who *had* sold out to the enemy, aroused any emotion in him, it was the satisfaction of one who could take credit for what had happened. When one of the guests, newly arrived from Shanghai, started to tell the others about the terrible things that had been happening in that city, assassination succeeding assassination, plot following plot, he was merely describing events with which Du Yuesheng was already familiar, having, indeed, been at the bottom of them himself. He thought to himself: yes, February had been dubbed Terror Month in Shanghai, with eighteen acts of terrorism, twenty-one dead and ten injured. He recalled, not without regret, many things about those who had had to die for their treason, but to his lunch guests he merely said something about the untrustworthiness of life.

'It's a scandal,' said one who had only just been rescued from collaboration himself, 'the way people hanker after jobs in Wang Jingwei's proposed government.'

'Sheer opportunism, of course;' another guest said, 'they only want to have a whack at being government officials and to line their pockets. They no more believe in this enterprise than you or I.'

'I wonder if anybody does,' said a man sitting to Du Yuesheng's left. 'I can't imagine how Wang Jingwei could have thought of it.'

'It's Zhou Fohai, you know, who put Wang up to all this,' remarked the first speaker, a large man given to leaning forward whenever he spoke. 'Zhou wouldn't jib at an alliance with the devil, if he thought his career could be helped by it. He's nothing but a shiftless rake. If Wang hadn't listened to him — if it had been Gao Zongwu he'd listened to instead — he'd be working for an honourable settlement and not for this absurd "peace government." Have you heard that they're all falling out? Zhou's camp simply can't wait to get rid of Gao. And the Japanese are only too willing to bump him off; probably tried to when he was in Tokyo with Wang last month.'

Zhou was certainly good at rallying support. One of the few things that just then disconcerted Du was the recollection of how, earlier in the year, Zhou Fohai had come to ask him for his support of the peace movement, and he and two fellow bankers had made a donation. Between them they had given fifty thousand dollars. It was a gesture of goodwill, not to be understood as connoting any political complicity. Still, he shouldn't have done it, though Du now reproached himself for nothing more than having been too ready with his donations. There were so many he hardly thought before he gave one. It wasn't as though Zhou was a friend, even if he had been a Guomindang stalwart, and had knocked about with Du's close friend General Dai Li when they were runing the Blueshirts together. On that point Du thought it a pity that two people in the same faction — one so close to Chiang Kaishek too — should now find themselves in opposing camps, each dedicated to the downfall of the other.

It only goes to show, one of his guests was saying, echoing Du's own thoughts, that politics is the game of intriguers. Though he kept his machinations secret, it had gradually become known that Zhou Fohai had created a security service to rival Dai Li's in Shanghai. He had dug up a lot of professional terrorists to staff it, and set them up with a headquarters at 76 Jessfield Road. Of course it was a matter of self-preservation — the traitors knew that Dai Li's agents would be gunning for them — but it was more than just a way of staying alive. It was the reflex of an intriguer and an opportunist given to advancing his cause through hidden, underhand means. Zhou knew well

No. 76 Jessfield Road, headquarters of Zhou Fohai's secret service (now the Jiandong Secondary School, 435 Wanhangdu), photographed in 1982

enough that 'power begins where secrecy begins.'

Japanese thinking at the beginning had been that the Imperial Army's Secret Service would provide Wang with the necessary protection. Wang declined the offer, for to him it would invite the suggestion he so greatly deplored, that he was their puppet. At the time, creating one's own service seemed as good a solution to the problem of security as any. He was not to know that No. 76, as this outfit came to be called after its location on Jessfield Road, would end up giving his enterprise such a bad name.

The two monsters that Zhou Fohai had dug up to head the organization must be held chiefly responsible for this. Between the two of them, Li Shiqun and Ding Mocun, they represented every shade of brutality and corruption imaginable. With the instinct of true time-servers, these two had procured a niche in Wang Jingwei's peace crusade in order to exploit it for their organized shakedowns of opium dens and gambling casinos. Li was an ex-Communist who had studied at Moscow University. While Ding Mocun, nicknamed Little Devil Ding for his diminutiveness (he was only five foot one), was not, his career was in almost every other respect identical to Li's, both men having worked with Dai Li in the Guomindang's secret police.

Wang Jingwei had come up against some very hard luck; allying himself with Li and Ding was his latest blunder. 'As if his reputation isn't bad enough already,' observed the men at Du's table. 'Who's going to join his peace crusade now, when all that it conjures up in the minds of most people is that chamber of horrors run by those two renegades?'

'But does he have a choice in the matter though?' one of them went on to wonder, picking up his cup of Dragon Well tea, which he tasted slowly, and found unimpeachable. 'Chongqing has put out a warrant for his arrest. He'd be shot like a dog if he didn't have some sort of cover. And anyway, Zhou Fohai was lining the pair up even before Wang was out of Hanoi. If anyone is good at the dirty end of the stick, it's Zhou; but he also knew how vulnerable he and Wang Jingwei were. Seeing what had happened to other collaborators in Shanghai, he had to counteract the terrorism somehow.'

Balance of terror, Du Yuesheng thought: yes, that was what it was all about, the crowd at No. 76 keeping up with whatever action his and Dai Li's agents took, the grade-one violence of the one matching the vengefulness of the other. Sometimes it was difficult to tell the two terrorist rings apart, so closely did their handiwork synchronize. And there was also the fact, dismaying and embarrassing to Du Yuesheng, that members of the Green Gang and the Constancy Society were going over to the other side in great numbers, so that you had a situation where one of the chief operatives at No. 76 happened also to be one of Du Yuesheng's most trusted disciples. People found it hard to believe that he hadn't been planted there as an undercover agent, so improbable did his defection seem. But he was only one of your more barefaced turncoats, that's all, and one Du Yuesheng had now to write off.

They grieved Du a little, these desertions, but as he now looked across the dining room, at the bankers and industrialists at his table, it gave him satisfaction to think that if many of his friends and followers had fallen by the wayside, more had been saved in the nick of time. These businessmen, for instance, an endangered species that was perhaps more at risk than any other — for a businessman by his very *raison d'être* sells to the highest bidder — had given the Japanese the slip. Not only that, they had left carrying all their assets with them — men, capital, machines, factories, the lot. Du had fixed it all, organizing planning sessions in Rue Wagner and Avenue Doumer, mobilizing protégés in Shanghai, and despatching runners to carry messages between Hong Kong and Chongqing. The evacuation had something of the quality of the massive hegira of the summer before, when mills, dismantled power plants, intellectual property and half the mainstays of coastal prosperity were lugged inland to the Nationalist stronghold in Sichuan. Moved over land and water by rail, steamer, junk and pontoon, and when these petered out past the swirling gorges towards Sichuan, by the callused hands of coolies in their thousands, these had tumbled like an avalanche upon the interior, creating instant industry.

Could such a manoeuvre have been repeated without Du? He doubted it. It occurred to him, as he left his lunch to take up his place at the mahjong table, that he and Chiang Kaishek needed each other as Chongqing needed Shanghai: the one gave the order, the other delivered the goods.

AT NIGHT the Peach Blossom Palace, the Good Friend and the other opium houses in Shanghai's Badlands (the quarter intersected by Jessfield Road, the Great Western Road and Yu Yuan Road) did even better business than in the daytime. Down the road the nightclub touts stood about, eyeing girls who, for all their urban artifice, moved with a waddle perhaps inherited from their peasant grandmothers. On the other side, gambling dens exuded warmth and avarice, while beggars methodically sifted the kitchen slops. Before morning at least one man would die violently.

Here a kind of thug free enterprise thrived. The Badlands — by now a byword in Shanghai — shared its water mains, electricity lines and even police patrols with the International Settlement, but because the land was originally Chinese, the place came under Japanese control. This accounted for its frontier character, and for its curious brand of law enforcement, which can best be described as ambiguous.

While Wang Jingwei would rather be living in his own house in the French Concession than at his new home in the Badlands, it must be admitted that the latter was a great deal better fortified. Standing in Lane 1126, Yu Yuan Road, it was one of a dozen or so houses that the Japanese had provided for his team. The previous tenants had been driven out the summer following Wang's arrival on the *Hokkōmaru*.

Wang Jingwei had not been idle in the six and a half months since his arrival. First he flew to Tokyo, where he was coolly received by Japanese officialdom and offered some peace terms that can best be described as derisory. The concessions the War Ministry wrung from him — the quid pro quo for his future regime — were a long way from what he had initially been prepared to give, but he was as putty when it came to negotiating with the Japanese. The harshness of the War Ministry's conditions, its continued insistence on concluding pacts with several other Chinese regimes in keeping with the policy of *bunji gassaku* ('separate governments working in conjunction', whatever that meant) struck him as dishonourable but unassailable.

In the end his stand for 'one government — one party' degenerated into squabbles over the use of the Chinese flag. It was on this sticking point, this fetish, that he lavished all his celebrated eloquence. He absolutely insisted on it, the right of his impending government to fly the Guomindang flag. The Japanese eventually agreed, but only on condition that he flew another flag with it to distinguish it from Chongqing's — a triangular yellow pennant bearing the words Peace and National Reconstruction (later the word Anti-Communism would be added). Zhou Fohai, likening the pennant to a pig's tail, thought it a compromise of the oddest kind. 'I'm going to have a hard time,' he added, 'explaining to my children when they ask me why the flag has changed.'

It was a mortifying experience, that trip to Japan; but as the summer progressed more failures would follow. Back in China, Wang addressed himself to campaigning for support. He had his eye on a warlord general, a political and military heavyweight whose support would greatly boost his cause. But the warlord, who having

General Kenji Doihara

been courted by Doihara, the Lawrence of Asia, was well acquainted with the pros and cons of collaboration, played extremely hard to get and in any case died that winter after having had a tooth pulled out by a Japanese dentist.

Of the others Wang worked to win over, two were the heads of the existing puppet governments, the ones which the Japanese Army had installed in north and central China. The northern quisling was a Shanghai banker once associated with the Banque Industrielle de Chine, a some-time politician whose greatest appeal for his people lay in his ravishing concubine, whose diamond-studded appearance on the theatre balcony crowned many a performance of Chinese opera. Wang Jingwei flew in disguise to Tianjin to meet him, but though their conversations were amicable enough, it was clear that it had never been intended for a moment that they should lead anywhere. At least not by the banker, who upon his visitor's departure called a press conference to announce that his government would not enter into any coalition. (In August he was to ask for American help to defect to Chongqing.)

With the other puppet leader Wang Jingwei had at least one thing in common: they were both devoted to classical poetry. But there the affinity seemed to end. If Wang had approached this gentleman with an invitation to an alliance, he came away without the promise of an acceptance.

From the beginning, Wang Jingwei saw his support as coming principally from the south, from not only his fellow Cantonese but from the Chinese communities in southeast Asia, which apart from being predominantly Cantonese would remember him for his association with Dr Sun Yatsen. It was therefore in a mood of expectancy that he made his appeal to these people that August. In an impassioned radio broadcast he spoke of the haphazard sacrifices, the unnecessary suffering which Chiang Kaishek's futile resistance was bringing upon the people of Canton, resistance which in the end would profit no one but the Communists, who wanted nothing better than to see Chinese nationalists and Japanese imperialists utterly exhaust themselves in combat. He made personal appearances and more speeches, but like almost everything else that summer these endeavours all fell a little flat.

Suppressing his despondency, he called a conference at 76 Jessfield Road. Billed for weeks by his press agents as the Sixth Guomindang Congress, it drew half the International Settlement's police, Chinese as well as Sikh, who now took up positions along the pavement, massing in a tight knot in front of the door by which Wang Jingwei and his companions were expected to enter. This was a side entrance, the main one being closed as a security measure. The delegates began to file in; altogether there were two hundred and forty of them — a figure considerably below that estimated by Wang Jingwei, who before the conference had claimed that from two-fifths to three-fifths of the Guomindang troops would desert to join his cause.

The ceremonies began with the orchestra striking up the national anthem, and the Chinese flag going up for the first time in occupied territory, springing tears to the eyes. What was remarkable about the meeting was that there was not a single Japanese present. Colonel Kasega, who had submitted to Wang's insistence on excluding Japanese representatives from the conference, felt apprehensive that without his own people there to keep an eye on things, the meeting would get out of hand and that he would lose his job. As it turned out, however, his fears were quite groundless, for the congress did no more than rubber-stamp the Japanese demand that the new government include some non-Guomindang members, a demand the War Minister had already dictated to Wang in Tokyo. Such passivity in the delegates arose as much from their sense of the inevitable as from their calibre: finer or stronger men would not have seen in Wang's enterprise a proper arena for their ambitions.

Wang as chairman made a long speech, and as his mouth formed the rushing words his eyes locked his audience in a gaze of heartbreaking helplessness that pointed up his pathos and his quandary: his personal distaste for treachery, the uncertainty of his position in the Japanese scheme of things, and above all the impossibility of ever going back, of becoming master once more of his own fate.

Chapter Ten

THE NANJING REGIME 1939–1940

OF THE THINGS that engaged Du Yuesheng's mind that autumn, two in particular stood out.

One was the death of his first wife. In September, when the first Mrs Du lay dying, her son and daughter-in-law arrived in Shanghai to be at her bedside. But she was already quite far gone, and had nothing to offer but a final relinquishing. Her end was unremarkable: she simply sank away, her lifelong desire for stupor gratified by death. Though in her opiate haze she was often lost to her son, her death still came, as deaths will, as a shock.

The husband who could not always remember to think of her when she was alive mourned her with many fond reminiscences now that she was dead. When he spoke to his bereaved son of what she was like when she was young, when he recollected the early days of their married life, he wept. These were respects paid not from hypocrisy but from some need to acquit oneself of the guilt of having behaved badly to the dead.

The other matter which preoccupied Du was Gao Zongwu's defection from Wang Jingwei's camp. Du knew about Gao's differences with the rest of the peace movement, but he had no idea Gao was actually thinking of deserting. The first he heard of it was through an unsigned note delivered to him by a Shanghai follower. It was from the chairman of that city's National Commercial Bank, and it said: 'Gao is set on turning around. Please make immediate contact with Chongqing.' It seemed that Gao, sickened by the way the negotiations were going, and especially by the way the Japanese kept breaking faith, was seriously thinking of forsaking Wang Jingwei, and was putting out feelers to discover how Chiang Kaishek would react. When the idea first came to him he consulted his mentor and friend, an old Chinese politician living in retirement in Japan, who in turn contacted the Shanghai banker, an intimate from the same native place. The two men then conferred, and agreed that the agent of Gao's deliverance had to be Du Yuesheng. Only Du could be trusted simultaneously to get Gao out of Shanghai, guarantee his safety, and make it look as though Chongqing had nothing to do with it.

Du flew to Chongqing the next day. Chiang Kaishek rushed back to the capital from his inspection tour of a neighbouring province and the two men met at once. Gao must be helped to escape, the Generalissimo agreed, and Du was to fix it. Was Gao privy to all Wang Jingwei's negotiations with Japan? And if so, would he be prepared to divulge? Once he had ascertained all the details Du was to come to Chongqing and report to the Generalissimo again.

Du Yuesheng was a bad air traveller and that rough flight back to Hong Kong was truly one of the most frightful experiences of his life. But shortly afterwards he would undertake that uncomfortable journey again, this time to bring Chiang Kaishek the news that promises had been exchanged between the two parties' intermediaries, that Gao would decamp with a copy of the demands which Japan had made and which Wang Jingwei was about to accept. Gao would give Chiang the draft, and it was hoped that this would unnerve Wang Jingwei into disclosing the Japanese terms himself, in all their greed and unscrupulousness. Chiang Kaishek's reply, sent back through Du, was simply, 'Come to Hong Kong.'

The draft unmistakably brought home the shabbiness of Japanese conduct in the entire affair. There was something incredible in the idea that Japan had all this while been meaning to hold China in thrall, but now that the draft had torn off the last shreds of Chinese sovereignty, the fact was undeniable. The talks took place in one of the houses on Yu Yuan Road, and every now and then the meeting place would be shaken by one of Zhou Fohai's hot-tempered harangues. But it soon became clear to Gao Zongwu, who was present throughout, that as far as the Japanese were concerned, it had never been intended that the Chinese should be anything other than fully compliant. He watched with foreboding the progress of Wang's capitulation. He now profoundly distrusted Colonel Kasega, whom he saw as 'just another Doihara'; and as one could read in a melancholy plaint he wrote at the time in the *tanka* form of Japanese poetry, he had ceased to have any illusions about the conclusion of it all:

The north
The south
The seas
And the mountains
None of them China's
Where shall the people live?

Indeed, he already knew what he had to do. The day the negotiations opened he had persuaded Wang to let him take the draft text home to study, and that night his wife had quickly made a copy of it. That was November. In December Du Yuesheng set the stage for his dramatic escape. The events that subsequently unfolded would set up reverberations sounding to the ends of China and Japan.

Four days before his departure from Shanghai Gao went to Rue Vallon to see his friend and colleague Professor Tao Xisheng. Tao, who before he joined Wang Jingwei's peace movement enjoyed a high reputation as Professor of Economics at Beijing University, was part of the team at the talks over the peace agreement. Like Gao, he viewed the terms of the agreement with distaste, so much so that he pleaded illness on the day of its signature.

His objections were not unknown to Zhou Fohai and the rest of the team, and for them, his and Gao's opposition had become too hard and too troublesome, to think of them as anything other than a nuisance. Tao knew this, and knew also that Zhou Fohai had a way of dealing with people he considered a nuisance.

'No. 76,' the professor said soon after Gao arrived at Rue Vallon, 'is after us. What are you going to do?'

'Run for it,' Gao told him, 'and so should you.'

It was a relief, to bring it into the open like that. The two men talked some more and then Gao left. When New Year's Day came around, the two men did what was customary: they called at Zhou Fohai's house to tender the season's greetings. The professor bore up well under the strain, but when Zhou saw him to the door, he remarked on the professor's wanness. 'You don't look well,' he said. 'You should have a good rest.'

Professor Tao said, 'I'm not even sure I'll live.' He might have been referring to his illness, or to the plans No. 76 had for him.

'Come now,' Zhou protested, 'there's no need to talk like that.'

Professor Tao then went to see the Wangs. Madame Wang did not bother to disguise her impatience, and told the professor it was high time he signed the agreement. When she said this her eyes flashed, and for an instant Tao wondered, stiffening as he did so, if it was his imagination, or did those eyes rest on him a moment longer than was necessary? Solicitous for his health, Wang broke in with a gentle suggestion that Tao waited until he was better; he had no premonition of the blow that was about to descend on himself.

At last they were able to leave. In a curious calm Gao performed a number of last-minute duties, cleared papers, packed. In the afternoon of January 4 he walked down the Bund at an even pace. The air was cold and his breath came in clouds. He considered, then rejected, the remote possibility of Du Yuesheng letting him down: there never was a better keeper of bargains than that mobster. Gao came in sight of the wharf, and there, down by the gangway, was the man's protégé. Du had seen to everything, down to the ticket for the liner.

At about the time Gao was suppressing his misgivings about Du Yuesheng, Professor Tao was leaving his house in the French Concession to drive to the Cathay Hotel. A short while later he arrived at Nanjing Road, and a smartly uniformed doorman admitted him to the lobby of the Cathay Hotel, that stylish landmark of Jewish enterprise in the Far East. He crossed it with outward composure, and within minutes he was out of the backdoor at the other end and speeding in a taxi to the *President Hoover.*

Darkness did not fall until Shanghai was left well behind. The two men had met up on board but both being a little dazed, did not speak much. Later the excellent dinner loosened their tongues and they talked lengthily of what they would say to Wang Jingwei and how they would get their families out. The next day the *President Hoover* delivered the two men safely into Hong Kong's incomparable harbour, and straight into Du Yuesheng's arms.

This was the telegram they sent to Wang Jingwei as soon as they had handed over the draft agreement to Du to pass on to Chiang Kai-shek: 'For the past three years we have believed in peace. We withdraw from your movement only because of the unacceptability of Japanese terms and the inadvisability of organizing a government. We would truly be dismayed to find these terms and that government made the basis of peace and national reconstruction. For China's sake you must abandon the movement at once: the success of your government can only mean the destruction of China. Please do not take our love for you as enmity....'

The professor then telegraphed Wang: 'Please guarantee my family's safety, lest I go to extremes.' A few days later Mrs Tao arrived by boat in Hong Kong with two of her five children, and explained that the others had been detained as hostages in Shanghai. She had gone to see Madame Wang the day Professor Tao left and had had a fraught interview with the lady. Claiming that she knew nothing of what was going on, she asked to be allowed to travel to Hong Kong to bring her husband back to Shanghai. When Madame Wang appeared unmoved, she said, 'I'm a simple woman; I do the laundry, I cook, I bring up children; I had no idea this was going to happen. I don't understand such matters but I cannot believe my husband will do anything drastic....'

Madame Wang did not so much as look at her; she obviously thought the request outrageous, coming as it did from a woman whose husband had betrayed Wang Jingwei. Luckily for Mrs Tao, it was at this moment that the professor's cable, pleading for the family's safety, was delivered; and at once, since there appeared to be no question of protesting the threat it contained, Madame Wang consented to let Mrs Tao go.

But Mrs Tao's ruse only half worked, for only two of her children were allowed to accompany her, while the others remained under heavy guard at Rue Vallon. If they were not exactly under house arrest, they were not far short of it. Du saw that to rescue them would take more than one underground agent, it would take three or four — it was that tricky.

Soon afterwards the professor's eldest daughter received a

telephone call from one of Du's most trusted protégés in Shanghai. Here is what you must do, the voice over the phone said; here it paused, before launching into detailed instructions, which concluded with the man saying that she was not to worry, he would be looking out for her.

She summoned her two brothers, told them what they must do. They asked, and received, permission from the guards to visit their aunt. The girl went off to school as she was expected. She entered the building, and as she did so a car drove up behind. Emerging from the backdoor she climbed in. No one thought to look up and the car just drove off, past the school, down Rue Lafayette, across the city, and into the neighbourhood where the two boys were visiting their aunt.

The car, having picked up the two brothers, then headed back east towards Avenue Doumer. It happened so quickly, before anybody could expect it. The passengers did not alight at Du Yuesheng's house, but at a briquet factory that had opened next door. It was dark in there, and milling with strangers. It was to cover their tracks that he had brought them here, the driver explained to the children; but they were not sure they understood what he meant. After a while they were parted and taken away in three separate cars to the Quai de France, and during the drive it was impressed upon each of them that when they met up again they were not to show any sign of recognition. At the pier another escort took over from the drivers. He led them up a gangplank and down a stairway, but it wasn't until their ship had cast off, and they were leaning over the side and looking down at the foamy wake, that the children lowered their guard and spoke to each other for the first time.

The ship docked in Hong Kong on January 20. The next morning the front page of the Hong Kong daily *L'Impartial* carried banner headlines proclaiming sensational disclosures of a secret agreement between Wang Jingwei and Japan. As the world thumbed through the morning editions it learnt that Japan intended nothing less than the dismemberment of China.

Zhou Fohai in Shanghai groaned aloud, and that night wrote in his diary, 'The beasts, Gao and Tao. I vow I shall destroy them.'

In Chongqing the beasts were instant heroes, Chiang Kaishek

hailing Gao in a letter as the 'genius of Zhejiang'. Japan branded the revelations as Chinese propaganda, and Wang's press denied that the agreement was authentic. (Later this denial acquired corroboration of a sort, for the document finally agreed upon made more concessions to Wang than were embodied in the one Gao published.)

Forestalling possible reprisals, Gao applied for a passport and sailed for the United States a few months later. Though that was the end of his career as a freelance confidential agent, he would one day be courted by American Ph.D. students wanting reminiscences and inside information on Sino-Japanese collaboration during the war.

Professor Tao continued to live in Hong Kong under Du Yuesheng's protection. The latter arranged for him to receive three thousand Hong Kong dollars a month from the Nationalist government, in return for which he was to edit an international news bulletin for distribution in Chongqing. He survived several narrow escapes from Japanese agents, whose interest in him was intense and understandable. Though he owed those escapes to the bodyguards Du sent to protect him, he was hardly ever aware of their presence. Once, after he had been to the cinema hiding his identity behind a false moustache, he received a note from Du Yuesheng suggesting that the fake whiskers would only serve to draw more attention to him.

At the time of Pearl Harbor Tao was still in Hong Kong. When Du, who was in Chongqing, sent a plane over to get his friends out, the professor's name was first on his list. The last years of the war would see Tao safely back in Chongqing, ghost-writing *China's Destiny*, Chiang Kaishek's master work. This was a xenophobic rationale of Guomindang rule which touched on national history, temperament and reconstruction, and was a bestseller in its day.

Throughout all those years of disquiet Du Yuesheng never ceased to look after Tao. Though the professor came through them unharmed, the months immediately following the defection cannot have been easy ones for Du, as there was the worry that the Japanese would seek reprisal in a wave of vengeful terror. His own safety was at risk, for No. 76's agents were all about his house and the Gloucester Hotel, and he knew that the prize they all had their eye on was himself. It was at this time that he heard from General Dai Li, who suggested that he bolster up his underground and underworld forces, urging upon him the idea of forming a secret-society consortium. All the elements were there: Du's leadership of the Green Gang; and now that he was in Hong Kong, where the Red Gang predominated, his growing links with that organization as well. Efficient as his men were, Du agreed that he could do with some cooperation with other gangland powerhouses, if he was to worst the combined forces of the Japanese terrorist ring and No. 76. He had always had a nice sense of balance, especially in the matter of violence, and he went to work to convene a conference of Red and Green Gang heavies in Hong Kong at once.

It was not so simple now, the mustering of gangland might. The war had made everything more equivocal, and collaboration had become the order of the day. Compromise had become part of Shanghai life, not least among the people in his own fraternity. Some had drifted into other allegiances; many more had yielded to what they saw as inevitable. Even his one-time partner and confrère, Zhang Xiaolin, was keeping company and doing business with the Japanese. Half a dozen times Du had warned his old friend to stay clear: for your own good, he would say, leave off before one of Dai Li's men kills you. But Zhang was never one to say no to big time, and when the Japanese offered to cut him in on their shady operations in Shanghai, in exchange for his connections with the dope market and the gambling scene, he said yes, he was interested; life was too dull and he could do with a little grandeur.

The gambling joints he ran in partnership with the enemy got swankier and swankier, numbering in their customers upper-world nabobs as well as underworld swells. Du was nervous for him, but away in Hong Kong felt hopeless to avert the day that was bound to come, the day Zhang would be called upon to pay his dues.

When they got him he was leaning out of the window of his house on Rue Wagner, just a few doors away from Du Yuesheng's. It was August, one of those steamy days when you waved your fan only to have its cooling effect erased by the heat your action created. Zhang, hot and bothered, was bellowing at his bodyguards, who were standing outside the house and making a racket. He could not know that he made of himself a perfect target, framed there on all sides by the rectangle of the window. The first bullet got him in the throat, the second in the chest. As with all such killings the sniper was one of the victim's own men, who, when he came inside to inspect his work, found Zhang on his stomach, a lake of blood beneath him.

JAPAN'S HEART was not much in Wang Jingwei's projected regime. She had hoped to buy a cheap peace by offering a course of conciliation to Chiang Kaishek, but Wang Jingwei was the nearest she had to a taker. Originally it was thought that he was in some way representing the Guomindang, and half of China believed him to be in league with Chiang Kaishek from the start. But whatever might have been the understanding between the two men, after the exposure by Gao and Tao, there was no way Chiang Kaishek would want to be associated with any course that even remotely suggested appeasement.

But the Japanese were nothing if not determined. And it was in the old mood of intrigue that they looked to another bridge to Chongqing. In Hong Kong one of their intelligence officers had come upon a man representing himself as T.L. Soong, brother of T.V. Soong and Madame Chiang Kaishek. There followed the bizarre fiasco of what would come to be known as Operation Kiri. This was the code name for the plot the Japanese military hatched to use T.L. Soong — if the man was really he — to get through to Chongqing. The man seemed willing to cooperate, and by March 1940, he and the Japanese were deep in talk.

The meetings were of course clandestine, taking place sometimes in a room above a Chinese business establishment in Hong Kong, and sometimes in a candlelit basement in the Portuguese province of Macao. At no time were the Japanese absolutely sure that the man they were dealing with really was T.L. Soong. He had been introduced to them by a Chinese reporter, who claimed to have been a contemporary of his at St John's University, their Alma Mater in Shanghai. Looking him up in their intelligence files, the Japanese had discovered that T.L. Soong was indeed in Hong Kong, working as the manager of the Southwestern Transport Company there. His appearance and behaviour seemed to fit well enough: he was short, something over forty, well-mannered, spoke good English, and given to an occasional puff on a cigar.

Though nothing was explicit the composition of the Chinese delegation at these talks — besides Soong it included a general from the Generalissimo's military headquarters and the National Defence Council's Chief Secretary — suggested to the Japanese that there was a genuine wish to open negotiations on Chiang's part. They took heart also from the rumour that Madame Chiang was often in town these days, assuming her presence linked to the talks somehow. Perhaps she was there to see which way the wind was blowing? Perhaps Chiang was resuming his cautious pursuit of a middle way between appeasement and resistance?

Japanese hopes for a *rapprochement* with Chongqing were high that spring, so much so that when it came to the inauguration of Wang Jingwei's government, they made all sorts of excuses to put it off. Wang was in the dark about Operation Kiri and much else.

Yet while he was kept dangling, nothing new was coming up about T.L. Soong either. Tokyo began to fear that the whole thing might turn out to be a hoax intended to confound the launching of Wang Jingwei's impending regime. It did not look to Tokyo as though the points at issue in these talks would be settled in a hurry. The Japanese, not wishing to find at the end of the day that Chongqing had all this time been leading them up the garden path, decreed that if a firm reply on those points were not received within four days, the ceremonies would go ahead on March 30. No reply came.

There was now no pretending that Operation Kiri would come to anything very much. But still its sponsors persisted, and meetings between the two sides carried on for another six months. By September, however, it had to be admitted that the operation was something of a lost cause. The Japanese never did discover, at least not until the war was over, whether the man who called himself T.L. Soong was an impostor or not. They did what they could to establish his identity and, with the Japanese aptitude for such things, they even went so far as to photograph the man through a keyhole. He was sitting in a room in the Grand Hotel in Hong Kong, his chair having been so arranged as to bring it within the focus of the camera behind the spy-hole. But when the photograph was shown to Zhou Fohai and another colleague, one said yes, the man *was* T.L. Soong, and the other said no, the chap was a fraud.

The mystery might never have been solved if, one day in 1945, the Japanese interpreter for Operation Kiri hadn't chanced upon 'T.L. Soong' in a camp for Chinese prisoners near Shanghai. Wanting to be sure, the Japanese went up and questioned him. The man admitted that he was not T. L. Soong, but a look-alike agent belonging to Dai Li's ring.

A COLD, wind-driven rain on March 19 stung Wang Jingwei's face as he set out with Zhou Fohai to climb the long slope of steep steps to Sun Yatsen's tomb, encouched in the Purple Mountains to Nanking's west. They had come as pilgrims to a sacred place, to pay homage to the patron saint of Chinese nationalism. In front of the mausoleum Wang Jingwei re-read Dr Sun's will through a blur of tears. The day, which had begun overcast and chilly, suddenly brought forth sun; and standing beside him, Zhou Fohai felt his spirits lift at this brilliant and unexpected augur of better things.

It was eleven days to the inauguration, or the 'return of the National government to the capital' — a phrase Wang preferred for its suggestion of legitimacy. They had come to Nanjing, he and Zhou, for the opening of the Central Political Conference to usher in the new government; and paying their respects to the founder of the Chinese Republic was in a way to give their present endeavour the seal and trappings of a restoration. For Wang was nagged by a sense of its not having had any endorsement by the people who mattered. He found himself wondering just which countries would recognize it. Italy probably, but not Great Britain. Count Ciano, Mussolini's Foreign Minister, had sent a congratulatory telegram, and had indicated that the Italian ambassador would be withheld from Chongqing so long as Wang's government was in the offing. But in England the Prime Minister Neville Chamberlain had said in a speech to the House of Commons that 'the only government in China recognized by the British government is the National government of China, of which General Chiang Kaishek is the president.' Germany would probably follow Italy but there appeared to be no question of any other Western power doing the same. What worried Wang most of all was the shoddy treatment he was getting from his sponsors, who even now were not prepared to say whether or not his government would be fully recognized by Japan.

That was one reason the meeting — the one he held the next day to herald the new government — was so lacklustre. There was something rather gimcrack about it, with superannuated officials left over from the Manchu dynasty and undistinguished Guomindang apostates taking up most of the table. When Wang Jingwei stood up to speak, some of them took their eyes off the documents placed in front of them and others took their glasses off to listen, assuming attentive and sombre expressions. He, as usual, was word-perfect. The hall, high-ceilinged and plushly draped, was fitted with klieg lights and telephone booths for the press conference that would presently follow. There had been an attempt by guerillas, General Dai Li's no doubt, to blow up one of the trains carrying the delegates to Nanjing, but beyond this display of violence the occasion offered little in the way of headline pyrotechnics, and reporters came away with nothing more interesting than a list of ministerial appointments.

Still, it was only a prelude to the great day itself, the day the flags would unfurl all over Nanjing like a sudden spatter of long-awaited rain. That day, March 30, came and the rain lifted. Zhou Fohai, who had expected to be sad, instead felt exhilarated, telling himself that he had not lived in vain. For such a sight, the Chinese flags all strung out like that, Zhou had reasoned, pleaded, agitated. In his negotiations with the Japanese he had made it a point of honour, but as so often proves true in the transactions between nations, symbolism would overtake substance. The final compromise pleased no one, for while it allowed the Chinese flag to fly, a triangular pennant advertising 'Anti-Communism, Peace and Reconstruction' was tagged to it like a negating suffix. On the morning of the ceremony Wang Jingwei ordered the loathsome pennant to be detached; but Colonel Kasega, who for a Japanese indulged the Chinese in much, did not do so in this, and before the ceremony began arranged for the appendage to be re-attached to all the flags.

The flag tapped a well of hatred. Catching sight of it, the Japanese soldiers all but erupted. It was as though all that shedding of Japanese blood, all those years of occupation had been for nothing, the way that Chinese emblem was reappearing everywhere. Men and women were cuffed and kicked for having hoisted the flag above their house. Japanese soldiers rampaged about, tearing the flag down, spitting on it and trampling it underfoot. In the mayhem created by this violence there loomed before the people of Nanjing the memory of the pillage of three years before, when the city bled from the savagery of the invading army.

The greatest and unwitting contribution made by the Japanese presence in China was to make patriots of those who would otherwise remain neutral. In attitudes towards the enemy there could be no indifference and, before it all Chinese stood conjoined in antipathy. What greater insensitivity and arrogance than the renaming of a Nanjing street after Matsui, that most hated of Japanese commanders; than the stipulation that all clocks be set to Tokyo time; than the holding of massive track marathons to celebrate Japanese victory and Chinese defeat, of sports meetings and school rallies where, the flags of puppet regimes flying, giant human formations shaped the characters *Dongya Xin Zhixu*, the New Order in East Asia?

So it was with mixed feelings that the crowds watched the flag parade pass through the streets to mark the inauguration of Wang Jingwei's government; few could be unmoved by national pride and sentiment, yet few could forget that the spectacle was by courtesy of the Japanese. There were free theatrical performances and lantern processions, and Japanese planes showering leaflets proclaiming the new government's programme. The crowds were drawn along in all this drama, but not many were beguiled into mistaking the fantasy for the fact, even though, being Chinese and greatly partial to public spectacles, they thoroughly enjoyed the show.

Now the ceremony began. The officials appeared, variously dressed in Chinese gown and Western suit, nodding to each other in greeting as they filed into the hall. The building, though generously proportioned in the way of government edifices, could have been larger or more imposing, but to insist on more space or grandeur would have meant dislodging the Imperial Army, which had commandeered the city's stateliest accommodation.

Addressing the Chinese assembly, Wang Jingwei's voice was sorrowful and, for normally so compelling a speaker, shockingly soft. He spoke of the Pan-Asianism that had been so much a part of the late Sun Yatsen's vision, making the most of this dated creed in his defence of Sino-Japanese cooperation. He himself believed in it still; indeed he had made himself do so, setting himself against whatever might cause his conviction to falter. The new realities of war had made Pan-Asianism an anachronism, and stretching it (as he now sought to do) to make it embrace the New Order in East Asia, Japan's latest watchword, only pointed up its hollowness the more. Yet he wished with all his heart that the 'good neighbourliness' enjoined by the New Order was not a sham, wished that the hopes of Pan-Asianism had not faded with the disillusionment of war. There are times when it is the death not of men but of their ideas that appears intolerable.

On the face of it, there was nothing unreasonable in the invoking of a bond of race and culture with the Japanese. Yet there was, in the military officers who really ran things in Japan, a lack of human and cultural reference that made them behave in just those ways that most repelled the Chinese. Deep down Wang Jingwei abhorred these young officers, the ones he described in a letter to a former comrade as ignorant, arrogant, profit-seeking and lecherous. (The letter fell into the hands of Japanese Intelligence, as it was bound to.) And it went against his instincts to enter into an alliance with a people who had staked their future on the use of force, on the way of the warrior that was not the Bushido of the past but the barbarity and violence of the present. Yet here he was, doing this very thing that he so deplored. How did he get into this situation? He felt hemmed in, tied down; we can act only a little according to our instincts and for the rest must submit to the forces that impinge from beyond ourselves.

To the press that greeted him as he emerged from the ceremony he gave an impression of exaggerated defiance that belied his own misgivings. For China to participate in the New Order, his press

Stone figures of Wang Jingwei and his wife on their knees — a reminder of the fate of traitors

statement said, she would have to regain her sovereignty and national independence. To Japan she might only prosper as part of a larger whole; to him she would only do so once she stood free.

At the same moment as he was saying this, a chain letter was circulating in Chongqing asking for contributions to a reward fund for Wang Jingwei's assassin, the money to be sent to the offices of the Guomindang. The night before, Chongqing had vividly demonstrated its feelings about Wang's treason: two grotesque cardboard effigies of a man and a woman kneeling had been raised in a public square, and torches touched to their base. The effigies, luridly illumined in the engulfing flames, had faces that were caricatures of Wang Jingwei and his wife. This enactment, of Wang Jingwei's public humbling and immolation, showed that the Guomindang could not see his latest move as anything but a baleful betrayal. Of the traitors that had followed him, Chongqing now demanded the arrest of another seventy-seven (on top of the twenty-eight for whom a warrant had already been issued). Chiang Kaishek's comment on the new regime was that it was nothing but an instrument of the Japanese Army, and that the world would never recognize it.

And that world, to Wang Jingwei's mortification, would seem to include even Japan. There was, to the Japanese, every reason to withhold recognition. To give their official seal to Wang's government in Nanjing would be to burn their bridges to Chiang's government in Chongqing, with which they still hoped to negotiate. The year had shown that Wang Jingwei was without popular support, and at home in Tokyo priorities were unequivocally shifting elsewhere. What if they offered the more generous of the peace terms to Chiang Kai-shek, leaving Wang only enough of a nibble to keep him ticking? If they scuttled him, would Chiang come round? These were the questions that now preoccupied Tokyo.

The terms of Japanese recognition were to be spelt out in a Basic Treaty. The man Tokyo sent to negotiate it was a General Abe Nobuyuki, whose rank was not exactly that of an Ambassador, but the lower one of Envoy Extraordinary. His instructions from the Imperial Army were to try and absorb Wang into its pet scheme, that of achieving a settlement with Chongqing. The two sides opened negotiations in July and, on August 31, when Wang Jingwei's team accepted the terms of the Basic Treaty, they found that they were agreeing to nothing less than the occupation of Chinese territory for a period of almost indefinite duration. Distasteful as it was, Wang Jingwei had submitted to the Japanese stand on the issue of troop withdrawal because it had simply been too intransigent for him to challenge it. Raising this issue with Colonel Kasega, Zhou Fohai had said, 'You claim that Japanese civilians won't come to China unless the army is here. If you'd only come as guests, we'd welcome you. But if your people feel they won't be safe unless they have guns, then that makes things very awkward for us.' In reply Kasega had said that Zhou was wrong to talk like that, of guns and guests. 'We did want to come as guests in our Sunday best, but your reception rooms just aren't good enough.' It wasn't as though Japan hadn't tried to get along with China, he added, but 'the atmosphere wasn't all that congenial and the peace wasn't kept very well. The kind of guests you want — good guests — won't come unless they can be assured of peace and order. You know that full well.'

It only remained for Japan to announce her official recognition of the Nanjing government. Weeks passed, then months, and still nothing happened. Even General Abe grew impatient, and one day travelled to Tokyo with Colonel Kasega to make an appeal on behalf of the new regime. Stationing themselves outside the Foreign Minister's residence, they announced that they would not budge unless the treaty was signed. 'We simply can't go back to Nanjing under the present circumstances,' Abe went on. 'If you don't recognize the Nanjing government we shall have no choice but to die here.' For an inheritor of a culture in which death is ever available as an alternative to dishonour, there was nothing incongruous or hyperbolic about this declaration.

But Abe did not die. After more weeks of equivocation the Basic Treaty was signed on 30 November 1940. Neither of the signatories could know that their timing was badly off, for on that very day, it was heard all over China that the Chongqing government had received a pledge from President Roosevelt for US$100,000,000 and fifty modern pursuit aeroplanes (with more to come). It was as handsome an aid programme as could have been hoped for. Of course it was not unprompted: the Japanese overtures to Chiang Kaishek throughout the autumn, and the fear of his capitulation to these, had evidently goaded the United States into this expansive gesture, intending by it a bolstering of Chinese resistance. Another thing which prompted it was the imminent recognition of Wang's regime by the Axis powers, Japan having signed the Tripartite Pact with Germany and Italy in September. Chiang said that Wang Jingwei was done for. It had started with his exposure by Gao and Tao in January. If that was his death, then the inauguration of his regime in March was his funeral; and this, this signing away of China and his own integrity, was the elegiac address read over his tomb.

The Nanjing regime itself knew the treaty to be ignominious. But the die was cast. Zhou Fohai likened the whole sequence to a seduction: 'Our coming to Shanghai, the heart of the occupation, is like a woman accepting an invitation to a man's hotel room. The man is aflame... it's all he can do to contain his desire. The woman, who might have seized the moment to extract certain promises from him, instead ruins her chances by starting to take off her clothes. With her dress coyly unfastened, her barricades down, what is there left to say?'

Though Wang would not have put it like that, he could not have been immune to the sense of not having done the right thing as he braced himself for signing the Basic Treaty that day. He was standing with his entourage in front of the hall where the ceremony was to take place, awaiting General Abe's arrival. Ahead, over Purple Mountain, white clouds were strung out against a timeless sky. He was staring into space. In profile his eyelids swelled against tears and his skin whitened over bone. Suddenly he began to tear at his hair, and there came from his throat a choking sound which in the silence of the day seemed to echo off the asphalt beneath him, scratching out the words, 'Damnable, oh damnable!'

For a time no one moved or spoke. Then the interpreter beside him said, very gently, 'Sir, Ambassador Abe is here,' and took out a comb from his own pocket to run it through Wang Jingwei's hair.

This simple physical fact seemed to bring him back to a sense of there being emotions other than anguish, and he quickly straightened himself, his dignity again a steel rod inside him. We must absorb this grief, his eyes said as his lips managed a smile, accept its punishing aftermath; none of it will get any easier, only more unbearable. Whatever might have been thought an hour or two earlier, when he was affixing his starched collar and putting on his tails, no one catching sight of Wang Jingwei now would say that he was a man for whom his supreme moment had come.

Chapter Eleven

TRAITORS AND GUERILLAS 1940–1944

MEN SELL THEIR COUNTRY for reasons never as bad or as good as one thinks. Never wholly out of greed, never purely for motives of ideology or loyalty. Treachery is never altogether despicable, or entirely forgivable, but a kind of corruption eased by a little push this way and that, sometimes well-intentioned, often miscalculated, going forward on the strength of the even greater difficulty of turning back.

So it was with the Nanjing collaborators. The regime was an employment exchange for the faint-hearted, the eccentric, the time-serving, the clever. There were also Madame Wang's Cantonese relatives, like her brother-in-law, the Foreign Minister and ambassador to Japan. Before he turned collaborator he was director of the Institut Technique Franco-Chinois. He was something of an eccentric, who had studied Pharmacology and Medicine at universities in France and had written his doctoral dissertation on the vaginal vibrations of the female rabbit. He was a genial fellow, at his best organizing ceremonial functions like the Belgian national centenary or Confucius' birthday. Immensely dedicated to athletics and health, he edited a widely-read health magazine and was very keen to promote shadow boxing as a popular sport. Had his notoriety as a traitor not swamped his earlier reputation, he might well have earned recognition for himself as the inventor of a mechanical sparring opponent for boxers, and have had his name linked to games like kite-flying and kicking the shuttlecock (of which he was very fond) instead of treason. Inexplicably he had come by the mummified liver of Dr Sun Yatsen, and when he was imprisoned for collaboration at the end of the war, he tried to bargain for his life by offering to return this diseased organ to Chiang Kaishek for enshrinement as a holy relic or a national treasure. The gambit did not work however, and when the time came he was executed with all the rest.

The Foreign Minister was not considered to have much of a mind for politics — Zhou Fohai never could take him seriously — but the Deputy Minister for Propaganda was thought to have a flair. Before he became Wang Jingwei's publicist, Hu Lancheng was chief editor of the *South China Daily* in Hong Kong. It was Madame Wang who, believing his talents to extend beyond the scope of the leaders which appeared under his pseudonym, recruited him for her husband's cause.

Hu Lancheng was born in Zhejiang Province, the son of a tea merchant. Before he came to Shanghai in 1937, it was his inability to stick to one job that saw him moving from his post at the Hangzhou Post Office to Yanjing University in Beijing, and from there to various teaching jobs in the southern parts of the country. For a time he was deeply interested in Marxism, but as far as his most ardent enthusiasms were concerned it can only be said that they centred predominantly on women.

He found it hard to be diplomatic with colleagues, and had no qualms whatsoever about snubbing the Japanese. The views he expressed in his articles were rarely tamed by tact or self-protection, and because he believed himself to be free of the prevailing shibboleths he was also estranged from their shelter. Still, until he fell out of favour he had the ear of Wang Jingwei and Madame, and because he was a man of letters he had his own patrons among the better read civilians of the Japanese consular service.

If the Nanjing regime was hospitable to the maverick, it was rich in opportunity for the time-server and the thug. No two men did more to discredit Wang Jingwei's cause, or struck more terror into the Shanghainese heart, than Little Devil Ding Mocun and Li Shiqun, the chiefs of No. 76.

Ding was thirtyish, and had the look of the consumptive he was. Li was lusty, and if one were to describe him, words like 'dilettante' and 'playboy' would come to mind. By the time Wang Jingwei appeared in Shanghai they had been recruited into Japanese espionage and organized vice. Li had defected first, having been talent-spotted by General Doihara, the master Japanese spy. Ding had at first been sent by Chongqing to try and win him back. In the course of his mission he had met Zhou Fohai, and because the two had been fellow members of the CC clique Zhou had greeted him warmly and talked him into joining Wang's cause. So Ding never did go back to Chongqing, but instead threw in his lot with Li Shiqun.

It was from Doihara that the two inherited the terrorist ring in Shanghai, when that Lawrence of Asia moved on to Beijing in 1939. Both were pros when it came to torture and the third degree, and at No. 76 you got a daily demonstration of this. At first it was hard to tell who had the more deadly innings in his career, but although in the days they worked in Dai Li's outfit Ding's rank was the higher, very soon it was Li who got the upper hand. In the handout of official appointments Ding was made Minister of Welfare, the job of Minister of Police, which the two had vied for, being assumed by Zhou Fohai, who thought this the only way to end the squabbling.

Both Ding and Li had implacable enemies, who would have liked nothing better than to see the two of them dead. The precautions they took steered them through some exceptionally treacherous waters, but there were some very narrow escapes.

There was the time Ding was out driving with his teenage mistress, a schoolgirl who had a Chinese father and a Japanese mother, and whose sympathies were assumed to lie on the side of the mother. In her way this under-aged paramour was quite a well-known figure in the French Concession: heads always turned when she rode by on her bicycle towards her home near the French Park. Since the street, as every espionage agent knows, is where the risks are the greatest, Ding would not normally have made an unscheduled stop. But when they came down Bubbling Well Road towards the Siberian Fur Store, the girl insisted that they got down to look at some coats. Just seconds before they entered the shop Ding realized that he had walked into a trap, for at the door were some men carrying brown paper parcels which would unwrap to disclose hardware he could very well do without. Though he managed to run for it, standard procedure demanded that the girl wound up dead. His suspicions that she was a double agent working for Chongqing were confirmed when he came across one of her calling cards inscribed with a Buddhist prayer for his painless death. Too squeamish to do it himself, he ordered one of his men to take her to a graveyard and shoot her. The young girl had the same effect on her executioner as she had had on Ding Mocun, and for a moment he almost saw in his gun-sight not an enemy target but a beauty it would be a shame to snuff out. 'Whatever you do, don't mutilate my face' were her last words to him. Nor did he, judging by the photograph taken of her remains (the rank immediacy of freshly executed traitors congealed into photographs, vividly suggestive of the effectiveness of terrorist techniques, was regarded as good publicity material by both sides in the secret service war).

In that war, Li Shiqun was pitted against not only a subworld of terrorists and spies but also an underworld of gangsters and secret brotherhoods. Not that the borders were all that distinct, but Li knew that No. 76 was no match for Dai Li's network unless he had somebody like Du Yuesheng for an ally. Du was a headache. Li's first thought had been to try and do away with the fellow and, in addition to sending some professional killers to Hong Kong, had endeavoured to get the authorities there to proclaim him persona non grata. Neither of these schemes had worked, however, and now he was wondering if he shouldn't try and find a rival to Du Yuesheng.

He chose Wu Sibao for the job. Big Wu, as this Green Gang heavy was known to many, was a swarthy, thick-set and lumpy-faced underworld arriviste. The son of a hot-water seller on Chengdu Road, Big Wu had worked as a groom at the racecourse and then as an Englishman's chauffeur. At some stage in his early career he was suspected of the murder of his wife's lover (in fact the real murderer was one of his disciples, who thought he was doing his master a favour), and he disappeared from Shanghai for a while, joining the Shandong warlord's army (the Three Imponderables mentioned earlier). He was thirty-nine when he returned to Shanghai six years later, and he was convinced that he was cut out for crime.

He was as gross as his second wife was refined. Mrs Wu was a stunning beauty: she wore sheer silk stockings and high-heeled shoes and her hair was drawn back in an S-shaped chignon at the nape of her soft white neck. Though to her admirer, Hu Lancheng, she suggested the orchid and the lily, there was yet a tautness to her stride and movement that hinted at something masculine within her.

Apparently as a little girl she had been dressed as the male child that her mother would rather have had. She was twelve before she was more appositely dressed, and that was only because her school friends laughed at her, not at the fact of her wearing boys' clothes, for that was not uncommon in China, but at their unbecomingness to her, and she had made a fuss to her father.

In addition to much else she had going for her the young Mrs Wu went to one of Shanghai's best girls' schools, where she showed herself to be bright but not conscientious. At nineteen she found herself pregnant by the son of a well-to-do comprador. The child turning out to be male, she was taken in by its father's family as a sort of second daughter-in-law (her affair with their son had actually preceded his marriage to the first daughter-in-law, but though love is important in a man's choice of mistress in China, family determines which woman he marries). She could have been upgraded when the first wife died prematurely, but since her son had died of scarlet fever when he was nine and she was already quite fed up with the family, she said she'd rather leave. Her husband begged her to stay. For so beautiful a woman she was not hardhearted, but she could not abide abjectness in a man and though she believed her husband to be sincere when he swore he would never remarry, she left and stayed clear of him for good. She was thirty-two.

She enjoyed the feeling of being wicked and fell to being Mrs Wu and the disciples' First Lady with gusto. There would be nothing small-time about her. When she celebrated her fortieth birthday, all the Nanjing government save Mr and Madame Wang came and the party had the panache of traditional underworld style — opera performances, hordes of guests, limitless food. Not since the dedication of Du Yuesheng's clan hall, everyone agreed, had Shanghai seen anything so grand. She herself looked lovely, in a rich ochre dress whose only adornment was a two-thirds opened peony pinned to the breast.

A pair of toughies, was how Shanghai described this husband-and-wife team. Under the aegis of No. 76, Wu Sibao's shakedowns and racketeering surged to such heights that many came to think of him as a lesser Du Yuesheng, and among them Tiny Du very soon became an alternative nickname to Big Wu. The large-minded saw him as another Green Gang potentate, as apparently devoted to the code of the *jianghu* walk of life as Du. But this was a misconstruction, for in truth Big Wu's lack of finesse was not Du Yuesheng's style at all. If there was one thing Big Wu didn't go in for it was scruples. The leather strap he used for flogging was stiff with unwashed blood and killing a man was to him like crushing a cockcroach under the heel of one's shoe. Whatever else Big Wu might be he was not one to slack off on a job, and after he joined No. 76 the carnage became so prodigious and indiscriminate that, away in Hong Kong, Du Yuesheng was moved to call a truce.

Originally the basis of the killing by the two sides of the terror war was an eye for an eye — which in practice worked out as a banker for a banker, or a journalist for a journalist, to name two of the most vulnerable targets — but by the first few months of 1941, No. 76 was killing even the clerks and cashiers of the banks Chongqing still maintained in the foreign quarters in Shanghai. It was then that Du Yuesheng decided that the time had come for a talk.

He sent an emissary to Big Wu. Wu to his credit took the gesture for what it was, the offer of a deal by one Green Gang member to another. A few days later Wu's emissary arrived at Du Yuesheng's house in Hong Kong, and during the weeks that followed political murder ceased altogether in Shanghai. Wu's emissary in the meantime was finding life very congenial in Hong Kong. Rather than go back to Shanghai, he asked Du if he might switch sides and enroll as one of his disciples. It would take someone less broadminded than Du to say no.

Li Shiqun, who had not been consulted, felt that all this was a challenge to his authority when he heard. It made him extremely wary, the way Big Wu could decide things for himself, and it made him realize how powerful his subordinate, the ex-chauffeur, had become. True to his word (for Tiny Du had this in common with his namesake, that promises weighed with him), Wu released the bank clerks held captive in No. 76, and as a goodwill gesture even gave them some money for their travel to Chongqing. Li found this intolerable, and thought to himself that without question Big Wu must go.

The first sign that Li was plotting his downfall came to Wu from

Zhou Fohai, who made it plain to him one day that he must resign from No. 76, he was giving the government such a bad name. The next sign came when his house was suddenly surrounded by the *kempeitai*, the Japanese military police, and it was a good guess that they were sent by Li Shiqun. While he went into hiding, Hu Lancheng as a friend of the family escorted Mrs Wu to see Li Shiqun.

Yes, he did know about it, said Li to Mrs Wu. The Japanese had a warrant out against him but, had he a mind to, her husband could avoid the worst by giving himself up. 'Tell you what,' he added, 'if you bring your husband to me I'll see to it that they don't go heavy on him.'

But no sooner was the husband produced than the *kempeitai* seized and clapped him in jail. At this Mrs Wu covered her face, her lovely face, and cried to Hu Lancheng that he must help her.

Li Shiqun was not an easy person to bring round, but Hu Lancheng made a great nuisance of himself, and in the end Li was so exasperated he agreed to have a word with the *kempeitai*. Big Wu was a sight when he emerged from prison two months later, bruised in several places and less overweight by far. When Li took him back to Mrs Wu he explained that the Japanese had only agreed to release him on condition that he, Li, took him into custody. As with all those just released from prison, the first thing Wu did on coming home was to have a bath and put on new clothes. Then he made obeisances before the family altar and reminded himself to order two hundred coffins to be delivered to charity in token of his gratitude to the deities. His gratitude to Li was as immense, and, struck once more by the narrowness of his escape, he all of a sudden went down on his knees and knocked his forehead on the ground before his saviour.

The next morning Hu Lancheng came to the house to say goodbye: at Li's bidding Big Wu was leaving for Suzhou, where it was thought he should lie low for a while. At the door of the couple's bedroom Hu was transfixed by the sight of Mrs Wu helping her husband into his clothes, the poignancy of the wifely ministrations. Two days later he would receive a call from Suzhou to say that Big Wu was dead. Some said it was the noodles he'd eaten at Li Shiqun's lunch, others said it was the fried sugared cakes. Whatever it was Big Wu was drawn into a tight ball after his meal with Li and very sick.

He was buried with considerable pomp by his wife and bereaved underworld following. Hu Lancheng arrived in Suzhou in time to accompany the coffin and the widow to Shanghai. The private railway carriage carrying the coffin was lined with flowers, and when Mrs Wu stepped down at the railway station she did not disappoint the inquisitive crowd. The funeral procession was long and drew half the city. On 9 February 1942, the obituaries in the morning editions said that a man known for his charitable works had died of an illness five days before in Suzhou. But if anyone's opinion had been asked, he'd have said it was murder by Li Shiqun. At the International Funeral Parlour on Jiaozhou Road Mrs Wu was seen in white. Beside her Hu Lancheng was wondering how he might avenge the death.

TWO MONTHS BEFORE, on Sunday, December 7 (or December 8, as it was in the Far East), the Japanese airforce attacked Pearl Harbor. From then on the Sino-Japanese conflict and the war in Europe were rolled into one, as the Second World War. That day columns of Japanese troops and light tanks marched through Shanghai's foreign settlements and proclamations were handed out to inform the citizens that Japan was at war with the United States and Britain. Hong Kong held out for thirteen days, and then fell. Being marked men to the Japanese, Du Yuesheng, Professor Tao and other Chongqing loyalists had to evacuate as quickly as possible.

What Pearl Harbor also interrupted were the elaborate arrangements Du had made for reviving the opium trade. These arrangements had come about not because Du needed the money so much as that the government did. The preparations were airtight, the connections trustworthy; but the timing was badly off. The produce, which could be had for the asking where the Chongqing government was, in Sichuan Province, would have been shipped from there to Canton Bay, whence smugglers could move it up the coast and abroad. But the operation was just one step behind the occupying power, and even General Dai Li, who as Du's partner in this enterprise would have been happy to facilitate matters through the Finance Ministry's Bureau of Freight Transport, which he happened to head along with Asia's most powerful secret police, could do nothing about it. It would be another year before the traffic got through to assuage the cravings of the thousands whom the Japanese-sponsored monopoly in Shanghai had for its clientele. By then, the load had passed through so many hands that if you subtracted all the rake-offs, there was nothing much left for Du.

In the end, all he got out of it was a house in Chongqing, presented to him by the authorities on whose behalf he had conducted the operation. It was in this house that he lived between Pearl Harbor and his return to Shanghai in 1945. It stood six to seven miles from the centre of Chongqing, on the south bank of the river close to where it runs into the Yangtze. It was too small for Du, whose habit it was to live surrounded by people, but it gave on to the back of a wood, and had a view of plum trees, bamboo and pine. The temperature was lower there than in downtown Chongqing, and more bearable, though the sky was the same leaden grey, the same dripping pall. Were the Chinese given to thinking of cities in this way, Du Yuesheng would have pronounced Chongqing ugly.

What was worse was the isolation, the boredom. Du still had his chairmanship of the Communications Bank, but until contact could be re-established with the Shanghai underground he felt that there was virtually nothing useful he could do. Chiang Kaishek, now that Japan had come into collision with the West (which was what he had banked on all along), was regarding the war as something to be retired from, China having in his view done quite enough already. This made of the wartime capital, once so full of fighting spirit, a place of matinee listlessness. Without pretending that it was a game he didn't play for profit, Du Yuesheng devoted his energies to mahjong more and more. Opium came next, but more as a prophylactic than an indulgence, for the grim climate greatly aggravated his asthma.

When he went on an arduous tour of the northwest in the autumn of 1942, in answer to a government call to businessmen to open up the interior for development, he had to skip the last leg of his journey because the attacks were so bad. The local notables who were his hosts along the way did all they could to entertain his party, engaging local opera companies or touring troupes and feeding him the harvests of the peasant's unpaid and prodigious labour. It was a world away from the normal life of the counryside, which was sunk in the misery inevitable in dearth. But the asthma took all the energy out of him, and when he cut short his trip and returned to Chongqing he was exhausted and far from well.

In Chongqing winter is the damp season into which the summer of steaming heat turns without transition. When his asthma came on again Du was attended by two specialists, one in traditional Chinese medicine and the other in the Western variety, both competent and well known (the latter the more so for having, as a medical student in Munich, tried to kill himself in unrequited love for a German girl by laying himself down on a railway track). The world did not crowd in on Du that winter, and he gave himself to observing. The newspapers which Du, being illiterate, had his secretaries read to him, told of Madame Chiang Kaishek going on a fund-raising tour to America and addressing crowds in Madison Square Garden and the Hollywood Bowl. The grapevine told of the antipathy between Chiang Kaishek and General 'Vinegar Joe' Stilwell, the man President Roosevelt had sent to Chongqing as Commander-in-Chief of the China-Burma-India Theatre to keep the Chinese fighting the Japanese, who might thereby be prevented from diverting their troops to the Pacific battleground. However, Chiang did not think it necessary for the Chinese to fight much more, and would rather, if the truth be known, keep all his best troops for a blockade of the area occupied by the Red Army. There was nothing novel or remarkable in this, since for all the talk of a united front with the Communists in resisting the enemy, Chiang had never relinquished the belief, long harboured also by Du Yuesheng, that the excrescence in the heart of China was Communism.

In contrast, the fighting between the Chinese and the Japanese in parts of the interior was by now quite half-hearted. While not actually growing friendlier, the two forces were mixing freely and busily engaged in trade. Cotton, cigarettes, car tyres, thermos flasks, textiles, enamel dishes, soap, medicines and buttons were flowing across the largely illusory Front from occupied China to supply shop shelves and meet scarcities in Chongqing and lesser towns in the Chinese-held territory. Beneath the propaganda of hate, profiteers and wheeler-dealers of both nationalities were thriving on the traffic. It was not always legal, but it was open and beyond official control.

Having developed some useful contacts on his northwest expedition, and being a shrewd businessman able to divine early the unwritten rules of the game, Du would bid for a large slice of the market himself. In the following year, when radio contact was re-established with his disciples in Shanghai, Du laid plans for a massive exchange of commodities between unoccupied and enemy-held China. Of course it meant dealing with the Japanese, but the way he put it to himself was: he drove a hard bargain, the trade would relieve a shortage of cotton goods and cotton yarn in the interior, and it was obviously highly profitable to Chongqing, so much so that it had the full backing of four government banks. Besides, the money he made on it could be used for underground resistance work.

The underground work, as his close friend Dai Li was happy to report, had lately become a matter of Sino-American cooperation. Dai Li was working in strange tandem with a Major (later Rear Admiral) Milton E. Miles to train and command a Chinese guerilla army for sabotage work behind enemy lines.

Milton Miles, who in his days at the Naval Academy was also called Mary, after a movie star named Mary Miles Minter, had been sent to China by the Commander-in-Chief, United States Fleets, shortly after Pearl Harbor to establish weather stations and bases in China and to prepare the coast for U.S. Navy landings in three to four years' time. Since, before setting out, he had learnt that Chiang Kaishek was going to place him under the care of General Dai Li, Miles had looked up the general in the files of the State Department and Military Naval Intelligence, and had been taken aback by what he found. Dai was, he discovered, a most unsavoury character who ran a Gestapo-like organization and his own concentration camp for political enemies, and whose particular *bête noire*, it so happened, was foreigners — few of whom he had actually met. (In fact Dai Li's phobia was focussed on the British only, having been soured by an encounter with them during a trip to Hong Kong earlier on in the war, when

Milton Miles and General Dai Li at a party for orphans of SACO's troops, Christmas 1945

at Japanese instigation the police Special Branch had detained him and treated him uncivilly. Finding nothing on him save a briefcase containing an American-manufactured sinus spray, they let him go in the end, though not before he had vowed never to set foot in the British colony again.) From Washington Miles learnt that the general was worse than Germany's Himmler, and his best policy was to stay well clear of him.

Yet out of the unlikely partnership of these two men there blossomed what was soon to be something approaching friendship. It was not until some days after his arrival in Chongqing that Miles was given the opportunity to size up General Dai Li himself. To anyone meeting Dai Li for the first time he must have seemed the most mild mannered of men: there he sat in his suit of whipcord khaki, a genial smile on his face displaying much gold bridge-work. He asked, by name, about each of Miles's children, and also about his car. This was obviously the sort of espionage he was good at — information about people's private life and tastes. When he invited Miles to dinner he served no poultry, having learnt from his intelligence that the American was allergic to feathered food. Almost from the first moment, Miles decided to throw everything he had discovered about the general in Washington out of the window.

For goodwill Miles presented Dai Li at that first meeting with a snub-nosed .38 identical to the one he himself was wearing, and the general put it into his holster at once. Dai Li loved pistols, machine-guns and firearms of every description as much as he loved cars — loved their mechanical perfection, their oiled responsiveness to pressure and, though he had no need for virility substitutes, the potency they passed to him.

The full range of his weaponry would unravel to Mary Miles as the weeks passed. The first glimpse came with a visit to a place which the major, having the American vocabulary for such things, termed a 'Special Devices Centre' or a 'Psychological Warfare Division' to himself. Nothing conspicuous marked the approach to this place, which lay in a valley some ten miles from downtown Chongqing, and there was nothing to suggest to the straggle of peasants toiling in the surrounding paddy fields the range of counter-espionage gadgetry that was being devised inside the dilapidated farmhouse. But Milton Miles saw everything: the camouflage equipment, electrical coding machines, spy projects with miniature cameras, devices for converting commercial radio receivers into transmitters — the adapters for this purpose disguised as fancy snuff bottles, ink bottles or cakes of soap — the telegrapher's key embedded in a fountain pen, and the antenna in an umbrella made in Shanghai. More ingeniously still, there were rolls of photographic gelatine, stripped from the film and written on in fruit juice, that yielded messages to no known method of photographic development but to the smoke of a special local tobacco. Amid a curious scatter of soaps and vitamin pills, Miles was amazed to discover masked poisons, incendiaries and articles for what he to his American self would call 'personal destruction'. That evening he returned to his quarters with his admiration doubled for the cleverness of the Chinese.

Further revelations came with an inspection trip to the front lines a week or so later. Travelling with Dai Li into the heart of occupied

China, where he was introduced to villagers either as the Salt Commissioner, a Chinese Maritime Customs official, or a missionary (but reported by Japanese intelligence as a Russian aviation adviser), the American to his wonder found that the coast was everywhere pitted with the general's underground scouts and guerillas, who as the two men travelled southwards kept arriving and slipping away again to Beijing, Shanghai, Taiwan, Canton and Hong Kong. It was an eye-opener, and it convinced the American that General Dai Li would be a very good ally.

These fighting men, together with a group of Americans sent over from Washington, would form the nucleus of the Sino-American Cooperative Organization, an intelligence and guerilla operation jointly commanded by Miles and Dai Li. This organization, whose contraction to SACO was always to be pronounced SOCKO for its hard-hitting suggestions, would in time be affectionately dubbed the Rice Paddy Army, the Cloak and Dagger Boys, the Jap's Wasp Nest, and the Allied Fifth Column. It was as odd an outfit as ever had its offices in Washington. By the time the end of the war was in sight, it was to have killed, wounded and captured some 25,000 Japanese, destroyed two hundred and seventy bridges, eighty-four locomotives, a hundred and forty ships, besides numerous depots and warehouses. Whenever its commandos struck, Japanese trains teetered off tracks, Japanese vessels laden with essential supplies capsized in billowing smoke, Japanese storehouses collapsed in a shatter of dynamite. In Chongqing it worked from its headquarters in Happy Valley, eight miles from the centre of town, where in genial irreverence and American breeziness it flew its white pennant marked with '???!!!***' in red, in elision of the 'What the hell!' it meant.

It inevitably grated on the U.S. Office of Strategic Services (O.S.S), the CIA's precursor in the Far East and proprietorial about behind-the-scenes operations in China. The two organizations saw things differently, and though Mary Miles was made chief of the O.S.S. in the Far East for a while, the accord did not last and each would go its own way. To the director of the O.S.S., Miles must have seemed the very image of an American gone native, consorting with Chinese Himmlers and commanding guerillas whose civilian backgrounds were such an inappropriate ragbag — coolies and merchants, pirates and bandits. In fact all was grist that came to SACO's mill — the Loyal Patriotic Army (relic of the commando squad which Du Yuesheng, chipping in out of his own pocket, mustered and armed in Shanghai at the start of the war), the Pudong Pirates Association, a force which, being indigenous to Du's native place, was also at his disposal. All was highly irregular, and well attuned to the ways in which Asians like to fight their wars.

By the time the accord formally establishing SACO was signed — by T.V. Soong and Dai Li for China and by the Secretary of the U.S. Navy and Miles for the United States — Miles' trust in General Dai Li was absolute. He found it difficult to understand why Dai Li's name was used in China to frighten children into behaving. His American trust, which had to it something eternally ingenuous and generous, would not credit the Chinese with the guile which enables that nation to cope with the realities of life. Once he visited a prison run by Dai Li's special services, and dismissed as so much nonsense the horror stories he had heard in Washington and Chongqing about their concentration camps. Here were no fetid cellars with prisoners stretched on a rack; instead, here was a camp where the guards were there to keep people *out*. Here was General Dai Li, who escorted Miles there himself, entering politely and exchanging bows with the inmates, and enquiring solicitously after an old lady, who was introduced as the mother of Wang Jingwei. It never occurred to Miles to wonder if the whole thing wasn't stage-managed, and he never did find out about that secret place in Guizhou Province, where four to five hundred detainees wasted away in nightmare conditions, or hobbled in pain from blood-curdling tortures.

Miles simply would not buy the standard story. To him Dai Li was not a man to inspire fear. He seemed utterly devoted to his mother, though not much was ever said about his wife. As regards women Miles supposed Dai Li to be as puritan as himself, for when a Chinese doctor suggested that the American boys in Happy Valley solaced themselves with local mistresses, the vehemence of Dai Li's opposition had been equal to his own. The truth of the matter was that the general was a sensualist of the immemorial Chinese kind, though his love affairs had usually been sequential rather than simultaneous. All this time he had been having an affair with the film actress Butterfly Wu, whose possession of an English name was the mark of a true star. The lady was married, but since Dai Li had given her husband a job affording ample opportunity for profiteering in Kunming, from the time of the fall of Hong Kong he had Butterfly all to himself.

Though Mary Miles got closer to the life and attitudes of the Chinese in a way that other Americans seldom could, it was never altogether clear to him which were the Chinese enemies he was fighting — the renegade soldiers who were employed as Japanese puppets but whose crypto-loyalties were to Chongqing, or the Communist soldiers who were supposed to be allies but whose sentiments were decidedly anti-Guomindang. When, towards the end of the war, Dai Li had his mind on the closer problem of clashes with the Red Army, Miles' troops found themselves killing Reds when they were supposed to be killing puppets. Understandably embarrassed by this, the U.S. Army Staff kept nagging Miles to stay clear of the 'fratricidal and internecine warfare' between the Nationalists and the Communists, and concentrate on the enemy. But Miles never grasped what Dai Li was up to (which was using SACO's American resources to fight the Reds instead of the Japanese), and thought that if their boys did kill a few Communists by mistake, why, it was because, as Dai Li no doubt assured him, they were somehow in league with the collaborators, for were they not always moving in wherever the Japanese troops were moving out?

The true treachery of it all escaped the American, sprung from a nation that goes round the world wanting things both ways — wanting both to vanquish its enemies and wanting to do no harm, wanting to pick the cause it champions and at the same time wanting that cause to be right. The wartime relationships between the Guomindang, the Japanese-sponsored regimes and the Communists were complex and cloudy beyond his imagination, and as it happened if anyone was in league with the collaborators, it was General Dai Li himself. Since early 1942 he had been in regular secret radio contact with Zhou Fohai in Shanghai. But whether this was because Zhou had decided to betray his Japanese sponsors, or because by seeming to be in touch with the enemy Dai was trying to play on American nerves about Chinese resistance staying the cause, or because the two men had more interests in common in their aversion to Communism than they were in opposition as regards the war, no one would really know for sure.

MORE THAN EVER NOW, when Japanese victory seemed no longer certain, Zhou Fohai cherished his links with Dai Li. The success of the several schemes by which he and Wang Jingwei had hoped to turn their regime into an independent entity provided only transient satisfaction. He and Wang had been pleased when their Central Reserve Bank opened its doors on the Bund in January 1941, and began issuing the Nanjing regime's own currency, the notes bearing the portrait of Dr Sun Yatsen on one side, and a picture of his mausoleum on the other. And being able, under the terms of a Japanese accord with Vichy France, to install their own judges in the Chinese courts located in the French Concession, had been a case for self-congratulation. But none of it convinced anybody, least of all the cynical Shanghainese, that the Nanjing regime was anything but hollow.

Pearl Harbor was a real shock, and there was something pathetic about the regime's declaration of war on the United States and Britain in January 1943 — 'It is our aim to liberate China from Anglo-Saxon tyranny, to build it anew and to fight for the liberty of the whole of East Asia.' — but Japanese pressure to bring this about had been irresistible. In exchange for it Japan did agree to the regime's repossession of the International Settlement, but though this was indeed a historical moment — foreign Shanghai becoming Chinese at last — there was no sense of a fresh start about it. Besides, President Roosevelt had been several steps ahead of the Japanese, having announced the abrogation of foreign privileges in China the year before.

In the Shanghai taken over by Wang Jingwei's government in the summer of 1943, there was a silence on certain evenings which had not been known in the city before. Men about to be interned walked with armbands announcing which of the Allied nationalities they were — A for America, B for Britain, H for Holland and so on.

The first camp to spring up was in the old British American Tobacco Company warehouses on the other side of the river in Pudong, but the best demonstration of Japanese torture was furnished by the infamous Bridge House on North Sichuan Road — water treatment and bamboo slivers forced under fingernails, and lighted cigarettes crushed out on naked chests. Here and there these tortures were countered by flickers of humanity and fellow feeling among the internees, as when, to give the women prisoners a measure of privacy, a ring of men would form, face outwards, around the one commode in the cell whenever any of them needed to use it.

Hitler's representatives went about the streets in fast cars and Germans nightly dined at Herr Riemer's Maskee Bar, breaking into song when drunk, particularly the *Horst Wessel Lied* so dear to Nazi hearts. At Joe Farren's Paramount Ballroom it was hard to imagine the elegant patrons of earlier times, drinking Scotch and vodka and feasting on the sight of flaxen-haired Russian dancers — Paramount Peaches they were called — doing their leggy act in sequins and net tights. Joe Farren himself was in Bridge House being given the water treatment or worse. If he ever did come out of that torture chamber alive, it was only to die in the car that came to pick him up.

A car was as much as could be hoped for at a time when charcoal gas in what looked like outsized samovars was used instead of petrol, which if available at all could only be bought at exorbitant prices from hoarders on the black market. You ate at the Parola because you had no servants by this time, and you ate by candlelight because that was at least less gloomy than the five-or ten-watt bulbs you were restricted to by the electricity supply.

Like Joe Farren, Parola's proprietors were Austrian Jews, hardworking and charming and about to be herded with fourteen thousand other Jews to the ghetto the Japanese set up under German instigation in the purlieus of Hongkou.

They knew it was coming. Three days before the ghetto was proclaimed the publication of a speech in a Shanghai daily as good as warned them. Jews were Bolsheviks, it said; lacking a homeland and abhorring nationalism in others, they never gave their allegiance to the countries that had offered them haven; in China and Japan they had made fortunes at the expense of their hosts. It was no wonder that Germany got rid of them, Wang Jingwei said.

Wang Jingwei had moved, in the year since Pearl Harbor, from humiliation to abjectness, and the thought that he could never be delivered from this was with him almost every day. America's entry in the war was a confounding of all he had done for peace. As is the way with people in the clutch of despair, he settled for living just for today. To his son he said, 'If China is saved, if she survives, then my life and honour will be lost, and you, and all our family, will be ruined. You must find the courage to face this.'

To his shame and forebodings was also added anger, the strains erupting in outbursts of violent rage. There was the time he lost his temper completely over some Chinese troops the Japanese had captured in a battle with Chongqing forces. When his subordinates, to whom the Japanese had turned over these troops, suggested that they be put into a prisoner-of-war camp, Wang Jingwei had refused to allow it. 'It's preposterous, unthinkable,' he expostulated, tears of impotent rage streaming from his eyes. 'It's all very well for the Japanese to imprison them. But these are men who have risked their lives for our country; it was for China that they fought. What in heaven's name are we up to, treating them like prisoners of war?'

In such growing disquiet did the days pass. There was a breath of impending disaster at Yu Yuan Road now, a touchiness and disaffection. The mood abetted petty squabbling and rivalry like no other. Since, in China, all it takes for two cliques to form is for three Chinese to be gathered together, schism further doomed the puppet regime to sterility. Tribal emotions, however much they may be adulterated, revert in such times to their original purity. The Cantonese clustered about Madame Wang, the Hunanese about Zhou Fohai. Zhou, the born schismatic, the realist whose eye had never lost sight of the value of factionalism in improving his political fortunes, surrounded himself with favourites and tirelessly jiggled the balance of power in his own favour, while surreptitiously keeping in daily touch with Dai Li.

And around the bickering and the double-cross, there was all the immorality and greed inevitable in the long tedium and stress of alien occupation and drawn-out war. Life's dullness was countered by a seemingly endless cycle of drinking, whoring, and grabbing. Only Wang Jingwei's private life was above scandal. For the rest there were the mahjong parties, the graft, the love affairs, the moments of intoxicated guilt and regret maudlinly passed, and all the fobbing off of reality by shuffling words about.

One day Zhou read in a newspaper controlled by Li Shiqun's faction an editorial attacking the corruption of the government officials, Zhou included. Li had just been passed over in an appointment to a coveted job in the lucrative government concern responsible for channelling Shanghai customs' revenue into the treasury, and had every reason to be disgruntled. But it was not a case for hostility, Zhou thought. Yet when he telephoned Li for an explanation Li denied responsibility for the article and accused Hu Lancheng of writing it. When he heard this, Hu thought, the man's asking for it, remembering the as yet unavenged murder of his friend Big Wu.

There followed some weeks of lobbying and private conversations between Hu and a contender with Li for the control of the espionage work, and between that contender and the *kempeitai*. The shifting loyalties were a perfect fluid from which to culture Li Shiqun's downfall. Two weeks into September the newspapers reported his death.

What had happened is this. Two nights before, a major in the Japanese military police invited Li to dinner. An invitation of this kind was not unusual considering that No. 76 frequently fraternized with the *kempeitai*. The meal ended with a beef dish the major specially recommended as having been prepared personally by his wife. The evening went by. Back at his home Li Shiqun was suddenly sweaty and feeling faint. A Japanese military doctor was called, and diagnosed food poisoning. Mrs Li went through a dozen towels wiping him down. I'm done for, Li said, and asked for a gun to finish himself off. Mrs Li summoned another doctor, but the dehydration would not stop. It was a slow acting poison, and took all of a night and a day to work. It was peculiarly Japanese, but the murder was widely rumoured to have been planned, if not actually perpetrated, by Hu Lancheng and Zhou Fohai.

The infighting remained, and for a time it looked as though the next casualty might be Hu Lancheng. He was going round saying that Japan and the Nanjing regime were as good as defeated already, and was said to be looking to an alliance with some civilian Japanese from another camp. Wang Jingwei, no longer trusting him, put him under detention, and there Hu might have remained had his Japanese friends not interceded and rescued him. He emerged from his incarceration unscathed, but also without a job. From now on he would be on his own, as a sort of freelance collaborator.

Wang himself was far from well. To the old diabetes and the bullet lodged in his back since 1935, there was now added an as yet undiagnosed lesion in the bone. Nevertheless, he went to Tokyo to attend a conference of the collaborating heads of State in Asia. Now, when it did not greatly matter, the heads had been brought together to glorify the Far Eastern Co-Prosperity Sphere. In the assembly Wang drew admiring attention. He listened while Subas Chandra Bose of India said, 'I do not think it an accident that this assembly has been convened in the land of the Rising Sun,' and 'This is not the first time that the world has turned to the East for light and guidance.' Wang smiled and bowed to Ba Maw of Burma, and exchanged polite words with Sukarno of Indonesia and Jose Laurel of the Philippines.

There was some comfort in collective treason, yet Wang Jingwei could not suppress the intermittent qualms, coming now like a sudden jostling from behind, about the future long with defeat ahead. His glimpses of what awaited him filled him, more keenly each time, with a sense of his own mortality, and the insight came to him that perhaps he wanted to die.

The conference couldn't have gone better, or more spectacularly. Leaving for Nanjing Wang Jingwei relived, in an instant, the welcome he had received as a head of state. Four months later he was to come to Japan again, only this time he would be heading for Nagoya, and coming to the end of his life.

WANG JINGWEI HEARD, from behind his door, the doctors' voices murmur and, muffled by the wall which separated him from it and by its heavy charge of emotion, the sound of his wife's anxious enquiries. The one word 'incurable', emphasized by despair, stood out. Then footsteps trailed off down the corridor, and heavy silence resumed.

Wang Jingwei knew he was dying. Bone tuberculosis, the august Japanese doctors had said, the ravages compounded by the old bullet wound. His joints were swelling, his body was aching. His back propped up, he stared at the walls enclosing his room in Nagoya University Hospital. But they had melted into a grey blur and as he brought his fingers to his eyes, where tears had left a dampness, he felt that life had failed him again.

A door opened and closed, admitting his wife. Standing by his bed she lowered her head over him so that her features were lit by the bedside lamp. They were features of such angularity that he still felt what he had first felt before her, in Penang: an admiration having a large part of its basis in alarm. He had always looked up to this fierceness in her, her capacity to compel servility. He remembered how she could out-fight, out-hector, out-scold the whole troupe of that roadshow — the ministers, advisers, generals, diplomats — in which it had been his fate to be a performer. Seeing her, an onlooker might put him in the company of a man who marries a termagant, a fanatic of a political course — a class to which many practical benefits accrue perhaps, but not one likely to entail much solace. Yet the onlooker would only be half right, for though Madame Wang was undeniably ferocious in battle, no woman was more docile in love. Behind his back people said that Wang Jingwei feared his wife, for did he not, strangely for a man with his looks and position, forswear sexual relations with other women? Yet was it in truth quite as simple as that; was he only that perennial figure of fun in Chinese joke books — the henpecked husband?

No, he would say, had he been challenged. How could they know, Wang's thoughts now lapsed into nostalgia, about those dreams we had, amidst the hibiscus and frangipani in Penang, or even in those early days in France, when everything lay before us still? Was it your ambition or my dream that made me take on the mantle of Sun Yatsen, you braced for glory as for martyrdom, knowing all the dangers, ready to stick by me through thick and thin? Who would have thought that the years would bring us to this pass, to the irremediable loss of face, the withering of dreams, to this white and absurdly short Japanese bed in Nagoya?

Wang Jingwei knew China would revile him after his death, and desperately for a moment, as he lay in pain in his bed, sixty-one years old and approaching his end, he longed for a chance to explain, to persuade his compatriots of his sincerity. In one half of him there had been some dim wish to do good, believing as Sun Yatsen and many of his generation did that China's best chances lay with Japan. Everything that happened, or did not happen, could be seen as having its roots, however obscured by the ironic turn of events and the passage of time, in the fallibility of that vision and in his growing sense of having been cornered into living on his own close terms with disillusionment. The actions that shape the future hardly ever shape their own intended consequences. One can no more guard against the thwarting of one's youthful urges, of love of country and culture, of service to one's history, than against the canalization of these impulses, once frustrated, into out-and-out self-interest, opportunism and expediency. The course of motives is seen as explicable only at the moment; in retrospect it is muddied, too much a matter of inexhaustibly unfolding ambiguities for simple explanations to be of much use. Of such is the sum of the history of individuals, of nations.

If he came squalidly out of hindsight, Wang thought, Chiang Kaishek surely would emerge no better. All along he had vied with Chiang, not only for the inheritance of the fruits of their early revolutionary endeavour, but in their loyalty to its mainspring, to — was it? — patriotism? The word could have no meaning for either of them now. Tempted by glory, they had both condemned themselves — one to the Japanese course, the other to the American one. For there had been no room in Sun Yatsen's vision of the future China for bondage, neither to the Western imperialists, nor to their replacement, the Japanese. Somewhere along the way both he and Chiang had misplaced their souls in the world they had helped to bring into being.

Thinking thus, Wang Jingwei closed his eyes and braced himself for the plunge into death. Death did him the favour of claiming him at 4.20 p.m., 10 October 1944 — the date, strangely enough, of the annual Double Tenth celebration, when all China united to commemorate the birth of the Chinese Republic. The events then set into motion — the arrival of the chrysanthemum wreath from the Japanese Emperor, the airlift of the corpse back to Nanjing, the viewing of the body, the public funeral — were run into a gaunt and hectic sequence whose most poignant image was the national flag, with its white sun against blue sky and its ground of rampant red, draped across the coffin, and whose climax was the stately procession of the funeral cortege, eight white horses leading, up the foothills of Purple Mountain. The funeral was conducted to echo the grandeur of Sun Yatsen's; such a spectacle had been against Wang Jingwei's wishes, for he had wanted to be buried simply close to the graves of revolutionary heroes in Canton. Mercifully he was not to know that nothing would go right for him even in death. For on 21 January 1946, under secret orders from one of Chiang Kaishek's most trusted generals, the commander of the 74th Army dynamited Wang's tomb with 150 kilograms of TNT, removed the coffin, and drove it to the countryside to be burnt.

Chapter Twelve

BETRAYALS AND HOMECOMINGS 1944–1946

IT WAS WHEN Wang Jingwei was ill that Hu Lancheng married Zhang Ailing. Marriages were for Hu Lancheng a large part of his existence. He had been married before, the first time when he was twenty. The girl had been picked by his parents from a suitable family in a neighbouring village. She did not attract him, this Yufeng, or Jade Phoenix, except in so far as she had the qualities that were attractive about women — gentleness, pliancy, shyness. He saw her only once before she came to him as bride; or rather, he saw the back of her as she flitted past the sitting room of her father's house, where he himself was being scrutinized as a prospective son-in-law. She was in indigo tunic and trousers, he would later recall, and had a basket laden with freshly picked tea leaves on her back. He was there because his mother, having heard that this was the new way, that nowadays people chose their own marriage partners, had thought that he should take a look at the girl.

But in the end Yufeng had had a better look at him than he at her. The courtyard where she sat with her sisters after lunch gave on to the paddy fields behind her uncle's house, and as she looked up from her embroidery, Hu Lancheng (who had been calling on her uncle), had been glimpsed in the distance, directing his uneasy curiosity at her. The girls, aware of the masculine interest, had fled upstairs; but she had peeped at him from a window, had noted his white cotton shirt and dark trousers, and had been well pleased.

Afterwards it was a question of go-betweens, the augur, and the exchange of gifts. From the groom's family to the bride's: a hundred silver coins, each decorated with the character for 'joy' in red, two lengths of satin, two jars of vintage wine, a box with two chickens, two fish, a cut of pork, several pairs of lychees, longans and lotus seeds, several packets of white sugar and the bridegroom's horoscope on a card. And from the bride's family to the groom's: the girl's horoscope, shoes she had made for her parents-in-law, dumplings, lotus seeds and sugar.

Hu Lancheng would have preferred someone better educated, more companionable; still, one could not always have exactly what one liked in the way of wives. On the night of the wedding, when the music had stopped, and the guests had departed, they had found themselves in their room alone, strangers who must somehow make conversation and discover one another. She broke the silence with something about her trousseau, over which there had been some misunderstanding and awkwardness. Then she poured him some more wine, undressed, and fell asleep almost at once. And so, in this manner, on a day in 1925, Hu Lancheng and Yufeng were made man and wife.

He was not unkind, but in the seven years they were married Yufeng saw little of him. First he was away in Hangzhou, earning his living as a Post Office clerk; then he was in Beijing, working and studying at the Yanjing University. Left at home, Yufeng went about a hundred menial tasks, sensitive to her mother-in-law's every need. When Hu Lancheng came home from Beijing in the year of the Northern Expedition, she presented him with a son. She would have done more, if he had asked for it — placidly ready, at the flicking of his hand. Her tenderness, while timid, had a monumental quality about it, as if it could do none other than squander itself on people more ungiving. She lived in fear of his publicly repudiating her, not minding that he had always done so in private.

When she was gravely ill he took more pains with her, feeding her tea and medicine. Up to the end she felt herself to be a burden to his family, that she had not been filial enough to his mother, who should surely have a daughter-in-law to serve her all her life. When it became obvious that her chance of recovering was slight, she said to him: 'You have been good to me. Only, I once heard you say that in all the time we'd been married, you had never been happy. That remark has been weighing on my mind ever since.'

'I must have been angry at the time; I didn't mean it,' he hastened to assure her. She took this without expression. It was an occasion when one said such things.

When the end came, he was miles away, frantically trying to borrow money to cover the expenses of the illness. It was when he was walking dejectedly home, having failed to raise the money, that news of her death came to him. He had three more miles to go when one of his brothers came running up to tell him. He did not grieve for Yufeng at once: it was too soon, and there was the money for the coffin to think of. It happened later, when he was viewing the body. Her face looked so small, like a twelve-year-old's. He made himself cry a bit, as he thought he should, then continued standing beside the board on which she was laid out. But it was not until later, when he leaned down to put his cheek against hers, groped for her hand under the cover, and in a low voice called her name, that pity at last burst from him in a torrent of felt tears.

Zhang Ailing, whom he married over a decade later, couldn't have been more different. From the first it was her brilliant mind that most deeply fascinated him. Leafing through a magazine in an idle moment in Nanjing, he had chanced upon a short story — entitled *Blockade* — she had published there. The piece struck him as being so remarkable that he thought he must meet the author. He made enquiries of another woman author, but to his question, 'Who is this Zhang Ailing?' he received only the cryptic reply: 'A girl.' Then he read another piece by her in the next issue of the periodical and was held anew by her fineness. Some days later he managed to extract her address in Shanghai from the writer to whom he had directed his first enquiry, but was told at the same time that Zhang Ailing received no visitors. Nothing daunted, he made his way to her apartment at the corner of Hart and Bubbling Well Road. He came away without seeing her, but he had slipped a note under her door, and next day she rang up to say she was coming to see him.

She was not in the least like what he had imagined. She was very young, yet he thought: one could not make trifling claims on such a person. She was like a sixteen- or seventeen-year-old schoolgirl, so seriously intent upon her own thoughts that, walking down the street alone, she could not even hear her friends call her. Yet this child's presence filled the room, and emptied his sight of everything but her, though she did not seem beautiful to him then, or even lovable. They talked for five hours; or rather, he talked and she listened: a foretaste, but complete in itself, of the pleasures to come.

Zhang Ailing was younger than Hu Lancheng by fifteen years. Her family pedigree was distinguished: her grandmother was the daughter of the famous Qing dynasty statesman Li Hongzhang. She was born in Shanghai, had moved to Tianjin when she was two, but had come back to Shanghai to live when she was eight. Her childhood, as evoked in her memoir of the period, was a far cry from the happier, airier rural boyhood that Hu Lancheng had had.

In the family home, a house in the foreign style of the early Republican period, family memories clustered thick about the rooms — 'like dozens of photographs superimposed on a single plate,' she recalls. A heavy drowsiness hovered where sunlight struck, and it was in the dark unlit corners, with their aura of ancient graves, that you felt cool and clear-headed. Only in the darkest heart of the house, where shadows shuttered a strange world apart, did Ailing feel altogether wakeful. But where light and shade met, there the glare of the sun, the jangling bell of a distant tram and the draper's sale announcements drumming and swelling all about, were curiously an inducement to sleep.

Ailing had a baby brother and he, from the start, was outrageously favoured by the nursemaids, who indulged and spoilt him in the unshakeable knowledge that boys must come first. Ailing had to bow to the inevitable underprivilege of her sex, not because she was docile herself in any way, but because, as far as her own nursemaid was concerned, that was the way things were: *she* yielded even if Ailing didn't. Ailing resolved early in life to surpass her brother in every way — an ambition easily achieved, as it turned out, her brother being a rather sickly child, and hapless and unaccomplished in a sadly touching way.

Yet despite the early rivalry, Ailing was protective towards him. He was a bit of a wash-out at school, and often came under adult fire. But she could bear to hear no ill of him, and would rush to shield him so vehemently that it was Ailing herself whom the grownups had eventually to console. Her brother did not feel his vulnerability as acutely, however, and once, when his father struck him at table, it was Ailing who felt the sting, who had to smother her sobs with her rice bowl, and who rushed out to cry her eyes out in the bathroom. Her brother forgot the slight in no time at all; and seeing him happily playing ball on the balcony through the bathroom window, Ailing was struck with the thought that after all he was used to such oppression (she herself was only spared by being away at boarding school), and it made her solicitude a hopeless and heartbreaking thing.

Her passion was all for her mother, a lady of great cultivation. Probably because her marriage was such an unhappy one, she was abroad in Europe for long periods during Ailing's childhood. Her husband's concubine moved in after she left, and Ailing in her memoirs recalls the house as being very gay for a time, with parties and courtesans — budding girls of fifteen and sixteen — summoned from the singsong houses to wait upon the guests.

Of the places Ailing had lived in, one in particular is remembered with rapture: the house of foreign design her mother moved into after her return to Shanghai. It was a place of flowers, dogs, books of fairy tales, cultivated friends and urbane relatives. Her mother and aunt would seat themselves at the piano, and dash into a take-off of a love scene in a current movie, sending all those present into fits of laughter, and Ailing, on the floor, rolling about in glee. Her parents were eventually divorced, and afterwards her mother left again for France. Then the only luminary in Ailing's gloomy life was her aunt, her father's sister, who had always been a close friend of her mother's, and an ally. All about her aunt's home Ailing could feel the presence of her mother, and it became a repository of all that she thought was best in life.

Life with father was cheerless and occasionally nasty. He was a man of virulent temper. As a husband he had been unfaithful, irascible, mean and selfish, even going so far as to withhold housekeeping money from his wife in order to make her fall back on her own savings, in the hope that she would exhaust them and be prevented from leaving him. As a father he was tyrannical, even by Chinese standards. Also Ailing was contemptuous of his opium addiction. He very nearly died once of an overdose of morphine injection. Ailing remembers him being very ill, sitting alone on the verandah, a wet towel on his head, staring blankly in front of him, while the rain descended in white solid streaks past the eaves, drowning his unintelligible murmurings. Her father's home became repellent to her, and she lived from day to day in languid apathy. She knew her father to be lonely; it was in his moments of loneliness that he seemed to warm to her, but 'in his room it was eternally afternoon,' and she always felt that if she didn't disengage herself soon enough, she would drown and suffocate. Yet now and then her spirits would lift at the opium fumes, the hazy sunlight, the tabloids scattered all about the house, and the gossipy chats with her father in some of his more companionable moments.

Her father remarried, a woman who exemplified all that was distasteful in the stepmother of popular imagination. Like him she was an opium addict. Being away at boarding school spared Ailing much unpleasantness, but it pained her, on the occasions she was home, to see her brother and her old nanny tormented so.

The year Ailing finished secondary school, her mother came back to Shanghai, and though she was unaware of it, this caused a change in her mood and manner. Her father noticed it, and found it intolerable: that after all these years of living with him, she should still have more affection for her mother than for him. When hesitantly she broached the subject of her going abroad to study, he snapped at her, saying someone — meaning her mother — had planted those thoughts in her mind. Her stepmother was more forthright: 'Your mother can't seem to stay clear of this family, can she, even though she's divorced. Why doesn't she come back, if she can't let go? Only she's left it just a bit too late; because if she does come back, she'll have to do so as a concubine.'

Their resentment was to well up and erupt one day in savage rage. It was when Ailing returned from a fortnight's stay with her mother. The war had begun in Shanghai, and as their house was near the Suzhou Creek the bombs had been keeping her awake at night. She had gone to her mother's just for a respite from insomnia. But when she came back, all her father's fury was unleashed, whipped up to a bizarre pitch by his own dark hatred and by the no less controllable rancour of his wife. Unremittingly the blows fell, the father kicking and slapping, the daughter reeling and flailing, and on the floor, in gathering pain, her mind so dissociated from the body that she could tell herself, as her mother had always done, that whatever she did she must never hit him back. Otherwise it might have been worse; even so, when he was finally coaxed away, Ailing staggered upstairs to the bathroom to find her body covered in bruises.

Her aunt came to the house the next day to plead for her, but the father vented his anger on her too, and hit her so hard she had to be patched up in hospital. But nobody reported the matter to the police, for fear of the taint on family honour. Ailing was locked up in her room, her attempt at escape foiled by a policeman at the door, who told her that the outer gates were locked, and that her father held the keys. The following were nightmare days, days in which she aged several years in a few weeks. Helpless, she heard the constant droning of the planes overhead and prayed for bombs to fall and life to end, for herself as for everyone else. Outside in the garden the magnolia tree bloomed, the flowers huge; like dirty white handkerchiefs, she thought, or wastepaper. Inside, anguish transformed itself into illness; she came down with severe dysentery, which laid her up for six months and brought her to the brink of death, her father adamantly refusing her treatment.

Autumn became winter. Recovered, she bided her time, until, her binoculars having told her that nobody was about in the street outside, she slipped out of her room and into the night, timing her exit to coincide with the changing of the police patrols at the gates. She fled to her mother's apartment, and some time later her old nanny smuggled sentimental knick-knacks and old toys to her.

Under straitened circumstances Ailing began to study for her entrance exams to London University, at no point certain that she was worth the sacrifices her mother was obviously and heartrendingly making for her. She passed her exams, but the war prevented her from taking up her place, and she went instead to Hong Kong University, where she remained for three years. Pearl Harbor interrupted her studies, and she came back to Shanghai before completing her degree. It was then that she started to publish her short stories and to make a name for herself; then, too, that Hu Lancheng came into her life, a tragedy no smaller in scale, if such things could ever be measured, than her childhood had been.

AFTER that first encounter Zhang Ailing and Hu Lancheng saw each other nearly every other day. Then he had to return to Nanjing, but about once a month he would come back to Shanghai and would go straight to her. That he was a man with wife and family, and many amours besides, hardly weighed with her at all; nor the frequent partings, which instead deepened the pleasure of their meetings, like the lantern festivals, which make the workaday seem new. Once she wrote to him in Nanjing: 'I've thought about it; if you just came and visited me now and again, that would be all right too.' Beyond that point she did not look. Earlier on she had been tempted, after their third or fourth meeting, to leave everything unhappened, sending him a message to say not to see her any more. But they went on seeing each other, and though they hardly talked about it before it actually happened, he married her, when he was free to do so, in 1944. He was thirty-eight and she a mere twenty-three. To give her a certain amount of immunity from the potential hazards of his politics, they held no ceremony, but simply wrote out their own marriage testimonial, he composing the one part, and she the other:

> Hu Lancheng and Zhang Ailing pledge for all their days to be man and wife,
> Wishful of good years ahead and peace and stability in this life.

But it neither changed the course of their life together nor made her any the less her own woman: as before he was more shaped by her than she by him. He was borne on discovery, acquiring perceptions that had so far eluded his experience. She was generous with her knowledge, and spoke to him with astonishing grasp of Chinese and European literatures. They talked, inevitably, of classical poetry, and he was amazed at the way she could, at one stroke, knock askew all his preconceptions and judgements. He, who thought himself well-read and uncompetitive, found himself pitted against her, groping always to strike the right note in her exacting ear, and yet repeatedly failing — 'stringed and woodwind strains emerging as clangour.'

He was dazzled by the beauty of her words and expressions, and quotations she made from known books and classics sounded new-minted, unnoticed before. He was pleased simply to be in her presence. Possibly he was also attracted by the improbable conquest of her person. He noticed in her a curious detachment from others' opinions and predicaments, and this lack of sympathy, in a person so obviously sensitive, intrigued him. The earth might be uninhabited, for all the reference her behaviour bore to people. He could not help thinking: how rational she is, as though purity of feeling is a matter of thinking things until she has thought the personalness out of them and the need for any sentimental response.

Their mutual delight held through the summer; enough of it was left to roll him along through the autumn when, at the bidding of his Japanese masters, Hu Lancheng left for Wuhan. He was to take over the running of a Japanese-backed newspaper there, the *Dachu Bao*, and in due course set up a school for political and military studies. The moves were factors in Japanese calculations that fitted serviceably with his own. Hu Lancheng's part in these grim twilight days of the war was apparently to make Wuhan, so strategically sited in the heart of occupied China, a secret centre of turmoil and Japanese resistance that could trip up the Nationalist Chinese army's recovery of the areas to its south and east. He was glad of the chance to exercise his talents once more for plot-hatching; among collaborators he was finding himself buffeted by eddies of conflicting opinions and factions, with most of which he was out of sympathy. Ever the maverick in politics, in his very first editorial in the *Dachu Bao*, he wrote witheringly of Japan's swagger, by now more hollow than ever.

Wuhan was really three cities in one: Hankou at the confluence of the Han River and the Yangtze; Hanyang across on the other side of the Han; and Wuchang opposite, along the Yangtze bank. Hu Lancheng and his three fellow newspapermen were put up in two rooms in the county hospital in Hanyang, from where they set out for their office every morning, crossing the Han River to get there and back. Staying at the hospital, they soon ran into the nurses who worked there. One of them, a slender, robust girl of seventeen, was to become the next woman in Hu Lancheng's life.

He noticed her one evening when a group of them were standing by the river, the hospital just behind them, watching the air raids on Wuchang. Somewhere in the distance, from under the stars, a bomber shot out and sliced across the air towards the edge of the water. Wuchang was ablaze, and as they all stared upward into the sky, the lights of Hankou and Hanyang below went out.

'I think it's picturesque,' said she.

'How callous of you,' said one of the other nurses.

'There's no one quite as wicked as our Little Zhou,' added the head nurse, teasing.

Little Zhou took no notice. Her next utterance, however, suggested that she had noticed him in the dark beside her, for she acknowledged him, in the polite, half-serious way one did: 'Director Hu.'

He asked her what her name was.

'I'm called Zhou Xunde,' she said.

'And I Hu Lancheng,' he immediately returned, only half a second before a peal of explosions rent the air above Wuchang.

Thus began, for Xunde, her first experience of Hu Lancheng's inveterate susceptibility to women. She herself was almost innocently open to it, as though it were all predetermined, giving her body to him with the courtesies due to a superior. Asked, later, what had made her take up with him, she said that there was no particular reason. But when he pressed her, she searched her thoughts to give him an honest reply. 'It's because,' she said, 'we saw each other every day.'

They were, indeed, much thrown together by the swirl of history around them. The world outside their own was being blown up by war, and every night there seemed to fade the age in which men could place their hearts' affairs first, could cherish expectations that anything would last. In a heavily blitzed city, the rift in the workaday quiet of life was endlessly widened, if not by a hurtling bomb then by its aftermath: ruins, dead bodies, piles of rubble and masonry, streets plastered with mud, clothes reeking perpetually of smoke however much you washed them.

Yet out of necessity and accustomed numbness the fear and tension resolved themselves into practical concerns: for Hu the long hours put in at the *Dachu Bao*; for Xunde the hospital, the babies to be delivered, the cooking and washing, the copying to be done of his writings. (For this last service he put her on the newspaper's payroll, a move which utterly compromised her and made her arrest for collaboration after the war ended that much more inevitable). Amidst the bristling nerves and the weary routines the sense, too, that life must have its diversions prevailed still. They went on walks and excursions, like the one on that fine late February day, when with the other nurses they paid a visit to Guiyuan Si, the Buddhist monastery famous for its hall of 500 *arhats* in northwest Hanyang. They arrived to find the place swarming with other sightseers, bent alike on enjoying themselves. Inside the hall the air was sweet with sandalwood incense and the smell of age. On their way home they stopped at a restaurant for lunch. Already the flagstones of Hanyang were captured by the afternoon sun. They ordered the carp for which the Han and the Yangtze are famous, and it came, gently braised in soya sauce and exquisitely fresh. Xunde, in a plain blue mandarin-collared sheath, was flushed with the walk and the afternoon sun, and he thought, how much I like this, without reflection or any accounting for taste, as someone might marvel at the deep pleasure that perfectly ordinary things could give.

It was all in the course of events. He did not feel guilty, in so far as Zhang Ailing was concerned, of any breach of good faith. If someone had reminded him that he could have kept himself aloof, that the affair need never have developed, it would have been meaningless to him. As for Xunde, young country girl that she was, she thought herself the beneficiary of something akin to privilege; so much did this seem part of the condition of being woman that, though for herself she assumed the faithfulness and circumspection of a bespoken woman, at no time did she think him all hers — that is to say, not Ailing's. One day he had said to her, 'Some day you'll marry me.'

'Oh no,' she had replied.

'Why not?'

'You are twenty-two years older than I.' And then, quite without pathos: 'Because my mother was a concubine, and the daughter mustn't be one too.'

The mother, when told of this man by the daughter, had said, 'His favour puts you in debt to him; you must repay his kindness.' There had appeared to be no question of his obligations to her.

In March Hu Lancheng flew back to Shanghai for a month and a half, staying with Ailing. He told her about Xunde, but only in a muffled sort of way. When he returned to Wuhan it was already less than four months to Hiroshima and the Japanese surrender it compelled. The city could cope less and less with the sirens and air attacks and machine-gun fire, and after the usual bout of unsettled weather in May a third of the population went down with fever, Hu Lancheng included. It was only the start of what promised to be a dazed and terrifying summer. At the height of his illness Hu was barely conscious, and even when the temperature subsided he was too tired to gulp down his terror and too overcome with lassitude for sustained work.

Then came August 14; and the Emperor Hirohito, unshaved, tearful, telling the assembled ministers of his cabinet in Japan: 'I realize how difficult it will be for the officers and men of the army and navy to surrender their arms to the enemy and see the homeland occupied. It is difficult for me to issue the order.... In spite of these feelings I cannot endure the thought of letting my people suffer any longer. It does not matter what happens to me personally. I shall endure the unendurable, and so must you.'

Flight was imperative if Hu Lancheng was to escape the fate that awaited all those who had collaborated with the Japanese. By dint of string-pulling by consular Japanese friends he was able to leave Hanyang, when all means of transport were immobilized, with a boatload of wounded Japanese soldiers, disguised as one himself. He took leave of a tearful Xunde, their world already a thing of the past — not so much shattered, as simply abandoned.

He arrived in Nanjing in intense summer heat, took the train to Shanghai and, still in disguise, found his way to Hongkou. To the high-up Japanese in Nanjing he made a plea for last-ditch projects, but they were stillborn, and indifference prevailed. The ensuing days held another disappointment for him: though his Japanese friends did what they could to get him to Japan, their efforts were unavailing. He was alone, and it dawned on him that to hold off capture by the returning Nationalist government he would have to go into hiding at once.

But where? Dangers were everywhere, the gears of Guomindang extermination campaigns — anti-communist, anti-collaborationist, it was all the same — re-engaged, the likes of Dai Li regrasping the levers. Then, as a fugitive looking for sanctuary, he thought of the mellow and watery landscape of his boyhood home. After spending only one night at Ailing's, he crossed the familiar waters of the Qiantang estuary to Shanghai's south and, slumping thankfully onto a bus bound for Shaoxing, the sight of his fellow passengers, hawkers, carpenters, village women, soothing in its simple reality, he found himself back, once more, amidst the rivers and valleys of his native Zhejiang Province. These would remain for a long time the scenes of his fugitive existence, as they had been the scenes of his youthful experience.

Now in his mind's eye he saw them again: the Hu village (for he shared his surname with all the families that lived there) where the girls coloured their fingernails with the blossoms of the angelica, and the hibiscus flowered under the wattle fence; where swallows came nesting under the eaves every spring, and the first buds of mulberry bushes were a tender yellow in the sun. He knew all about rearing silkworms then, and picking tea leaves and digging up sweet potatoes, and edging close to the streams to pluck river snails from their banks. He remembered his mother and her care: how, after each downpour, she would hang up the mulberry leaves on clothes lines inside the house to dry, swabbing them one by one with a towel, and even fanning them. And when, halfway through the night, she found that the silkworm grubs had already crunched their way through the last pile of leaves, she would wake him up from his sleep and send him out into the dark, to pick and load up with more. Then when the snowy white cocoons were formed at last, to the village would come city buyers with gold rings and bars of aromatic soap, milky white face flannels and things enthrallingly foreign; and the younger of these visitors would try flirting with the Hu village girls, as ignoring them and not ignoring them they went about washing their clothes and vegetables by the stream.

And as the year unfolded, fluidly in the passing of the seasons, fitfully in the effervescence of feast days, so immemorial life moved forward in the village. Brought by this yet undigested turn of events to the brink of certain captivity and probable death, Hu Lancheng took comfort in it now. He thought back to the festivals: the Pure Brightness Festival when ancestral graves were visited and rape turnip dumplings were made; the Dragon Boat Festival when the calamus was stuck on doors and newly married women came home for longed-for reunions with their parents; the Lunar New Year when every child's pockets bulged with melon seeds, peanuts, roasted beans and sweet potato slices, and the ancestral altar in every home creaked under the weight of red candles and tiers of sacrificial foods. Then came summer nights lived through by the stone bridge, where against the wooden parapet and in the full shine of the moon, local men fanned themselves into sleep as the dew seeped through, and dawn was always marked by the strains of a distant bamboo flute. Then came the autumn and the harvest, and when the reaping was done and the days had turned cool, hand in hand with the thanking of the gods the village stage would be put up for the arrival of the Shaoxing opera troupes, which annually performed with drum and gong in the tenth month, when the tallow tree was redder even than the maple.

It was all up with him now. At a distance of some thirty to forty miles from remembered soil, he wondered if the place would be hospitable to him again. Already it was the end of September and the weather was perfect. He would seek out the family of an old school friend and see if they could shelter him for a while. Passing a temple on the way, he read the graffiti on the walls: 'Eliminate Japanese Collaborators' and 'Exterminate Communist Bandits' in new red paint; and legible still, though time-faded, the words, 'The War of Resistance *Will* Triumph.'

He found the Si family home; the father had died, but the widowed mother, and the equally widowed young concubine took him in. Then followed nightmare days, in which the bark of a dog at night was an invitation to fear; all around him, in Shanghai, in Hangzhou, in Shaoxing, he could feel the hunt for collaborators hotting up. He knew he could only hold off capture by being constantly on the move, but all he could do was to surrender himself to his host, as he himself had run out of places to hide. His plight condemned him to months of wandering, staying for a brief period here, lying low for a short spell there. Always he had to prevail upon the sympathy of the Si family's friends and relatives.

The kindest of all was Fan Xiumei, the widowed concubine. When all possibilities of shelter were exhausted, she offered to take him to Wenzhou, way down south by the sea, where her seventy-year-old mother, not seen for over twenty years, lived in indigent obscurity.

They set off before daybreak on December 6, and as they reckoned the journey would take three days, hired two rickshaws to take them. First light stole across the country just as the city gates fell behind them. The wind, merging with the heavy frost on the ground, was cutting. Hu had a rug in his lap to keep him warm and Xiumei a pan of hot coals by her feet. They stopped only for the rickshaw pullers to change their straw sandals, as the ones they started off in had worn to a frazzle by the time they had travelled two miles, and for food and hot stewed tea. Hu noticed that Xiumei's hand warmer had scorched her dress and there was a large brown patch in the purple silk. But she didn't seem to mind and made light of it, out of consideration for him.

Jolting they went, crests to one side, brooks to the other. From the fields the sounds they heard were mainly of water. Now and then they would walk a little, ahead of the rickshaws, to stretch their legs. It was during these moments that Xiumei told him, because he asked, about herself. It hadn't been easy for her, it seemed, though Mrs Si, the first wife, had been irreproachably kind, not pouring on her the scorn normally due to a concubine. Still, it couldn't be helped if sometimes the maidservants and the children disparaged her, if there were hard words and withering looks. Now in a way she had broken through into their regard, into their respect even. During the war when the family was hard up she had put up the capital from her own savings to start a business, a travelling trade between their home town and one further up the river. She was quite without misgiving, and even when the business flopped after only a few trips and all her savings were dissipated, she still didn't think that there was anything to begrudge.

As for romance, there had been a man in the silkworm farm where she worked before the war. They had cared deeply for each other, and when the war drove them back to their separate homes, had remained in touch by letter. Three years into the war they had met again when he happened to be in the area and had called on her at the Si home. With her own savings she had bought him some wine and had killed a chicken for his lunch. They could have got married when his wife died but somehow they never did. She did not look upon this as a possibility squandered, so much did parting and separation and loss seem to her a part of the condition of life. For in China the woman is the survivor, who performs generation after generation the immemorially assigned role of continuing to exist, to be pliant or steely to order, to accept her lot.

At her disclosures Hu thought: only the Chinese are capable of such detachment in attachments. If it had been the Europeans, such affairs of the heart would take on an entirely different light: they would either make heavy weather of them, or dismiss them as not worth the fuss; invest them with either too much intensity, or too little. It is only in China, he thought, that love arranges itself so neatly into the scheme of things. Is this the Golden Mean of Confucius — joy, anger, sorrow, delight all aroused and expressed in their proper degree, from a sense of the harmony of the whole, of composure? The Japanese wouldn't be able to keep Zen out of it, to respond to garden, wood, rock, the beauty of men or women without some degree of sublimation. But people like Xiumei don't lapse into Zen, or Buddhist release. They test their feelings against their sense of proportion, shape them according to the good tried forms of expected behaviour. By their lights, Xiumei's and her suitor's, they have both behaved with utter correctness, with the Chinese's traditional uninsistence, and with blame attached to neither side.

And so talking, Hu and Xiumei grew confessional; and confessional, he grew bold. By the time they were on the boat to Wenzhou they had become lovers — or, as Hu Lancheng put it, husband and wife (feudal at heart, he took it for granted that a man could have more than one wife). Partly it was the circumstances that had brought them together, and partly it was his not wholly disinterested intention to use her; but mostly it was his inclination to alight on the nearest perch. He did not tell Zhang Ailing, whose remittances from Shanghai would see him through his first three years on the run, and nor did she suspect. So it was with some consternation that he greeted her sudden appearance in Wenzhou the following February.

He knew it was the most natural thing in the world for her to come. She was his wife, after all, but he couldn't help feeling a perverse disappointment that his idea of Ailing as someone who did things for reasons unlike anybody else's should turn out to be false. Ailing met Xiumei, and even without being told, had a definite, piercing sense that she and Hu Lancheng were lovers. She thought Xiumei quite beautiful, more like a Central Asian than a Chinese, and sat down one afternoon to sketch her. But the features as they came out seemed to her more and more like Hu Lancheng's and she could not bear to finish the drawing. Her misery came as a surprise to him: he had thought her someone who was untouchable in her core, who, in the last reaches of her unhappiness, was above being wronged.

It was not long afterwards that Ailing spoke to him of his earlier love in Wuhan, Xunde. They were taking a walk down a winding lane and, rounding a bend, Ailing put it to him that he must now make a choice between her, Ailing, and the girl he had left behind in Wuhan. Hu Lancheng demurred, saying that for all he knew he might never see Xunde again. It was unimaginable that he should desert Xunde now that she was in trouble for collaboration. Why should Ailing expect it of him? He could not love singly; and of all people Ailing should be able to resist feeling aggrieved. But for her part Ailing did not believe, as he evidently did, that their relationship was proof against his betrayals of it. She stood her ground, and insisted: 'I do realize, as you say, that the best things in life are not amenable to choice. And yet I would ask you to choose.'

But he still held back; and when she saw this, she saw further, as clearly as if he had told her, that it was irredeemable. She sighed very deeply then, and wondered if her heart would wither. Before three weeks were up she left Wenzhou for Shanghai. It rained the day he put her on the boat. She sailed in sadness, alone, the rain running off the rim of her umbrella as she stood on the deck. And then as the sea journey wore on she was weeping with the emptiness of first grief: they had been married two years, and it was over.

He would see her one more time after that. It was when he was on the run again: soldiers were scouring the country towns for Communists, and rather than risk being ferreted out in the general hunt, he had left Wenzhou, and after lying low for eight months with the Si's, had resurfaced in Shanghai, there to take the boat back to Wenzhou. The night before he sailed he spent with Ailing. They passed it in mutual censure, self-exoneration and wretchedness, the shadows of last winter's memories hovering. He, in a churlish mood, demanded Ailing's interest in an account he had written of Wuhan, but she could not bring herself to give it, crushed by its teeming references to Xunde. In a madness of disappointment he struck her — a gesture which, though not entirely serious, drew from her a cry of such shock that it stung him. That night they slept separately. When he woke the next day, just before daybreak, he slipped into her room, and as he bent over her she reached up her arms to him. Then he saw her face stream with tears, heard her cry his name.

After another seven months he received a letter from her, the very first sentence of which shocked him like a thunderclap. 'I no longer love you;' it read, 'you had long ceased to love me. It has taken me a year and a half of hard thinking to arrive at this. As you were in enough trouble at the time, I hadn't wanted to add to it. Don't come looking for me. If you write, your letters will be unread.'

As before she enclosed money, but it was the last time she did so. To that letter he knew better than to reply; he wrote instead to her closest friend in Shanghai, not really expecting an answer, and getting none.

ON 25 JUNE 1945, Du Yuesheng was returning to Shanghai after an eight-year gap. His mission, a highly confidential one, was entrusted to him by General Dai Li, himself travelling part of the way with

Du, and with a cook, laundryman and Milton Miles in tow. The long and hazardous journey could only be undertaken after much preparation, and already eighteen of Du's men had preceded him into enemy territory. Du Yuesheng was to follow with his retinue, of two bodyguards, a physician, a secretary, and a valet-cum-masseur. They were to go by plane from Chongqing to Guiyang, and from there to an airfield in Hunan Province, where another plane would fly them to Fujian. Their final destination, to be approached by road, was a place called Chun'an, in Zhejiang Province, up the river from Hangzhou Bay. There, from Dai Li's listening post in the Western Temple, Du Yuesheng would direct his operations against the Japanese. The Japs, they all knew, were about to decamp: orders had been received from the Emperor to wind down the war in China. And all along the coast from Shanghai to Hong Kong, Miles, for once clearing his plans with Washington, with General Wedemeyer (who had replaced 'Vinegar Joe' Stilwell as the Commander-in-Chief of the China-Burma-India Theatre), and with Chiang Kaishek, was already launching a series of what he called 'hit-and-run' attacks on the retreating Japanese troops, aimed at keeping them on the defensive and off balance.

The region to which Du and his party were now venturing, though bristling with Japanese troop movements and well beyond the Nationalist government's defence lines, was actually well plumbed by SACO's agents and guerillas. It was Miles' belief that the Japanese were preparing to create a last havoc in Shanghai, to wreck the place before quitting it. It was the sort of wantonness, as the sack of Nanjing had well attested, to which the Japanese were peculiarly prone. Against such an eventuality, only one man could secure Shanghai. Better than anyone in Chongqing, Dai Li knew the power Du Yuesheng wielded in Shanghai. Besides, in the man he had singled out for his purpose he saw someone scarcely less of a strategist than himself, someone, moreover, in whom a hunger for political consequence was tinged with a certain shade of patriotism.

For Du Yuesheng himself, this mission was to provide the slipway from which his reappearance in Shanghai would be launched. Here, too, was a chance to redeem his public image, which had been smudged, to his great chagrin, by the gold scandal of only a few months before. It was all over Chongqing that he had bought 500 taels worth of gold bonds on March 28, the day before the government raised the price of gold from 20,000 to 35,000 Chinese dollars per tael. The bonds were something the government had introduced as a measure against inflation, available for purchase to anyone who had deposited the right amount of money in the bank six months prior to their issue. Du Yuesheng's large purchase, made just before the price of gold was due to go up, savoured scandalously of political promiscuity, suggesting not only that the news had leaked (as indeed it had, causing a rush to the banks the night before), but that it had been disclosed to the privileged glimpses of those able to milk their closeness to the political centre for their maximum personal enrichment. His name, after an investigation into the matter, had been among those found guilty of misdemeanour by the government, and published. If events were to run their course he would be prosecuted. All of a sudden, the ignominy which he had guarded against all his life was about him in a flood.

Dai Li, by proposing this timely mission, had snatched him from the worst of this embarrassment. It was doing them all some good. While it gave Du the opportunity for a *coup de théâtre* that would blot out his disgrace, restore his public poise, and provide a boost to his political fortunes, Miles needed it as evidence that he was fighting the Japanese just as much as the Reds, his efforts on this score having recently given the U.S. Army much cause for suspicion. Miles imagined in the army's criticism, and in the displeasure of General Wedemeyer with the methods of SACO, a characteristically military stuffiness, a distaste (to Miles quite unfounded) for Dai Li and his un-American murderousness. As for General Dai himself, he was merely anxious to discover the lie of the land, for the purpose of coming upon the Japanese, for knowing what the Communists were up to, or just for the pleasure of killing.

And so they were three quite purposeful men that met to board the C-46 for Hunan. Du had to steel himself for the ride, his asthma and the thought of the primitive living ahead more than slightly troubling him. A rattan chair, installed on board specially for him, and held down in position by his two bodyguards throughout the flight, made the journey less uncomfortable than it might have been. Even so, the hours of the flight merged in his memory with the sensation of a dry tautness in the chest, and a dull soreness in the seat.

The plane as it lifted itself from the earth yielded an array of landscapes, seeming now a vista of ribbed surfaces dabbed with sun, now a perspective of rimmed fields, now a green hill and a clot of trees, and then a distant river sinking from sight into the shadows of a valley. This is the land which centuries of poets and disillusioned men have discovered to be the reality behind life's illusions. But Du Yuesheng was unseeing, having, indeed, little taste for the country, far preferring the opportunity and experience of the city. He was not at home in the country; the lack of amenities disconcerted him, and the stamp of the peasant's hopeless toil and unending effort made his spirits sag.

It was not until July 15 that the three, after a dusty overland drive that was as rough as it was long, arrived in Chun'an. Installed in Western Temple, Du set about laying his plans at once. It was, as he saw it, a matter of mobilizing the Eight-Legged Bands, the men employed in the public utilities — the tramway systems, communications, water works and electrical and gas authorities — the stevedores, and the dock workers, not forgetting the coolies and the loafers. These, combined with the units of Dai Li's Loyal Patriotic Army and secret police, the regular forces of the Chinese Army and the pirates of Pudong (whose allegiance he also commanded), would make Shanghai and its environs, if not impregnable, then at least forbidding, to Japanese sabotage. There were plans to go further: to bring a hundred and fifty men over from Shanghai, to be put through a rigorous anti-sabotage training programme, and then insinuated back into key places in the city.

But the training school became an anachronism before it even began, for the dramatic news of the atomic bomb and Japan's unconditional surrender to the Allies reached them on August 14, and dwarfed all other events and obviated the need for the school. Du Yuesheng, grasping the momentum of the situation at once, sent most of his men back to Shanghai that day, with instructions to lay the ground for a takeover by the Nationalist government.

Du followed with his retinue on August 29, travelling by tugboat up the Fuchun River to Hangzhou, there to take the train back to Shanghai. A sense of anti-climax hovered over the journey, and Du felt somewhat like a relief team come too late to a beleaguered city, good for receiving the survivors and evacuating the wounded, but missing the participation in the fighting, the glorious intervention. Still the feeling took little toll of his avidity for card games, which kept up his spirits all through the voyage, or of his appetite for the reeves shad, the exquisite fish for which the Fuchun is deservedly famous. By the time he reached Hangzhou he was looking forward unreservedly to his arrival, a triumphant homecoming to be attended by much publicity. He could already picture the grand spectacle at the Shanghai North Station: the ceremonial arch erected for the occasion beckoning, the obedient crowds cheering, the whole thing stage-managed by his minions to run like the good theatre it was. That night, lavishly entertained to dinner by Ding Mocun, formerly of No. 76 and a turncoat overnight, Du could afford to be generous with his host, tactfully keeping the conversation off the subject of collaboration and war crimes trials.

Shanghai was already euphoric with the victory, and Du Yuesheng counted on his homecoming being greeted in the same mood. But as the Ningbo-Hangzhou-Shanghai Special sped homeward across Zhejiang Province, something happened to change the whole tenor of the occasion. Two men, bearing a message from Shanghai, scrambled on board the train at a stop close to the final approach to the city. When Du Yuesheng heard what they had to say, he decided on an abrupt change of plans. Instead of going all the way to the North Station, he alighted quietly at the West Station, the stop before. From there he made his way back into the French Concession, not to his own house at first, but into the obscurity of his bodyguard's home. Meanwhile the Ningbo-Hangzhou-Shanghai Special pulled into the North Station. In the drizzle the expectant crowds waited. They did not look welcoming, and revealed by the pamphlets they were distributing and the placards they were holding that they were in fact demonstrators. 'Down with Du Yuesheng!' and 'Du Yuesheng Is An Evil Influence,' the placards read. A straggling group of curious passersby peered. A

The Glen Line Building on the Bund,
taken over as U.S. Navy Headquarters in 1945

leaden air hovered over the station. The time passed. But no Du Yuesheng materialized.

Yet it did not matter: the damage had been done, and the man had been denied his hour of triumph. How had it come about? Privately, among Du Yuesheng's followers, there were instant recriminations. To them the identity of the person responsible for the demonstration was never in any doubt: it was the recently appointed Deputy Mayor of Shanghai, a man whose shifting loyalties, before they finally settled upon Communism, had swung the full arc from the Guomindang's extreme left wing to its extreme right wing, taking in a temporary allegiance even to Du Yuesheng himself. The act was a deliberate challenge to Du's power in Shanghai. His men, to whom the idea of anyone defying him with impunity was not only repugnant, but utterly inconceivable, urged him to pick up the gauntlet. Whatever else might happen, Du Yuesheng must never be upstaged.

But Du, his face set in its usual expression of wryness, did nothing. What happened at North Station had the quality of a siren going by in the night. He hazily grasped its deeper meaning. The Shanghai to which he now returned was not the Shanghai of eight years before. Though he was not sure what he had seen he thought he had glimpsed the forces that were ushering in the end; he thought he had glimpsed the inevitable.

But as yet the end, sighted by Du from his higher perspective, was remote to a Shanghai just loosened from the grip of an eight-year war. The visual trappings of liberation took all its eyes. Rear Admiral Miles, arriving on September 4, added not a few of these. Borne on a manic wave of activity by a diet of benzedrine and atabrine, he began to spread across Shanghai the paraphernalia of American might. Up the Huangpu channel minesweepers were sent; onto the Glen Line Building on the Bund American ensigns and the logo of the U.S. Navy were hoisted; at the Cathay and Park Hotels American servicemen were billeted. The British, no longer pre-eminent in Shanghai, were invited to step aside from their traditional mooring berth at No. 1 buoy to allow an American cruiser to take their place. (The No. 2 buoy, traditionally occupied by the American fleet, Miles graciously assigned to the Chinese, who just as graciously yielded it to Admiral T.C. Kinkaid's flagship, the U.S.S. *Rocky Mount*, having no ship of their own to take up the mooring.) Wherever he went Miles presented the American image of abundance, energy and largesse. And Du Yuesheng helped by putting at his disposal a limousine that had belonged to the now absconded collaborationist chief of police. Made originally, it was claimed, for Al Capone, the car had all the familiar fittings of the class, including bulletproof glass and Venetian blinds of quarter-inch-thick steel slats with openings on top for guns. Declining Du's offer to SACO of any, or all, of the de luxe hotels in Shanghai, Miles had moved, Du's gift of champagne and caviar marking the

The arrival of the U.S. fleet in the Huangpu River, 1945, seen from the southern end of the Bund

occasion, into the mansion of the car's original owner. The gold brocade interiors seemed strange after the dust and rural deprivations of the weeks before, the opulence unbelievable.

Everywhere American popularity was monumental. As the conquerors passed before Shanghai — General Wedemeyer and Ambassador Patrick Hurley on September 19, and Admiral Kinkaid and his magnificent white fleet on the same day — crowds cheered, children waved banners, girls presented bouquets. It seemed as if to nearly everyone Americans were *dinghao*, the very best, the source of every luxury from Del Monte canned peaches to penicillin.

Nearly, but not all. There were people in Shanghai to whom they were indistinguishable from the disliked British, those white people who, so they had learnt from Lenin and Mao Zedong and the Japanese, were forestalling the doom of Western capitalism by their imperialism and exploitation. Only a few weeks before, the order had come from Yan'an for the Shanghai Communists to quit the area for a thousand-mile march to Manchuria, there to rally with the Red armies north of the Yellow River for a decisive military offensive against the Guomindang forces in the spring. The Shanghai Communists, for the moment, stood to one side. They were shadowy, but linked to the country's deepest core, the inheritance of exhaustion, deprivation and frustration that had been bequeathed them by their fathers and their forefathers and that they, and the vast elemental forces of revolution, were destined to shatter and redeem.

Chapter Thirteen

JUST AND UNJUST DESERTS 1946–1948

FOUR DAYS AFTER Hiroshima was bombed, two contradictory sets of orders were issued to the allied Communist and Guomindang troops. From Chiang Kaishek the order to the Commander-in-Chief of the Red Army, renamed the Eighth Route Army after the formation of the united front, was: 'Remain in your positions and do not accept the surrender of any unit whatever of the Japanese army;' and that from the general of the Red Army to the Chinese forces in the liberated areas: 'Disarm all Japanese and puppet troops immediately; seize and take over cities and communication lines previously held by the Japanese or their Chinese lackeys.' As far as Chiang was concerned if anyone was going to take over from the army of occupation, he was. The Communists, considering themselves allies, saw no reason why they shouldn't get into the act too.

Until the American airlift of Guomindang troops from southwestern China to the key centres of Japanese-held territory to the north and the east, and until the landing of American marines on the coast, it was not altogether apparent that Shanghai would be taken over by Chiang Kaishek's forces and not by the Red Army. To the north the Communists were powerfully pursuing their own manifest destiny from their guerilla base areas, and rumour had it that they, and not the Guomindang army, would step into the vacuum left by Japan.

In either case there was bound to be contention and disorder, added to which there was the likelihood of the Japanese Army setting the place to the torch before leaving it. Anticipating such an emergency, Zhou Fohai, who since 1942 had been drawing closer and closer to Chongqing, wrote a letter to his former patron Chiang Kaishek. He understood the Generalissimo was planning a counterattack, it said; 'I am in the tiger's den. The groundwork for such an attack is bound to be complex in the extreme: if we delay, we may be caught unprepared; if we make haste, we may reveal our hand. Whatever your orders, they shall be my first priority. When the day of victory comes, I will submit myself willingly to the severest punishment. Even if I die.'

Zhou Fohai was not the only collaborator to have felt the change in the wind, recanted, and gone back to the Guomindang, but he was probably the one Chiang Kaishek most welcomed, at least until such time as he had exhausted his usefulness. For the moment he could help Chiang to beat the Communists to it when it came to taking over Shanghai; for one thing he had swung his troops behind the Guomindang forces, and for another he was keeping a tight rein on Shanghai. To General Dai Li, who could be seen in Zhou's house practically every other day, it was a matter for mutual congratulation that they were now in the same, instead of opposite, camps. When Chongqing appointed Zhou the Commander of the Nanjing-Shanghai Area Special Action Unit in recognition of his actual and impending usefulness to the Guomindang forces, Dai Li couldn't be happier for him.

Japan's defeat had thrown everything out of alignment, and now it was not so much Chinese versus Japanese, as the Guomindang colluding with the Japanese Army and the collaborators against the Communists. There is nothing puzzling or unusual, given the nature of politics, in shifting allegiances; and Chiang readily accepted offers from collaborators and Japanese commanders — the very commanders who several years before had ordered their soldiers to 'kill all, burn all, destroy all' in China — to help him secure cities, communications lines and installations to prevent them from falling into Communist hands.

It only went to show, said Mao Zedong in an acrimonious press release from his stronghold in Yan'an, how much Chiang had been in collusion with the enemy. To the traitors he said, 'We tell you gentlemen of Nanjing frankly: you are war criminals, you will be brought to trial.' All the witch-hunting, the extermination campaigns, all the struggles and uneasy alliance of two decades had led at last to this: within a few years of the Japanese surrender it was finally to be decided which was the stronger — the nationalism backed by American power of the Guomindang, or the nationalism riding the wave of mass mobilization of the Communist Party.

That Americans were powerful everyone in Shanghai could see. The Huangpu River was choked with men-of-war of the U.S. Seventh Fleet; U.S. dollars were flown to Shanghai from San Francisco, Pearl Harbor and Guam by the ton. SACO men, pouring into the city the summer before, had made whoopee with their greenbacks in all the nightspots. Even children were made adult by the expectation of American deliverance, tugging Yankee sleeves and saying, 'Hey Joe... Shoeshine, Joe? Want nice girl, Joe? Very cheap, Joe?'

Shanghai, war-damaged and looted as it was — the Japanese had gutted the insides of hotels and apartments, ripping out door knobs, fixtures, fireplaces, piping — still restored American standards of comfort and consumer supply to the returning soldiers and civilians. After the dearth and provinciality of the interior, Shanghai seemed cornucopian to the returning bureaucrats from Chongqing. With the Japanese gone, the sluices were opened to rapacity and plunder; there was no stopping them, the grabbers, profiteers and carpetbaggers. Assets confiscated from collaborators, contributions made by the United Nations Relief and Rehabilitation Agency, American surplus — all was grist that came to their mill.

But the backwash of war, moving through the city, did not only create opportunity; it brought privation and injustice, and all the things that privation and injustice make people do. Awakened to nationalism by the war, people were now further goaded into it by social inequality, by the American presence, and by Communist subversion. There were demonstrations, students marching to show that they wanted less corruption and the Americans out. There were anti-Guomindang slogans scrawled on walls. Inevitably, there were also clampdowns, arrests, and witch-hunts.

SACO HAD BROKEN UP and Mary Miles was back in the United States. Miles was unhappy because General Wedemeyer had wanted Dai Li's organization, the Bureau of Central Investigation and Statistics, dismantled. Miles thought it shortsighted of the general, since the bureau was China's best hedge against the Communist menace. But the U.S. Army never could get over this idea of the man being some sort of ogre. Miles, whenever he thought of Dai Li, did so warmly, remembering the man in his more relaxed moments, as at that Christmas Eve party for instance, the one the Chinese members of SACO gave in the Paramount Ballroom in Shanghai last year, where to everyone's delight Dai Li fell to doing La Conga on the dance floor, being taught it by one of the American Navy radio-men. There was also the time he threw a Christmas party for the orphans of agents and soldiers killed in the line of duty. It was something to see the man, whose name was said to be a bogey used to frighten children into behaving, handing out presents from under the Christmas tree, and playing with the orphans and making them laugh.

For further evidence of the man's goodwill, one need only quote from the letter he, Miles, had just received from him (written in Chinese, it had been translated into English by government interpreters in Washington). 'The achievements of SACO and the everlasting friendship between the two of us,' it said, 'not only concern the welfare of a small proportion of our peoples, but will also have a great bearing on the friendly relations of the people of both our countries. China, after eight years of bloody warfare, after long suffering and much bitterness, should from now on make great strides in her work of construction, thus rejuvenating her strength. However, being backward in many ways, both technically and economically, we will continue to need the helping hand of your friendly nation. Furthermore, judging from the situation in the world at large, the destinies of these two great nations are certain, henceforth, to be deeply interwoven.... You and I... will continue not only to value the joint successes we have shared in the past, but also work for the future benefit and welfare of our two countries.'

The letter was so full of hopeful purpose, so unshadowed by any portent of disaster, that when news of Dai Li's sudden death reached Mary Miles, it was nothing short of a bombshell.

On 17 March 1946, the military plane carrying Dai Li from Beijing to Shanghai disappeared into the clouds above Nanjing and crashed on the hills below. Everyone on board was killed. The plane, a C-47 belonging to the Chinese Aeronautical Commission, had made a stop at Qingdao, where it had taken on extra oil in case the bad weather reported from Shanghai necessitated a detour and a landing in Nanjing. Two hours after take-off the pilot, flying without radar, had radioed the aeronautical station, first to say that he was turning back, then to say that he was landing; but after that nothing more was heard from him. The search went on for three days — during which time it rained continuously — and in the end turned up eight corpses, so charred and rained on you could scarcely tell one from the other. Dai Li's body, which had the right hand and leg blown off it, could only be identified by the gold bridgework, some shreds of woollen underwear, and the American pistol Mary Miles had given him four years before.

He had been in Beijing to set up some additional links in his intelligence network, but was hurrying back to Shanghai on private business when the fatal accident occurred. The matter which the crash disrupted concerned his mistress Butterfly Wu. Dai Li was anxious to get to Shanghai to discover what success Du Yuesheng had had in arranging for her to be separated from her husband so that he could marry her himself. A deal was involved, and some very delicate dialogue. In the conduct of this affair Dai Li benefited greatly from Du's generosity. For one thing, by turning over his mansion on Avenue Doumer to the general's East China operations, Du Yuesheng enabled Dai Li to have a base in Shanghai.

Du could scarcely credit that Dai Li should die just when things were going so swimmingly for him. Nor did it seem credible that someone who had worsted death so often should be felled, not by the poison cup, the bullet, or the dagger, but by the play of arbitrary forces. Du felt the loss keenly, and was not surprised to hear that Chiang Kaishek had wept at the news. Most people thought of Dai Li as a person who could kill without batting an eyelid, but to these two friends there was much more to the man than that. Du would agree with most of what *Time* magazine said of the general when the news of his death came out: 'He was hard and he was tender. He personally succoured victims of Japanese atrocities, established orphanages for Chinese waifs. For Communists and fellow travellers, he maintained concentration camps. He was an honest man, scorning the traditional "squeeze". Once he discovered a close friend's malfeasance, invited him to dinner, had the police arrest him, testified against him in court, and had him shot.'

Dai Li's other admirer, Milton Miles, would also judge this description fair. Miles turned up in Shanghai that September as the commander of a cruiser, the U.S.S. *Columbus*. He had received a message from Generalissimo Chiang Kaishek about Dai Li's funeral, which he was very keen to attend. But the matter was not so simple. At a time when American diplomacy was trying so desperately to bring about a coalition government, reconciling the irreconcilable — the Guomindang and the Communist Party — it might not be politic for Miles, as a representative of the U.S. Navy, to be attending the funeral. For the Communists hated Dai Li above all others; and General George C. Marshall, the presiding architect of this ephemeral truce, was afraid that if Miles were allowed to pay his last respects to such a man, the fact might be damaging to the goodwill he was trying to foster between the Communists and the Guomindang. The matter could only be resolved by Miles attending as a private person; and so, when he took the train up to Nanjing on the day with all the other mourners, he was in civilian clothes. The U.S. naval attache would have awarded the deceased the Legion of Merit medal, with the accompanying citation extolling his 'notable spirit of loyalty and unswerving cooperation and devotion to the needs of the U.S. Navy,' had he not been given orders not to do so at the last minute. To some extent Miles made up for this by presenting the deceased with a pair of plum trees, which he planted at the foot of the grave.

The burial ground, up on a hill to the east of Sun Yatsen's tomb, overlooked the Valley of Spirits. The site was chosen by Chiang Kaishek himself, and the geomancer having pronounced it properly positioned, it may be assumed that the deceased's descendants would not suffer any evil effects. It had taken the Generalissimo two trips up the hill to find it; the first time he was accompanied by his wife, whose Italian heels unfortunately gave way before they reached the top.

The obsequies were performed in a leafy bower raised not far from this spot. Milton Miles could follow the Chinese rites because a major general, acting as master of ceremonies, intoned the directions: Hats off, Bow three times — one, two, three, Hats on, Three minutes' meditation, Three minutes up, Present incense, Present flowers, Present coins, Present wine, and so on. At the end of the ceremonies the principal mourners bore the coffin away, climbing up a winding path to deliver it to its subterranean vault in the hills. That night it rained heavily, the downpour greatly impeding the work of the Shanghai contractor who had been commissioned by the Guomindang government to seal the vault up with cement, as a precaution against exhumation of the corpse by body-snatchers for vengeance or desecration.

AT THE NEWS of Dai Li's death, Zhou Fohai thought: 'I am finished. And I was so close to besting fate too.' From the first Dai Li had taken personal charge of him, assuring Zhou of his protection. Things seemed to go right in those first few months after VJ Day. He had done what he could to secure Shanghai for the Guomindang, commandeering enough raw materials — cotton, newsprint, gold — to finance Chongqing's projected counter-offensive; it was accepted that his allegiance had switched to the Guomindang; it really looked as if he would not go the way of the other traitors. He had not known what to expect when Dai Li flew him to Chongqing in October, but as he said to Little Devil Ding, who was on the same flight (having, on the strength of his past service to the Bureau of Central Investigation and Statistics, been taken under Dai Li's wing too), he was reasonably confident that the general would testify for him if his case should come up for trial. In Chongqing he was remarkably well treated. It is true that he was under house arrest, but he was denied few comforts and his wife and son were allowed to visit.

Now, all of a sudden, the man responsible for his safety was dead. Zhou Fohai's awakening to this fact, the fact that here was where his hopes ended, was rude and terrifying. For a moment there was disbelief too that, having come so far, one should abruptly find oneself back where one began — unless our existence was ruled by freakish influences, and accident was the force beneath the apparently rational order of things.

It was not until he collected himself that another thought struck him, that you could retrace the footsteps of your life and set off again in a different direction once, or maybe twice, but you could never do it three times. This being the case, he reckoned that it only remained for him to be condemned and thrown to the wolves.

And that was what now happened. As soon as the guards appeared at the door he knew that that was it. They took him to another part of Chongqing and looking up, he saw for the first time the gates of Earth Bridge Prison. A cell door was unlocked, he was thrust inside, and an iron bolt slid between him and the world.

By the time his case came up for trial, in September 1946, some 2,700 civilian and military collaborators had been executed and 2,300 sentenced to life imprisonment. Hated collaborators like the chief of the Japanese-run secret police in Hangzhou were marched through the streets and lynched. The newspapers went into the minutest details of the last hours of the condemned, the Chinese appetite for the facts of death being very large, and undiminished by all that opportunity the war had provided for satisfying it.

For his trial Zhou Fohai was flown to Nanjing; the court had to be moved to the main hall of a temple, the crowd of spectators was so large. There was no dock and Zhou, in a grey silk robe, simply stood in front of the presiding magistrate, who happened to be someone he could once call a friend. The accused's name, age, native province and county established, the proceedings began. Zhou Fohai was charged with high treason, and in the course of the cross-examination much interest was shown in his financial dealings under the auspices of the Japanese-sponsored regime he worked for. He pleaded not guilty, and reminded the court in a long defence that once he discovered the Japanese to be insincere in their quest for peace, he had returned his allegiance to Chongqing. He provided details. Among others he invoked the name of General Dai Li. Hearing him speak like that, with confidence and seeming sincerity, one felt like letting him off. When he was led out after the session, he was besieged by reporters and asked for his autograph. He gave it, scrawling in a handwriting characteristically graceless, the words, 'You will know the real me in ten years' time.' He had been found guilty of treason, a charge carrying the penalty of death.

The impact of this verdict upon his wife was, to say the least, a cruel one, especially in the light of his earlier immunity. As a woman, she had a hundred reasons to quarrel with him (not the least of which was his infidelity); as a wife, no one could be more loyal. She sought out Chiang Kaishek, who alone could commute the sentence, and sinking to the floor before him, sobbed out her pleas. The Generalissimo, holding within himself many possibilities, including the exercise of executive clemency, remained impassive, not wishing to run the risk of inviting further accusations of the Communist press, that his slowness in bringing the collaborators to justice was the very proof of his collusion with them. But when Mrs Zhou went on crying, he leaned forward to ask her to get up, and in a tone not ungentle, said that her husband must stay inside for a year or two, but that he would be released in good time, and she was not to worry. Her tears dried to a surge of gratitude, but the words of thanks stuck in her throat, and she remained there on her knees, to touch her forehead to the floor. On 26 March 1947, Chiang Kaishek issued an order commuting Zhou Fohai's sentence to life imprisonment.

Nanjing's Tiger Bridge Prison was notorious for its deliberate brutality in the days when the Japanese *kempeitai* used it. But nowadays the warders could all be bought and the rigours of imprisonment softened by money spent in the right places. Had there still been hope of a last-minute reprieve Zhou Fohai would not have found life intolerable there. In the part of the camp where the wards were named Gentleness, Goodness, Respectfulness, Thrift and Submissiveness, he had a cell to himself. While rice and soup were delivered twice a day through a hatch in the wooden door, he mostly ate in the canteen, where under a special arrangement more palatable meals could be made available. At Tiger Bridge he and one or two other collaborators constituted a sort of elite, of a distinctly higher class than the other inmates, most of them ordinary criminals, and towards him the warders showed a certain amount of deference — the ingrained deference of the Chinese towards a member of the official class.

Of all the fellow captives, Zhou thought Little Devil Ding the most pathetic. Ding had done exactly what he himself had done — that is to say, he had turned coat twice — yet Zhou could not help despising him, this man who never burdened himself with even half a principle. Wan and underweight with galloping consumption, Ding had a miserable look about him that grated on Zhou whenever the two met up at drill.

Ding had been sentenced to death, and when his executioners came for him, a few minutes before noon on an early July day, Zhou in his cell heard them. Lying there, with his arm beneath his head and a magazine splayed on his chest, Zhou heard their footsteps stop at a cell, heard the grind of the opening door and the queasy moan of Ding's fear as, limping and staggering, he was half-lifted and half-carried down the corridor. There was an interval of silence before he heard the last thing, the crack of a firing squad's rifles as it might sound in a yard round the back. Zhou pictured Ding's face in that brief instant before death, seeing it glazed and puckered in fear. Later he was not surprised to learn that Ding had met his end drivelling and squealing, he always knew the man to be a coward. What a loss of face, how different it was from the equanimity with which some of the others in their team had faced the firing squad, or from the dignity of the defeated Japanese soldiers, for that matter, who before they went to their deaths bowed at an angle of 90 degrees while facing east.

Anyone seeing Zhou would have said he looked pretty wretched himself, his hair shorn, his skin the colour of the surrounding cell walls. Every now and then glints of the old wise-cracking self would still show through, but if the truth be known he was a man at the end of his tether. When the summer abruptly ended he woke up every morning chilled; and he was getting very thin. Existence gradually became simplified by the inability to rise from the bed. A Chinese saying has it that good fortune awaits the man who survives a calamity. Zhou found this hard to believe, and thought instead of the Cantonese story of the old man who survived the flooding of his village only to fall into the neighbourhood cesspool, dying in excrement when he might have died in water.

As the autumn and winter wore on sleep became impossible. The only position in which he could even half-rest was on his back, propped up by quilts and blankets thickly piled up underneath him to hold him above his pain. He knew that he must die; it was what would release him from the bondage of his tearing flesh.

One day in February 1948 the papers announced that Zhou Fohai, aged 51, ex-Guomindang cadre and traitor, died in his cell in Nanjing's Tiger Bridge Prison of a heart attack. This was followed by a rumour that he died by his own hand.

IF IT HADN'T been for her, someone had said, Wang Jingwei would not have succeeded; equally, he would not have come to grief. Madame Wang's trial on 16 April 1946 opened to a courtroom filled with people curious to discover the truth of this remark. What they saw was a bulky figure in black, the hair mannishly cropped, the famous glare masked by smoky glasses. From her carriage and the way the head was tipped she might have been a general about to accept an enemy's surrender.

Since her husband's death she had lived, it was known, in Canton, the city in whose day-to-day administration during the occupation she had always had a firm and steady hand. It was there that she was arrested. It did not happen all at once. First a government agent came for her, solemnly telling her that arrangements had been made for her to fly to Chongqing. He must have implied that his mission was benign, for when she was doing her packing, she thought to include a basket of peaches — these being in season in Canton at the time — to present to Madame Chiang Kaishek on arrival. But when they were on their way, somehow, suddenly, she found herself not being taken to the airport, but to a bridge on the Pearl River. She passed, in the next hours, from the company of the agent come to fetch her to the care of a launch and a large number of unsmiling men from the Bureau of Central Investigation and Statistics.

All through the journey she harangued them, threatening a tantrum, the sort nobody could withstand. 'Even old Chiang knows my temper,' she breathed, 'Who do you think you are?' But it was no use, and only made them hurry the more to reach their destination. This, Madame Wang discovered, was a house on the other side of town, a two-storey building with grounds guarded by armed men. She understood that she was to be placed under house arrest, and, resigning herself to this, she took to her room upstairs, locked herself in with her maid, and passed days and weeks reading poetry and playing chess.

Later, on being moved to a detention centre in Nanjing, Madame Wang said, 'I have the courage to face execution, but I can't say I have the patience to sit it out in jail.' Her case was now abandoned to the machinery of Guomindang justice, the grinding of whose gears had already extirpated her brother-in-law, the eccentric Foreign Minister of the defunct Nanjing regime. From Nanjing she was taken one midnight to Suzhou; there, on the following morning, she appeared at a building which, for an indication of its purpose not otherwise apparent from its homely exterior, had a vertical board proclaiming 'Suzhou High Court'.

OUTSIDE WAS a dragon-contoured crowd. Inside, spectators were taking up seats in rows. Though most of them seemed inattentive, some scratching themselves, and others chatting, their mood in sum was one of curiosity. Of course the woman hadn't a leg to stand on, not a few were thinking; but then there was also this, the widely rumoured story that what Wang Jingwei did was done with the tacit approval of Chiang Kaishek all along. As for Wang's own motives, some thought him prompted by ambition and jealousy; some thought him moved by a genuine sense of the usefulness of appeasement to his country; some did not doubt that it was this woman who had put him up to it all along. Few of them came wanting to see justice done, for treason is not a crime particularly abhorred in China; if not actually commonplace, it was so often the recourse of the ambitious, discontented, or simply hopeless that it was held in no particular horror. The road to treason is in any case paved with good intentions, and the swift changes and equivocations of the Chinese political scene can make any distinction or condemnation false at almost any moment. No, these people had come not to clamour for an evil-doer or a hero; they expected to hear a little truth and to see some guilt brought home, but they also expected a great deal of the reverse.

And now, through the door of the courtroom, there entered the lady herself, wearing on her face the straying attention of the arrogant. 'Here comes the empress,' someone caustically whispered, as she was led up front to face the stiff figures of those who presumed to judge her. The indictments against her, Case No. 396, a member of the political control commission of the treasonous puppet government, were read out. She had further offended, it seemed, by her complicity in the murder of underground resistance workers, by her engagement in espionage, and by her traitorous wire-pulling in Canton.

Her pride could never allow contrition, nor her convictions the sense that she was wrong. Single-minded in her loyalty to her husband, she was spared the self-questionings of conscience: out of allegiance to him, she simply put everyone else in the wrong. The prosecution could not put questions to her; rather it was she who, in a voice that conjured her Cantonese origins and was like a quick-firing gun, demanded to be heard. 'Are you, in your patent mediocrity and ignorance of the real world of politics, qualified to judge me? Don't you know that the thankless task of conciliating a powerful victorious enemy is not for the faint-hearted? Let me remind you that we went to the enemy empty-handed. As for Mr Wang selling his country, just tell me how he could possibly have done this, when there was not an inch of territory to sell: what Chongqing had was not ours to give; where we were was occupied land; whatever we did have we had wrested from the enemy; how could we have given anything away?'

'You try me today,' she continued, 'in the name of a victor country. But what if Japan had dropped her bombs on Siberia instead of Pearl Harbor, what would be the issue of the war then? Wouldn't our course be vindicated then? Mr Wang sought nothing for himself. If you consider as traitors those who, for the defence and survival of their homeland, allied themselves with the enemy, then treason in China was not confined to Mr Wang alone.'

Behind her she heard a hubbub grow louder, a tide of coughing and scraping feet from the public area thunderously magnified by applause. The cross-examination continued at some length, but she refused to be shaken on any point of her defence. This, for all its circularity of reasoning, held together remarkably well. Western imperialism, Soviet Bolshevism, Japanese expansionism — among these three threats to China, was there, truth to tell, all that much to choose from? Her husband had stood at the right hand of Dr Sun Yatsen. If he wanted to see Western imperialists ousted from China, no less was he concerned that Communism should not reap the harvest of a protracted war. Her husband cherished his countrymen as much as any patriot; it was because of their suffering, and not in spite of them, that Mr Wang had agreed to negotiate with the Japanese, for he could not stand by and watch that suffering intensified by a needlessly drawn out war. If we opposed brutality only by fighting the men who caused it, we should merely keep the wheel of brutality turning. That was not saving China, it was subjecting her to further cruelty.

She had a gift for trenchant invective, which being in the dock did not in the least inhibit her from displaying. At the same time as she offended her auditors she compelled respect. Yet though her demeanour was not a bit forlorn she aroused sympathy for being nevertheless a woman alone. When the session was over and she was marched out of the room, the ushers had to hold the crowd back. She held her chin high and declared, in answer to a question a reporter shot at her from across the throng, 'I didn't come here to show I could still hold my head up; it's never been bowed.'

She was sentenced to life imprisonment. She considered the penalty unjust, 'but I won't appeal,' she said, 'because it will be the same verdict whatever I do.' And now she would have to do the more difficult thing, the thing she said she had no patience for — marking time in jail. Her cell was on the ground floor of Jiangsu's Number Three Detention Centre, known colloquially as Lion Bridge Prison. One of the first things she did when she got there was to tick the wardens off for calling her by her maiden name — 'Even Sun Yatsen never called me that,' she complained. So afterwards it always had to be Madame Wang, or something equally deferential. Beyond finding fault she had nothing at first to help her through the days, but as time went by she came to like some of the other women prisoners and began to derive some satisfaction from teaching them to read.

If she got used to widowhood it was not by effacing her husband's memory. Of all that had been taken from her, her home, her freedom, her husband's honoured place in Chinese history, it was the loss of the last that she minded most.

One day a friend leaving China for good came to visit her and left her with a few mementoes of the world she had done with.

Amongst them she found an old photograph, a blurred snapshot of a couple about to sail for France, leaving behind a city, not pictured, with which Wang Jingwei's fated enterprise would be inextricably entangled.

She never expected to see Shanghai again. Yet she did see it, one day in 1949, when, along with a languishing economy, a thoroughly demoralized populace, the victors of China's Communist revolution also inherited her. After the founding of the People's Republic she was moved from Suzhou to Shanghai's Tiered Basket Bridge prison. It was there that the widow of Sun Yatsen, the vice-president of the new republic, came to see her. She brought with her a message from Mao Zedong, offering to discharge Madame Wang in exchange for a signed confession of error. Madame Wang replied, not brusquely, 'One cannot deny to Mr Wang the acknowledgement that what he did in occupied China was in the service of his people — least of all I, who knew him as no one knows him, and therefore have a responsibility to speak up for him. You cannot say that the present regime's friendship with the Soviet Union is in the interests of the people of China without raising the question of how different that is from Mr Wang's cooperation with the Japanese.' She ended by saying that she was quite happy to remain where she was.

She died, aged 69, in the thirteenth year of her imprisonment, on 17 June 1959. Her children, in Hong Kong, travelled as far as Canton to collect her ashes, despatched from Shanghai in a rosewood box. From Hong Kong they then took a boat, and when it slipped out of a passage into the sea, leaving harbour, bay, island and international shipping, they scattered the ashes over the water, saving only a pinch for themselves. It was the closest they could come to exalting the *jingwei*, that bird of monumental longing and tragedy, whose remorseless destiny it is to be forever filling in the sea.

IN ANOTHER Shanghai prison Big Wu's wife was unsparing in her efforts to maintain refinement in the face of squalor. Not to wear clean clothes, sleep in laundered sheets, comb her hair into a smooth bun flattering to her round, fair face, taper her fingernails and brush her teeth until they shone — not to do all this was to be cast down by the brutish meanness of prison life. Lacking basins and running water, she scoured, with broken bits of tile, the stained concavities of the one lavatory bowl so clean she could think of rinsing her sheets in it. And for a looking-glass she used the mirroring surface of an upturned biscuit tin held in a certain angle in the light. In those days she went to the courthouse a lot. She went as a witness, and always in high heels, and with a touch of a little excitement, a little expectation of something interesting happening.

Soon after her arrest General Dai Li had come to see her, and promised to help get her let off. But like everyone else she was undone by his plane crash. She got seven years, but announced this with a smile and a turn of the head — as if to say, I don't care, life is long yet.

As it happened she was out after three and a half years for good behaviour. The day she came home to her adopted son and daughter she looked so well and happy no one could guess what privations she had endured. When, soon after her discharge, her birthday came round, Big Wu's gangland protégés said they would give her a party, she being their matriarch and all. It was a do in the old style, down to the cake — the biggest and most expensive of course — from the bakery at the Sincere Department Store. She came on like royalty — it was something to see her queening it again.

Life proved a hard business all the same. Runaway inflation wore away what little money she had saved from confiscation. Her adopted daughter, unequal to the stigma of an unmarried mother (of an offspring fathered by a married doctor), one day took an overdose of sleeping tablets and killed herself. Yet Mrs Wu took what came without letting it weigh on her; and she continued to look on the bright side.

When Communism took Shanghai and there could be no question of her staying, Mrs Wu went to live in Hong Kong, where she found among the exiled gangsters from the old world the same ampleness of means and willingness to share it as they had exhibited in Shanghai.

Some years later her name turned up in the papers in Tokyo in connection with illegal entry and heroin trafficking. She was ever the leading lady in underworld drama. She had been down, she had hit bottom, but like a rubber ball she bounced right back towards the headlines. The publicity subsided and she found purpose and relative obscurity running a bar. Of the events that followed perhaps none more fittingly completes her story than her reunion with Hu Lancheng, her late husband's friend. Like her he had found in Japan a haven from Communism and the retribution generally visited upon the traitor. His romantic instincts were still functioning and his admiration for her was quite as robust as before. Accepting the measure as an almost inevitable expedient, given their circumstances and feelings for one another, they were married in 1954.

Two years before, Zhang Ailing, Hu Lancheng's wife in an earlier time, left Shanghai for Hong Kong. From there she emigrated to the United States, where, hailed by a professor of literature as the best and most important writer in Chinese in contemporary times, she became something of a literary cult among the younger generation of intellectuals. In her writing she comes very close to the heart of individual experience, and bares the squalor veiled by surface decency. For many years she has lived in California, a virtual recluse. 'People tossed about by troubled times must just get by,' she was to write, 'they have no place they can call their home.'

FOR SOME TIME, Du Yuesheng must have been aware that he was past his peak. But what really brought it home to him was the discovery that he had not been appointed chairman of the provisional Shanghai city council, a post he long considered his own. Chiang Kaishek had gone and appointed somebody else; and he had not been able to protest. Indeed, in the aftermath of war, in the ousting of the old by the new, and in the gestation of that soon-to-be-born juggernaut, the Socialist State, he had not been able to prevent a serious challenge to his power from ranks above and below. In any confrontation with the new powerhouses, it was beginning to be clear that he would not always come off best.

The business clout was still there, his boardroom stature was still unassailable; he was a director of some fifty to sixty large companies, including Shanghai's leading newspaper; he was president of at least four trade associations. But where was the pre-eminence in public life that should go with all this?

In the summer of 1946, an election returned Du Yuesheng and 180 others to the city council. Du's election to the council was easy, but the speakership — which was what he wanted — was another matter. Perhaps it was his vanity that made him crave it, or perhaps it was the sycophancy of his followers, who flattered him into an illusion of popularity; but for a moment he imagined the appointment to be within his grasp, and that he could rise to it like the kingpin he always was.

Something must have made him pause, for he began to entertain the notion that if he could only get everybody to elect him, to show that he was still capable, as it were, of sweeping the stakes, then he'd gladly renounce the speakership in favour of somebody else. But their support must appear to be total: that is to say, there was not to be a single dissentient vote. When the time came he would step aside, but for appearance's sake the proceedings leading up to this magnanimous gesture must be conducted on his terms.

His disciples set to work conveying this idea to each councillor. It was in everybody's interest, they said, that he agree to this; indeed the master would be most grateful. They were quite sure that the honourable councillor, being the gentleman he was, would not spoil things by obstruction. The lobbying left no stone unturned. Some gentlemen were grudging but not, Du Yuesheng felt, beyond the exercise of suasion. And when the day of the election arrived, and Du was being led up the assembly hall by the mayor, he was agreeably secure in the expectation of unanimous support.

He looked at the rows of seats, and made for the bloc reserved for him and his entourage. The ballot box was opened, and like everyone else's in the room, Du's expression assumed the impassivity demanded by the occasion.

'Du Yuesheng...'

'Du Yuesheng...'

A single voice was reading out the name marking each ballot paper. The name was always the same, and it was assumed by more than one person in the audience that there would be no other, it having been so pre-arranged. The voice went on; the audience was quiet; it was going like clockwork. After a while of this the voice abruptly halted: here was a blank piece of paper, and here was another. As the minutes ticked by it gradually emerged that out of a hundred and eighty ballots some forty and more were unmarked. Du Yuesheng sat still, but his breath came and went rapidly, and his face had turned quite grey. In a moment or two he would have to rise and deliver his carefully prepared speech. But who could face an audience after so monstrous a piece of treachery? What honour was there in bowing out of an election that was so obviously half-hearted?

Amid the polite hand-clapping he got to his feet. He had won an overall majority, it was true, but as he took the microphone his murmur of thanks and apology was in his own ears caught by an amplified echo that seemed only to compound the impression of defeat. He managed a rueful smile and, abandoning the wording of his prepared speech, he muttered something about his failing health, which to his regret prevented him from accepting the onerous duties of the speakership.

He could not deny it, this sense of his power passing. One comes to expect different things at different times in one's life; but one comes to it by learning, quite often painful. In the early months of 1947 Du Yuesheng was learning that the world was changing, and that he could not stop it from doing so. In early February he made a trip to Hong Kong. The reasons were mysterious; the *New York Times* made out that he was contemplating a prolonged stay. From the sudden haste of the departure it was assumed that some urgent political matter was at stake. His recent fortunes having been seen to falter, it was also speculated that some sort of crash was imminent; and a rumour ran through Shanghai that Chiang Kaishek was poised to strike him down and that Du, taking precautions against such a time, was in Hong Kong to make a bid for British protection.

In fact, what had summoned Du Yuesheng to Hong Kong was more ominous, or at any rate profounder in its implications, than the threat of Chiang Kaishek's displeasure. A trusted protégé, an office holder in the Chinese Labour Association, had turned Red. Specifically, he had absconded to champion a radical labour movement in Hong Kong; worse, he was proposing to go to the international labour conference opening in Geneva claiming to be the rightful representative of Chinese workers. He spoke of 'democratic rights' and 'free trade unions' — words which were becoming synonymous with Communism, which of all political complexions was the one Du Yuesheng distrusted the most.

Things looked very bad. Du had decided to go himself and impress upon his protégé the error of his ways, and also the intensity of his own objections. 'You must come back with me to Shanghai,' he said. 'I know very well — we needn't mince matters — I know quite well that disciplinary action will be taken against you by the government when you get there. But I shall ascertain most thoroughly the intentions of the government; and I give you my word that only when I have satisfied myself, only when I have extracted a promise that you will come to no harm, will I come for you.'

Du spoke paternally, and with the confidence of one who knew himself to be dealing with a kindred creature of an ancient fraternity — one equipped, that is, to understand the sanctity of a pledge such as this. Du Yuesheng's word had always been his bond; you could count on him to act honourably as you could on no one else. That had been his reputation for so long he had no reason whatsoever to expect it not to take.

But it didn't work. The protégé would not take his word for it, would not give in, and would not go home to Shanghai. Instead he proceeded to speak for Chinese labour in Geneva and London, and was next heard of in the spring of 1948 joining the Reds up in Harbin.

What stayed with Du after he regained his composure was the unexpectedness of the affair, the unexpectedness of finding the seeds of Communism sown, and taking root in his very midst. It was much, much more than he had bargained for. It was nothing short of a hint that it was time to come to terms with history. As if to rub this in, Shanghai was shaken in May by strikes and rioting, people getting up to protest against the hunger and the high cost of living. And in the summer it was learnt that the Red Army had crossed the Yellow River. Indeed, as Mao Zedong was telling his Party, 'The revolutionary war of the Chinese people has reached the turning point... a turning point in history.'

However, the swamp of present distractions rendered these events no more than distant rumours, and for the moment Du Yuesheng's day-to-day concerns were those of a man about to celebrate his sixtieth birthday and court another opera star.

It was a dazzling gala, the birthday celebration. The event lasted for days, and some five and a half thousand guests were invited. In the street outside the Lido Ballroom — where one of the dinners was served — bystanders pressed forward with that collective curiosity which only an extremely drab life coupled with a Chinese love of crowding produces, for a good view of the guests as they spilled forth from their American cars. Of the women, many were elegant and bejewelled; gowns then were slit sheaths that came down to the ankle, hair was drawn back or done the way American film stars had it in the movies. Of the men, most looked as though they enjoyed their success.

The occasion, which was to be marked by ten days of opera performances, brought to town two of the nation's greatest stars, Mei Lanfang and Meng Xiaodong, maestro and prima donna of Beijing opera. Five of the ten days of their engagement were in aid of flood relief in Guangdong and Guangxi Provinces, two of Du Yuesheng's best-known charities. The tickets sold for thirty to fifty thousand Shanghai dollars apiece — hefty sums even allowing for the leaping price index. When Meng Xiaodong sang her famous aria 'Searching for the Orphan, Saving the Orphan,' people paid a million dollars each to hear her.

That she and the maestro would be seen in the same town was itself a phenomenon: the two had been lovers, bitterly parted. It might have been a brilliant partnership, in life as in art. But the affair had degenerated into a national scandal, with Mei Lanfang being threatened with a gun by the lady's crazed former admirer, and his own wife threatening him with hysterics. Mei Lanfang had then relinquished Meng Xiaodong, perhaps in the belief that marriage to such a commanding stage personality must at some future date require a little stepping down.

It was on the plane of gossip rather than that of art that the Shanghai press took up the appearance of the two performers. There was no need, in any case, to tell the readers what they already knew: that as the nation's greatest singer of female roles, Mei Lanfang could deploy

Mei Lanfang in one of his famous female roles

the eyelids, the iris, the feet, the hands, the fingers and the wafting sleeves with a perfection achieved by no one else before him; that his consummate mimicking of feminine gait, in its imagined shimmy on crushed 'lotus' feet, had been mastered at the cost of blisters and pain walking on stilts across winter's ice; that on his resoundingly successful American tour he had met Charlie Chaplin and stayed with Douglas Fairbanks and Mary Pickford in Hollywood. His fans knew by heart the scenes that he had made famous, and while not consciously excited by their transvestite aspects, thrilled to the spectacle of the beautiful heroines in lush gowns that he conjured up before the footlights — now an empress making herself drunk in an agony of spurned love, now a maiden feigning madness to avoid marrying an emperor. As once before, when they saw him perform at the inauguration of Du Yuesheng's clan hall in 1931, many in the audience marvelled at a touch so sure. Others were seeing him for the first time in eight years, for, shortly after the outbreak of war, Mei Lanfang grew a faint moustache — a patriotic gesture which, putting paid as it did to the possibility of female impersonation, absolved him from having to play for the Japanese and their puppets.

Meng Xiaodong, the nonpareil of the *pihuang* opera — the style of singing in which she had been rigorously trained — endeared herself to her newspaper critics in the special way great actresses believed to lead unromantic backstage lives do. She had been on the stage since she was twelve; she was now a shade past her prime, but when the whine of those extenuated syllables cut its great crescent through the air, you could hear golden carillons, it was said.

Du Yuesheng, who had pulled off a great coup in bringing these two luminaries together before the footlights, shook off the doldrums of the past spring though not the bedevilment of his asthma. At the same time he felt a stirring of new desire. While the tabloids buzzed with innuendoes about an offstage reunion between Mei and Meng, Du Yuesheng asked the diva if she would like to become his fifth wife. For propriety's sake the press was fobbed off with an impression that nothing newsworthy was happening. The lady returned to Beijing after the birthday party, waited some weeks for the gossip and rumours to subside, then quietly caught a plane for Shanghai and moved in with Du Yuesheng and his fourth wife.

She crowned a last display of the old flamboyance, the all-too-human conceit of having made it to the top and having everything for the asking. Yet however splendid the occasion, and unequalled the scale, the birthday party was in a way a swan song. Nothing would ever be quite the same again. Du himself, who had so loved the noise and pomp of that other not dissimilar event, the dedication of his clan hall a decade and a half ago, found it harder to keep his spirits up this time, for one thing because he was more than once overcome by bad attacks of breathlessness. There seemed to be a cloud on the horizon, and in one way the occasion was soberly adapted to that sense of darkening: the guests were treated during the festivities to Buddhist vegetarian fare, as though the host saw all of life to be illusory, felt the shifting sands beneath, and knew that time was running out.

Chapter Fourteen

RED STAR OVER SHANGHAI 1948–1952

FOR MOST PEOPLE in Shanghai, the autumn of 1948 was turning into a nightmare. The price index had skyrocketed from 100 before the war to 10,300,000 by the end of 1947 and would soon go up to 287,000,000. On the black market the American dollar was fetching a value fifty times greater than what it was at the beginning of the year. To go shopping you carried great wads of worthless money in bundles. Red Army victories were in the headlines of every newspaper: Luoyang had fallen, Kaifeng had fallen, and now, in September, the defeat of the Guomindang forces in Shandong Province was making all of the lower reaches of the Yellow River fall into Communist hands. Before six months were out the Guomindang would be defeated in the three great battles — of Manchuria, of Huaihai, and of North China — which would put an end to Chiang Kaishek's China once and for all.

And yet in the shops the buying was frantic; on Nanjing Road, in the department stores, people were jamming the doors and pushing past each other to snatch up the Rolex watches, the Parker pens, the jewellery and the fabrics — spending their paper money as fast as they could, converting them into goods that would cost far more tomorrow than today. Refugees were arriving at the rate of six thousand a day; and the streets were an unlovely mess, clogged with hawkers, beggars, destitutes from the country who, weak with hunger and disease, had come in despair to a city which even then had the highest concentration of wealth in China.

The month before, the government had all of a sudden announced the replacement of the currency by the 'gold *yuan*' at an exchange rate of 3,000,000 to 1 — the new currency being backed, so the government claimed, by a hundred per cent reserve made up of gold, silver, bonds and securities, government-owned properties, and foreign exchange. At the same time the public learnt that all privately held gold, silver and foreign currency were to be turned over for conversion to the new currency, all foreign assets held abroad to be registered at once, and that there were to be strict economic controls, a price and wage freeze, and a ban on strikes, hoarding, speculation and black marketeering. Chiang Kaishek's own son had been put in charge of the crackdown — the locals called it a tiger hunt — and under the terror of his capricious justice, violators of the new laws were intimidated, arrested, and even publicly executed.

The measures hit financiers and businessmen both big-time and small. Many were cowed into behaving, for it really was 'reform at pistol point'. The ordinary people liked nothing so much as to see the high-ups brought low, and especially to see their heads roll; and for a whole month it looked as though the reforms might actually work — inducing order in a situation whose ungovernable character was reflected in the popular saying, 'Business is better than working; hoarding is better than business, and speculation is better than hoarding.'

Certainly any lingering doubts as to whether Chiang was serious about these reforms were dispelled when it was learnt that no less a business corsair than Du Yuesheng had been hit by them. In the popular mind that name still suggested inviolability — weren't Du Yuesheng and Chiang Kaishek the joint impresarios of Shanghai's burgeoning capitalism? So when the September 8 editions revealed that Du Weiping, third son of Du Yuesheng, had been arrested for a bear sale of shares on the eve of the currency reform, the fact took time to sink in. Yet there it was — even the *New York Times* carried the story — the revelation that the younger Du was in deep trouble for having dumped 30,000,000 shares on the market the day before the government announced its economic programme. Selling short is only for the speculator with strong nerves — or very reliable information; where else could the younger Du have got that information if not from his father? The publicity ripped into the miscreant, and Chiang Kaishek, who had needed just such a scapegoat, issued a statement saying, 'Those who love money more than their country cannot expect their country to be lenient with them.'

It could not be helped, and Du Yuesheng faced what there was to face. When his son came to talk the matter over with him he was in his bedroom, propped up stiffly on the bed. He leant back against the pillows, closing his eyes. When he opened them and looked at his son, very gravely, like an employer interviewing a prospective recruit, it was not possible to tell which way his thoughts were going. He said dully, rather as if he was repeating something tiresome he himself had heard many times before, 'It will be all right. They're only doing it because the Economic Supervisory Office wants a little credit and publicity. The thing will be pure theatre, but we'll have to go along with it. There's no honourable way of getting out of it, and we shan't even try.' Another crack had run through the foundation of his life.

At the trial the judge pressed repeatedly for the source of the younger Du's information, but the latter adamantly denied previous knowledge of the government reforms. At the conclusion of the proceedings he was sentenced to eight months' imprisonment, not on the count brought against him — which was the use of improperly obtained intelligence — but on the technical count of having dealt in shares outside the regular stock exchanges. The spectators in the public gallery looked across to see how the father was taking it; he seemed to be following the proceedings closely, but without any expression of alarm or pain, except that now and then his chest heaved rather rapidly. He had looked at the son when he was brought into the chamber, and then had turned his eyes away.

Then the campaign was past its peak, not a few speculators had been hauled out and shot; but the confidence in the gold *yuan* cracked, the inflation and hoarding resumed with renewed frenzy, the shop counters were besieged, and the city's economy threatened at any minute to fall apart. Now the disintegration was so far past the point of rescue that nothing would redeem the campaign from disarray and the currency from total collapse.

At the same moment as Du Yuesheng's son was being led through the corridors of one of Shanghai's overcrowded prisons to begin his eight-month term of imprisonment, the sons robbed of their fathers by his father in the great coup against the Left in April 1927, when Du Yuesheng set his toughs upon the city's workers and labour unionists, were returning to collect their blood debt and claim their birthright. Underground revolutionaries were waiting to surface, to seize that moment when China would be upturned to disclose another land, of land reforms and Great Leaps Forward, and Cultural Revolutions for the remaking of man. Against such a time, those of the moneyed class that recovered their instincts enough to feel how the wind blew began to put feelers out and move their capital to Hong Kong and Taiwan. Two years before Mao Zedong had reckoned it would take five years to wrest China from the Guomindang; now he brought the estimate down to a year. In the event it took the Red Army eleven and a half short months to sweep all the way down from Manchuria to Canton, and proclaim a new State power over an exhausted fourth of mankind.

Ten months before that climax, Chiang Kaishek enlisted the services of Du Yuesheng for the last time. Du's People's Action Committee, formed in league with Dai Li's secret police at Chiang's instigation during the Japanese war to organize gang leaders and keep them, in a manner of speaking, safe from collaboration, was now resuscitated. Renamed the Association for the Reconstruction of New Chinese Society, it was turned into a fraternity of adherents bound to the Generalissimo in this hour of need in an oath of blood. Chiang, plunged now into the stealthy removal of gold stock, gems, antiques and entire museum collections to Taiwan, in preparation for his retreat, gave Du to understand that he was to raise money for the ultimate defence of Shanghai.

As if what we do now would make the smallest difference to the outcome of the civil war, Du thought. This call for yet more funds was something he'd heard over and over again. As many times before, he would respond to it; out of sheer habit he would deliver as he was expected to, but it wouldn't be with anything like the old enthusiasm. The larger issues were beginning to seem remote now, in the immediate concerns of his own personal safety. For a moment he imagined with regret the passing of all that Shanghai had meant to him and to all those who had shaped its dream, the dream that you could grow up in that place and bamboozle your way to riches and glory. But in the end, he thought, it would have to go, that was the shape of things in store, no gesture of mine could prevent that from happening. When the crunch came he would have to get out faster than anybody else.

It was widely rumoured that he would stay. To go by hearsay, Du Yuesheng was vacillating between continued loyalty to a moribund Chiang Kaishek and cooperation with the about to be triumphant Communist power. Though Chiang had invited all the most important and able people to retreat with him, both to buttress his own ranks and to deplete the Communists' (and because in politics the appearance of support counts as much as the fact), there was no knowing, so the rumour ran, what Du might do, considering how many other men of means had plumped for life under Communism in the imagined cosiness of a mutually profitable compact between State Socialism and what the Communists called National Capitalism.

In fact, however capricious Chiang might have been of late, to Du it was far more hazardous to put one's faith in the Communists. They were not likely to forget what he did to them in 1927, whereas the worst that Chiang could do to him was to snub him. So far, in the messages that the Communists had passed to Du under a sub rosa arrangement with several of his friends (the ones who had decided to give Communism a try), they had expressed the utmost goodwill, intimating that should Du agree to cooperate, he would not only be extremely welcome but would be given a special role to play in the new China. To these emissaries Du would say, 'That may be, and you may vouch for my safety, but from what I know of Communists they are not the sort to honour personal undertakings; indeed, I wouldn't even take Mao Zedong's word for it. I simply can't bank on their not wanting to square accounts, pay off old scores.' Though he didn't say so aloud, the kind of future he would have in the impending State had him shuddering already, just the idea of it.

He saw Chiang Kaishek for the last time in April 1949. On May 1, he made ready to leave Shanghai for Hong Kong. Hundreds were leaving too; you could see them all over the teeming waterfront — people and all of their liquid assets moving from cars and pedicabs, past the ticket and passport controls and over the gangplanks leading up to the black hulks massed along the Huangpu River. For Du

Yuesheng the journey to the harbour ran through Route Cardinal Mercier, across wide streets with tramlines and grey walls, past alleys sweet- and evil-smelling (as he would always remember) with the mixed odours of profuse humanity and preserved bean curd — Shanghai specialities both. In the speeding car he said almost nothing to his two companions, his fourth and fifth wives, but felt a pang that was perhaps a presentiment of nostalgia when the waterfront announced itself by the sounds and smells familiar to him since the time he was a fruiterer's apprentice new to this great dying metropolis.

This place had been important to him; it had made him, and he it. He knew some pride in Shanghai's vitality and in its apartness from the rest of China, feeling that the energies and genius of his people, his several peoples, had here an expression and monument of no less consequence than the poetry and traditional achievements of that other, inland, immemorial China. Here was China as she could be if she had opened up to the rest of the world. Here was the true Western-Chinese hybrid, that most transient of integrations that had only a generation in which to grow and mature, expressing itself as much in the broker who kept abreast of the London and New York Stock Exchanges at the same time as he followed the fluctuations of the Zhejiang market, as in the left-leaning intellectual familiar with the ins and outs of Marxist theory.

Du was sad to be leaving the city then; but here was the ship, its Dutch flag snapping in the wind. And here was the cabin, all polished and impeccable. The engine was throbbing now, and visitors who had come to say goodbye were leaving. The hawsers were released, people waved, or held their handkerchiefs to their eyes. The Bund moved back, as a deep and purple sky was lowered over a pale and orange one. The ship moved forward, steered through an archipelago of ocean liners, tankers, barges, freighters, junks and swirled about by muddy waters. In the distance, neon signs pricked the darkness ahead of the stars. Could anyone have guessed that in a time of Maoist austerity yet to come, a whole generation would grow up not knowing what a neon sign looked like? In his cabin, feeling Pudong left behind him, Du Yuesheng had had a stab of regret, seeing in a flicker of memory the sun striking the flaring roofs of his clan hall

— that monument to all that he had won, and all that he was about to lose.

In Hong Kong Du Yuesheng took an apartment on Kennedy Road. From newspapers read to him in the next few months, he learnt that the territories lost by the Guomindang troops covered no less than half of China. Throughout, Mao Zedong had clearly kept his end in view; on October 1, before an immense crowd gathered in the Square of Heavenly Peace in Beijing, he proclaimed the People's Republic of China, saying, 'Never again will the people of China be enslaved.'

Shanghai did not fall in apocalypse. On May 26 red flags suddenly appeared over factory buildings. The People's Liberation Army had simply walked in in their sneakers and straw sandals the night before. You could see them the next morning lying quietly in rows on the pavements, young soldiers curled up as though they might be under a tree by a river, but spread out with almost geometrical neatness all down the sidewalks. But for these, and for the announcement on the radio on the 27th that the People's Liberation Army had taken Shanghai over, you could hardly have known that Shanghai had fallen to the Reds.

Many citizens shrugged their shoulders and said, 'Well, you had the Japanese from '37 and Chiang Kaishek from '45. Mr Mao can hardly be worse' — the devil you don't know being always preferable. Like most innocents acquiring knowledge, Shanghai would come to know Communism through painful experience, in phases that might have been decreed. At first it seemed that youth, zealousness and discipline seldom combined so happily as in the case of the Red soldier. His was the manner of uncommon gentleness and modesty; he was honest, courteous and incorruptible. No soldier, it seemed, would think of riding in a tram without buying a ticket or of jumping the queue. And he was, strangely for a man in uniform, not predatory: he did not commandeer rooms but continued to sleep on the pavement; when requisitioning firewood he would weigh it out carefully and then return the exact amount — of a quality that was usually higher; he hesitated even to accept a drink of water, so undemanding was he of the local people.

The Red soldier had come to Shanghai as a virtually unknown

quantity. Of course Guomindang propaganda had tarnished his image ahead of his arrival, but that had been damaging in direct ratio to the credibility of Chiang Kaishek's government; and no one, as the civil war progressed, had put much faith in what that regime said. In any case, though the war had been the frame of the city's life, it had been something a long way distant, a succession of rumoured names which had a life in the rural hinterland but not here. In the teahouses they could not smell the stench of sweat-soaked khaki, or see the straw fraying on the tired sandalled feet dragging through slime or parched earth. You heard Mao Zedong spoken of, you knew his name, but you didn't altogether understand why it was pronounced with so much awe. In Shanghai the popular mind was much more concerned with the resumption of business just as soon as possible.

It was a relief, now that they were here, to find the Communists going along with your wishes. No revolutionary programme of the sort aimed at rapid social transformation darkened those summer days. There was the utmost goodwill between the Party and the business leaders; together they would plan for the future, and industrialists and accountants felt a sense of being appreciated, and of life moving soundly forward. The *New York Times* reported that 'Red Moves Please Shanghai Bankers', and the *Liberation Daily* said that 'Only with the speedy restoration of all public and private industrial enterprises in Shanghai and their normal operation will a real revolutionary order be set up.' The businessman assumed it would eventually become clear to him how he, what the new order had termed the 'national capitalist', would contribute to the economic reconstruction of Shanghai. He did not worry unduly: the Communist Party must, it seemed to him, walk a middle path to begin with, for how else could it get the economy going again? So close, indeed, were his own interests to those of the new regime that he could not imagine the sacrifice of the one without the damage of the other. The Communist Party seemed to like nothing better than to solicit the opinions and advice of the financiers, technicians, administrators and officials of the old regime — the ones they did not class as 'active counterrevolutionary enemies of the people.'

Only occasionally did it occur to the businessman to wonder if things might take a different turn, if a Communist takeover might imply his own downfall. After all, just before it happened people were saying, 'The Communists will ruin Shanghai and Shanghai will ruin the Communists.' Cities were a puzzle to these peasants, the ones who had taken it over. Whereas a more familiar environment might have elicited appropriate approaches, here they found themselves running a place of whose workings they were ignorant, whose sophistication they could not appreciate, whose complexity was a mystery. With his proneness to condescension, the businessman quickly saw how these peasants, finding it all to much for them, could feel suspicious and endangered. Mao Zedong himself had warned of the 'sugar-coated bullets of the bourgeoisie' and the trap of their deadly allure. Like those who, wary of liking a thing too well, make it a point of not liking it at all, the Communists did approach this 'lair of imperialists, compradors and bureaucrats' with deep puritanical distrust. Yet the reality of Shanghai was more mixed than the preconceived idea, and it could not be instantly seen how the corruption, the love of luxury, the bourgeois practices could be expunged without displacing what was healthy and helpful to Socialist reconstruction.

That summer the new rulers of Shanghai decided they would go about their tasks quietly until they had got the lie of the terrain.

DU YUESHENG HEARD how gently the capitalists were being treated by the Communists in Shanghai, but he did not for a moment trust it — he was too used to man's inconstancy for that. It wouldn't last, he thought, this seeming comradeship between the two classes; sooner or later the reservoir of goodwill would run dry. He thought it a pity that Shanghai, a spring of so much enterprise and modernity in a land so laggard, should have all its stuffing taken out of it, for he had no doubt, knowing how Communists felt about *laissez-faire*, that the new rulers would ruin it.

He would stay put in Hong Kong. Both before and after his departure from Shanghai his friends and business connections had urged him to follow the Guomindang to Taiwan. The previous autumn, while making a last stand in Canton before finally decamping to Taiwan, Chiang Kaishek himself had sent for him. But he had politely declined, though deep were the regrets he both felt and voiced. This attitude of a neutral did not stem from rancour but from a weariness with politics and a wish to be left alone; the underlying loyalty, though it had been increasingly unrequited, indeed abused, over the years, remained intact. But for once his active support of the Guomindang could not be had for the asking.

At the same time, however much he might also wish to sever his ties with Shanghai, to people's surprise he compromised himself by sending his eldest son there that winter, damaging his appearance of neutrality. At the younger Du's departure there was widespread speculation about his reasons for making the trip and it was supposed by many people, Chiang Kaishek included, that it was a preliminary step towards a *rapprochement* with the new regime, and that the son was making a reconnaissance of the conditions for the father's return.

The truth of the matter was in fact quite different. The younger Du would not have gone for anything; only, the banking business which in the haste of his departure from Shanghai Du had not had time to wrap up was causing something of a headache just then. What brought matters to a head was the sudden resignation of the branch manager. The bank's trading being not inconsiderable and there being no trustworthy replacement for the manager, it fell to the younger Du to go and take temporary charge.

It took him six months to sort things out. When he came back to Hong Kong his father made him sit down and recount everything — all the transactions, the conversations with friends, the encounters with officials and the taste of the new China. In sum the discursive reports told Du Yuesheng that the days of his cronies in that city were numbered.

They will have a difficult time of it, the younger Du said; the Communists reckon the Shanghainese had it coming to them. The city, they said in one of their papers, was parasitic; it was a criminal city, a refugee city, a city where consumption was greater than production and where waste was greater than consumption. 'These Communists, they talk of transforming Shanghai by thrift and economy,' the younger Du continued, 'but what they're doing is to create a system in which it is impossible for wealth to belong to anybody.

They talk of giving the old moneyed class a place in the people's government, the ones that prove to be capable and ideologically acceptable, but what they're really out for is your blood. They may befriend a certain person, or class, or even a certain country; but they will eliminate you the moment you've outlived your usefulness to them. They talk of defending national interests against imperialism and its lackeys, but you should see the giant pictures they've put up of Marx, Engels, Lenin and Stalin: if that isn't truckling up to foreigners, what is? When Mao Zedong went to Moscow there were pictures of the Great Meeting between him and Stalin everywhere, and there is even this song they sing — with the line "Mao Zedong! Stalin! They are shining as bright as the sun in the sky!" Whatever next....'

At this point in the tirade the father interrupted him. 'Did you,' the elder Du asked, 'see to your godmother's funeral when you were in Shanghai?'

The son said he did. His godmother, Inspector Huang Jinrong's wife and Du Yuesheng's first patroness, had died that spring, a lonely forsaken woman. Some twenty-five years before, Inspector Huang had taken a concubine half his age and she, his betrayed wife, had risen manfully above the outrage, had simply sorted out the keys to the household safes, and left, taking only her due. She wanted nothing but the clean break, and to keep her self-respect. It was Du Yuesheng who, coming to her aid, found her a place in Seymour Road to move into. There, waving sympathy and alimony aside, she had sat out the remaining decades of her life, in solitude and seclusion. No one mourned her death more than Du, who even now looked warmly upon her as benefactress. On hearing of her death, he had sent word to his son in Shanghai at once, instructing him to take charge of the burial arrangements and pay for them. Everything thereafter, so the son now reported to the father, had taken place much as he had wished it. The coffin was a box of high-quality wood, and it was expected that in it she would find the repose denied her in the latter part of her life.

Inspector Huang's new liaison had turned out, as such liaisons will, to be a summons to doom. He worshipped his young concubine, but she fell for someone more her age and, taking the contents of the household safes with her, left the poor besotted husband three years after he married her. She had apparently not intended to cast herself away on a man well past his prime, even if rich. Inspector Huang, distraught, did not have enough presence of mind to go after her, but his partner Du Yuesheng did. Not above a little well-aimed intimidation, Du recovered all of the loot from the lady.

This sad episode turned the inspector into an old man, with laboured breath and a certain distance from life. When the Communists came and Du urged him to quit Shanghai he said that at eighty-one he was getting to the end of his life. And whatever might be said in favour of Hong Kong it cut no ice with him; for one thing it could never sustain his three daytime occupations: opium, steam bath and gambling.

Like most Chinese of the commercial class he would leave politics alone if politics would leave him alone. But in a society where no one escapes being classed as a landlord, bureaucratic-capitalist, Guomindang reactionary and henchman, worker, peasant, petty bourgeois or national bourgeois, and being treated according to one's category, it was difficult, as Inspector Huang would soon discover, to be left alone by politics. The new regime would give him no quarter. There would be no respite or receding quietly into retirement.

INSPECTOR HUANG was wondering if people didn't grow tired of the parades that came down the streets week after week. There was always a crowd to watch them, though it seemed to him there was nothing to see but more portraits of Mao Zedong and Stalin, and banners exhorting the worker to take his place in the reconstruction of China. He supposed that the girls were nice, the ones in pink trousers who came drumming and dancing the *yang ge* down the street, but he should hardly have guessed that it was a peasant folk dance they were doing, so daintily did these Shanghainese urbanites execute the footwork.

Huang Jinrong wouldn't dream of thrusting his way into the crowd. In fact he seldom went out of his house, but people came and told him things, and he knew that rallies and demonstrations were now part of your daily existence. People used to take them for a lark, but there was something sinister in spectacles that could so change the expression of people — faces shining like the lights coming on. A neighbour's daughter had been so carried away watching she said she'd give her life for the Chinese people; 'How little do I matter,' she had come home and said, 'when I see them out in the parade ground — thousands of them, an ocean of humanity.' Her father had not liked that sort of talk, and had wondered if she wouldn't go and denounce him to the Party officials one of these days. Kids did this with so much blitheness you wouldn't think there was a time when filial piety meant something deeper than you can imagine.

Huang Jinrong was getting used to the street and lane committees and the new vocabulary, though he still found that words like 'popular masses' and 'model workers' sounded strange in his own mouth. And he was not entirely sure of their meaning; he'd been told by one of his nephews that some words — 'voluntary', for example — had a reverse meaning in the new China. What really got the inspector down was the enforced austerity. He was not accustomed to conserving scarce commodities, since in the past they had never been scarce to him, even if they might be to other people. Now you had to eat an ounce less of rice a day, or eat gruel twice a week instead of rice. You couldn't use electrical appliances because you had to save energy, and all over town neon illumination faded from the shop-fronts and doors.

In Shanghai in the winter of 1950, austerity was certainly the order of the day. Even the clothes bore this out. Lenin suits, a beacon of the wearer's disdain for adornment and therefore his progressiveness, were all the rage. (In its way Socialist snobbery sets styles.) Like all fashion the Lenin suit imposed restrictions on accessories and lifestyle; and as the papers pointed out it was not meant to be worn with a necktie and it was unbecoming to unclean living of the sort displayed in dancing and gambling. Actually it looked not all that much different from what used to be called the Sun Yatsen suit — matching jacket and trousers in a style which the late father of the Chinese Republic must have picked up from the Japanese, who must in their turn have got it from the Shanghainese tailors who emigrated to Nagasaki the century before. Now young girls coveted the suit with as much ardour as their elder sisters, in hero-worship of the

American commander of the China theatre, had once wished for what they called the Wedemeyer jacket just after the war.

Shanghai that winter was certainly no place for the frivolous or leisured; most emphatically it was no place for the indolent. If it wasn't the political classes it was the small-group reading sessions, and if it wasn't the reading sessions it was the campaigns. The campaigns. That was what finally broke Inspector Huang, these mass movements that swept the country every so often and flushed out the enemies of the State in a tide of hysteria. People would come to know them for what they are: the Communist Party's lifeblood and the means by which it gets things done. They would learn to distinguish between the ones that had no human targets from the ones that did. In the Patriotic Cleanliness and Health Campaign aimed at eliminating the Four Pests, for example, the targets were rats, bedbugs, mosquitoes and flies. In the Campaign to Suppress Counter-Revolutionaries launched that autumn, the targets were Dregs of the Old Society — 'the landlords and their lackeys, reactionary officials and their lackeys, reactionary secret societies, mercenary bandits and thieves and other bullies and hooligans.' The likes of Huang Jinrong, in other words.

In such a movement, thousands must be gathered, to shout 'Eliminate all counter-revolutionaries!' or 'Long live the Chinese Communist Party!' beneath rippling red flags. On the rostrum, or beneath it, a pen might be erected, and in it placed, like caged animals, the men the masses had assembled to Struggle Against, each newly defined to himself by the long white cloth pinned to his chest, proclaiming Bully, Ruffian, whatever. On his bowed head there might be placed a dunce's cap. Then the whole monstrous thing would be set in motion, and beyond and above the shouting, chanting and cursing, the loudspeakers would boom, the complainants accuse, and then the mob with a vengeful convulsion would roll over the pen.

At the moment when the Campaign to Suppress Counter-Revolutionaries moved towards its brutal climax, teams of Party interrogators, skilled practitioners of the form of intimidation known as Expose and Criticize, were coming to Inspector Huang's house everyday in relay, one taking over as the other flagged. The inspector himself, however, had no respite; it was the third degree throughout. He was looking swollen in the wan electric light, and his head kept moving from side to side. Try as he would, he could not convince his interrogators that there was nothing more to be said. Such a thing had never happened to him before, this cross-examination that went on for days and nights on end. The very effort of understanding the questions that were being shot at him was exhausting. He shivered in the first pale light of an icy dawn, and through a haze of fatigue, stared remotely at the interrogators easing themselves back into their chairs. He for the moment was standing, had been made to stand or kneel at whim, and occasionally to perch from a high chair, so that his feet felt like twigs that had half broken off from the trunk and yet were made to bear accumulating weights.

In his stunned condition it did not anger him, as it might ordinarily, that these callow fellows to whom apparently he was to entrust his confession were so clearly younger than he. They had expressionless eyes, life or history having as yet left no deep marks on them. In his extremity of fright and sleeplessness the inspector was docile, and, motioned to a chair and table sat down and wrote, as they had told him to, about his past crimes, business deals, friends, the money he had stashed away. In this last item his questioners were specially interested, and demanded details — where, how much, and in what way retrievable. He was not good at financial accountings, and was inclined to be forgetful besides, but these young men wanted everything spelled out, and surprised him in being able to coax from him figures he was not aware of knowing or remembering. Lacking a way with the written word, he looked to them to supply the vocabulary, phrases of a prescribed code which seemed not like real words but more like counters with a bargaining value: the more he used them the less his interrogators harried him. His confession grew, its catalogue of wrongdoings set out with an accountancy so thorough as to seem a feat of superhuman memory.

He put his signature to the sheets and awaited his sentence. The curious fact was that, now that he had been made to face up to his past, he looked back on it with something like real shame. So much was being dug up, dug into; and he was made aware, in a strange and sentimental fashion, of the hurt and damage he had caused people in the course of his long life. Here lay the essence of Expose and Criticize: at the end of it all it always drew forth a grain, however small, of conscience and shame.

As sentences went, his was not harsh. The official enmity towards the Dregs of the Old Society sometimes went hand in hand, paradoxical as it may seem, with a respect for age and position; and for the next few months the inspector was to be seen sweeping the streets in front of the Great World, the fun palace he once owned on Avenue Edouard VII. The punishment was advertised, bombastically and at length, in newspapers which decried the sins of other bourgeois offenders with no less bombast and no less prolixity. One learnt that the onetime kingpin of the Shanghai underworld had repented of his ways, and that the State in its leniency had spared him his life.

THE SECRET BROTHERHOODS came off badly in the class struggle. Of the five to six hundred members of the Constancy Society left in Shanghai, a very large number suffered some form of persecution. Du Yuesheng kept loose count of the casualties as news filtered to him from Shanghai. Huang Jinrong's case especially upset him; he could not think how his old confrère could have borne the insults and the humiliation, and coped with having to get up so early in the morning, he who never rose before noon. The picture of the palsied old man bending over his broomstick outside the Great World, published in a newspaper in Hong Kong, had given Du a jolt, and brought on paroxysms of hampered breathing.

Nowadays the lamp he used for diffusing some moisture in the air against his asthma was always burning in his room. For hours he would lie quite silent, with his eyes closed. His youngest wife, with the solicitude she once showed to her ailing singing master, would come in from time to time, shift his pillows, bring him broths, and even sit up with him through the night. Often his chest would ache with the effort of respiration. Vague memories would float through his head; he had friends who were dying, who were dead. It was no longer unimaginable that he should follow them.

It did seem incredible that he, who once had money to burn, was now, in a manner of speaking, poor. Money had always run through his fingers like water. Not to squander it, to give it away, to flaunt it, would have required a character very different from his, and a tradition not rooted in the secret society and banditry. True, the sale of his house on Avenue Doumer to the United States government had brought him eight hundred thousand Hong Kong dollars, and he had left another hundred thousand U.S. dollars with T.V. Soong's younger brother to invest in America; but the sums were paltry when one considered the huge medical expenses, the four wives and the ten children. There was hardly enough to meet all their needs, let alone to bequeath. Yet no real regret went with this realization, except perhaps a certain disappointment at the absence of sycophants from his house. Indeed it now sometimes occurred to Du that, drained of the means and impetus to make any substantial changes to his life, it might be better if he were despatched from dependants and financial worries, and from this hardly endurable infirmity. What action could he himself take that would greatly alter the material circumstances of his existence, he whose light was already faded, whose legend history was already waiting to pass on?

He was, towards the summer of 1951, nearing the end of his sixty-third year and a very sick man. He had the best doctors, and any amount of oxygen inhalation. But the fits of breathlessness were wearing him out, and he was sleeping very little. When he had one of his asthma attacks he gasped for air conscious only of his body contorting to the jamming in his chest. The very rise and fall of breath seemed a miracle. In quick succession he lost, first, hope, then the use of his legs, and finally any sense of the world. On August 16 he went into a coma. That afternoon an official of Chiang Kaishek's government arrived on a plane from Taiwan almost too late to convey to him a message of concern and comfort from the Generalissimo. Du, on receiving the message, murmured something which the emissary took, for the purposes of future Guomindang propaganda, to be an expression of hope for the recovery of China and the return of Chiang Kaishek's government to the homeland. It passed, the instant of lucidity just before the end. At 4.50 p.m., twenty-four hours before his birthday, Du Yuesheng died.

The coffin, of the finest *nanmu*, the yellow West China cedar, was priced at fifteen thousand Hong Kong dollars but was procured at fifty per cent discount, the undertaker being a friend. The funeral parlour, hung with blue lanterns and draped with white crepe, was transformed by banks of floral wreaths — out of which the florists did very good business, there being more than seven hundred of them. The mourners, who had arrived during the last three days at the Luk Kwok (Six Nations) Hotel, paid their respects and took up places in the appointed restaurants nearby. Countless condolence telegrams from prominent persons and corporate bodies arrived from Taiwan, but nothing was heard from the presidential palace until just before the casketing on August 19, when, after repeated appeals by Du's friends, Chiang Kaishek deigned to send an inscribed tablet paying tribute to the dead man's 'conspicuous loyalty and integrity'.

The funeral procession would have been a bright pageant, had the rain not dulled its colours and tinged it with melancholy. It left the funeral parlour at two o'clock in the afternoon, the bands playing, the monks and nuns and Taoist priests chanting, the hearse coming out, bedecked with pine and cypress foliage, the symbols of mourning and virtue.

There was a sense of an epoch ending, of chapters closing and the need to make another start. The deceased left seven sons and three daughters, but none of them would ever follow in his footsteps, or know again those heights of splendour. The eldest and youngest sons would eventually settle in Taiwan, the one a banker, the other an official in the Ministry of Defence. The second son, who had studied education in the United States, would one day end up as an international bureaucrat in New York. The third son was to emigrate to Brazil and to start up a stockbroking business there, seemingly undeterred by the trouble a similar venture had once landed him in Shanghai. The fifth and sixth sons had returned to China with their mother, the second Mrs Du. She, long estranged from her husband, had decided to keep her distance in Shanghai. The daughters are said to have grown up into nice girls and to have married well.

The obituaries were fulsome, and dwelt on themes of honour, heroism and chivalry. In Du Yuesheng the *jianghu* spirit, good and bad, had found its grandest embodiment — loyal, magnanimous, altruistic, brave. He might have been brutal, he might have offended, but in all his years in clover and out, he had never been mean. He was not an official and yet a public man, not high-born and yet highly regarded, not tolerant of enemies and yet indulgent towards friends. And he was not the sum of these qualities either, but a fusion beyond them all.

He was a man, the newspapers said, who transcended his origins. Yet they might have added that he was also a by-product of his time. Had he been born in any other period of Chinese history, he would not have emerged as he did. But it happened that when, at the turn of the century, he came across the Huangpu River from Pudong, a new kind of society was coming into existence in Shanghai, and it was in this raw, dynamic, vulgar, crudely materialist and astonishing society that Du Yuesheng found his perfect opportunity. His life had exactly spanned the age of China's openness to the West; and only by seizing his chance in that oriental-occidental mix at once so encouraging of enterprise and commerce, and so fuzzy about law and morality, could Du Yuesheng be what he was.

The newspapers took up the tribute Chiang Kaishek paid to his loyalty, but forebore to mention that though he remained faithful to Chiang throughout, Chiang did not really play fair with him. Nothing gave Du greater satisfaction that to serve the Guomindang, translating to that Party and government the ancient obligations and almost unquestioning allegiances of the secret society. To the end he remained the Guomindang's man, however tirelessly the Communists had tried to make him theirs. Yet in his last years he found his loyalty unrewarded, his services to Chiang Kaishek disowned. For to Chiang he was fundamentally and ineradicably a gangster, and all his life he was bedevilled by the wrong kind of fame.

Yet though his reputation was to remain ambiguous, to the man in the street he was not all that villainous a gangster, as gangsters went. He was the last of the old kind of Chinese bandit, and would pass into folklore with all the rest, the image of his brutality balanced with patriotism, in the way of popular Chinese accounting. It is a curious truth that people secretly like and respect killers, if only because they add colour and variety to the drabness of human lives; and there was killing enough for most tastes in Du Yuesheng's life. Once it was realized that he died a not particularly rich man, that his bank account was not stuffed with the profits of carpetbagging or the opium trade, Du acquired even greater merit in the popular mind. His renowned prodigalities, his irrepressible munificence, and now his relative impoverishment all went to confirm the conclusion that at heart Du Yuesheng was an unmercenary man. Money matters were trivial beside the sweep of the high old style.

On 25 October 1952, Du Yuesheng's body was taken under the watchful eyes of the Hong Kong police to a pier and put on board a boat bound for Taiwan. Not having lived for eight years in Hong Kong, Du was denied a burial there; and so it was upon a cleft in the hills behind Taipei that his tomb was finally to be erected. Under the dappled shade of pine and bamboo, the setting was tranquil, its silence broken only by a cock's crow or the tolling of a nearby monastery bell. In it his mourners fancied they saw, most probably because they wished to, the contours and colours of the deceased's native Pudong. As a gauge of worldly pride and success the tomb is too modest, as a monument to a vanished era it is poignant beyond words.

AS DU YUESHENG became a ghost or a memory, so, in a spasm unprecedented in strength, scale and pain, did the China that he stood for. While the world, following America, revised its conception of China in indignation at her fighting in the Korean War — picturing the Chinese once more as a menacing 'yellow tide' — the Chinese themselves began to modify their earlier views of the Communists.

In the first half of 1952, the Five-Antis Campaign flushed out the Five Poisons of bribery, tax evasion, the stealing of State property, cheating on government contracts and the stealing of State economic intelligence, together with the last of the urban business class. Things were following a certain pattern, and it was a good guess that at the end of it all the bourgeoisie would be wiped out as a matter of Marxist principle. There had been the Three-Antis Campaign of the August before, which was said to be aimed at ridding the Party and State of the corrosive influences of the bourgeoisie, chiefly its propensity for Corruption, Waste and Bureaucratism. Now its sequel, the Five-Antis Campaign, had got under way in Shanghai. The mayor himself launched it on March 25, saying, 'I consider this city's Five-Antis struggle to be the key to the success or failure of the entire nation's Five-Antis Campaign', because 'Shanghai is China's bourgeois centre.'

From their experience of mass movements, moneyed people were feeling jittery months before the campaign began. Their apprehension grew with the stages of organization and mobilization: teams of propagandists touring the city and preparing factory workers and shop assistants for action; a rash of posters appearing; loudspeakers blaring outside shops and above major intersections, continuously pouring forth slogans and that chilling question, 'Hey, boss, have you confessed yet?' The Party leaders' barrage of speeches and publications left no one in doubt of the writing on the wall: 'This is a fight against the enemy, a fierce counter-attack against the trap of corruption prepared by the enemy... the lust for gold has led the bourgeoisie to sink to such depths that they are more poisonous than snakes, more ferocious than tigers and wolves.' The only means of salvation was to confess one's guilt in time and to denounce other miscreants as a demonstration of one's own conversion to the people's point of view.

For three months the movement had been hatching, then rapidly it rose to its climax. The campaign cadres were putting their training to good use and the propaganda was growing. Meetings proliferated; one class was pitted against another; the government pledged protection to those who would denounce their neighbours or bosses; investigative teams scoured shops and factories. Confessions spilled forth. Then the businessmen themselves turned informer, in pursuance of old grudges or in the interest of their own skins. Soon the authorities could claim that denunciations were running in the tens of thousands. In the mutual suspicion and recrimination that these engendered the old values of regional and guild solidarity cracked. So the ground for private capital's conflagration was being prepared.

The authorities now had a lot of information. From the denunciations, confessions and investigations, they had learnt almost all they wanted to know about the city's 163,400 business establishments and 110,000 hawkers. Leaving aside the latter they now sorted the business enterprises into the five predetermined classes: the Law-abiding, the Basically Law-abiding, the Semi Law-abiding, the Seriously Law-breaking, and the Completely Law-breaking. This in turn translated, by another formula, into a distribution of business enterprises by the amount they had to cough up to the State.

By such levies did the government tap the wealth in Shanghai, break the back of private capital, and enrich the State treasury. The businessman woke at last from his dream, his illusions of his place in the new society trailing away in folly. All that spring and summer, business tycoons cracking under the pressure were taking their own lives, hurling themselves from the tallest buildings on Nanjing Road. In Hong Kong their exiled counterparts followed the developments in horror, their view of Communism turning completely sour. Often the pressures for the return of improper earnings to the State spread beyond the Communist frontiers to Hong Kong, where relatives or branch managers suddenly received telegrams demanding ransom money for their kinsmen or principals in five, six or even seven figures. Hong Kong felt the trauma in other ways. Its trade with the mainland halved, its intimate mercantile links to Shanghai came under strain and above all, its business dealings with China had to adapt to the growing realization that now the only real entrepreneur in China was the State.

Now everybody condemned the Communists for their duplicity; only now, people said, are they showing their true colours. Now people believed the earlier benignity of the Red Army to be a hoax, not recognizing in this benignity a stratum of the truer reality: that the actions of Communist powers are all determined, at the deepest level, by clonus — by the alternating spasms of contraction and relaxation, of cracking down and loosening up that the Chinese Communist himself, in his down-to-earth way, terms the condition of 'being cold at two ends and hot in the middle'. Things go up and down: it has to happen that way, in China as in Soviet Russia. The soft-pedalling in the initial stage is no more duplicitous than the allowing of a grace period to elapse between one phase of a revolution and the next.

It was something inevitable, the extirpation of that lush and transient world. The campaign was not just what the cynics called it, a device for extortion and enriching the State; it was not just the squeezing of the rich until all the money ran out for the State to sop up. When all is said and done it really was class struggle, the supplanting of one tyranny by another. Perhaps the purges and persecution were necessary for the cleansing preparatory to the fulfilment of a new destiny. Perhaps Shanghai was being stripped for a new existence. Certainly what happened was the very negation of the city's *raison d'être*. Vice will not breed here. Worlds will not meet here. The likes of Du Yuesheng will not be seen here. The chapter had begun to wind up with the man's death, and now the campaign was closing it, with convulsion and thoroughness. A revolution is a draught which must be drained to the last bitter drop. Everything in the land that Du Yuesheng's heart knew was in that summer erased, save the turbulence and the silent timeless cry, 'China, China, what cross must you bear now?' It is a myth, the deep stability of that land and its people. In China you are outlasted by turbulence.

INDEX OF NAMES